# 老外最想与你聊的
# 中外文化

金 浩 | 编著

[美] Nellie Connolly
[美] Logan M. West | 审定

中国宇航出版社
·北 京·

图书在版编目（CIP）数据

老外最想与你聊的中外文化／金浩编著．--北京：中国宇航出版社，2011.7

ISBN 978-7-80218-968-3

Ⅰ．①老…　Ⅱ．①金…　Ⅲ．①英语－口语　Ⅳ．①H319.9

中国版本图书馆 CIP 数据核字（2011）第 095867 号

策划编辑　李士振　　装帧设计　03工舍
责任编辑　李士振　裴燕娜　　责任校对　王静

出版发行　中国宇航出版社
社址　北京市阜成路 8 号　　邮编　100830
(010)68768548
网址　www.caphbook.com/www.caphbook.com.cn
经销　新华书店
发行部　(010)68371900　　(010)88530478(传真)
(010)68768541　　(010)68767294(传真)
零售店　读者服务部　　北京宇航文苑
(010)68371105　　(010)62529336
承印　三河市君旺印装厂
版次　2011 年 7 月第 1 版　　2011 年 7 月第 1 次印刷
规格　787×960　　开本　1/16
印张　16.75　　字数　390 千字
书号　ISBN 978-7-80218-968-3
定价　28.80 元（附赠全文 MP3 光盘）

本书如有印装质量问题，可与发行部联系调换

# Preface

As China's economic status rising in the world, more and more foreigners come into China and learn more about China. Economic cooperation and cutural exchanges between China and foreign countries become more frequent too. Therefore, the importance of English learning has been further improved, and more people eager to improve their English level so as to effectively communicate with foreigners.

In order to meet the needs of many English fans to practice their oral English, this book provides a wealth of new and practical topics and compiles these topics into separate dialogue covering almost every aspect of social culture, including Media, Literature and Films, Sports and Games, Love and Family and so on.

The format of this book is in English-Chinese and there is background knowledge in each chapter, which is convenient for the readers to study. As to the useful expressions, we list them separately so that the readers can learn them by heart as basic sentence patterns. All the new words and phrases in each dialogue are added with explanatory notes, which are easy for the readers to accumulate their vocabularies. In addition, this book is appendixed with a CD recorded by experts from Beijing Foreign Studies University. You can imitate to read and recite after the CD while learning, which is quite helpful to improve your spoken English and listening comprehension.

Each topic is independent in this book, so there is no need to follow the original chapter when you are learning. You can choose the order according to your own interest flexibly. You can learn by yourself, playing two parts at the same time or you can invite a partner to communicate with each other and practice together and finally reach the goal of mutual promotion and progress.This book can also be used as a textbook for small-class oral teaching with the teacher and all the students participating together and discussing the differences between Chinese and western cultures. It can help everyone enlarge their views.

In order to be more authoritative and idiomatic in the English language, we particularly invited some American linguistic experts Nellie Connolly, Logan West and Graham Paterson in Beijing Foreign Studies University to take part in compiling and revising this book. They made great contributions to the publication of this book. Therefore, we'd like to express our heartfelt thanks to them all!

We hope you can enjoy the idiomatic spoken English and meanwhile learn about cultural knowledge both at home and abroad after reading this book. We also hope it can arouse your interest in English and train your excellent language speed and sense. We believe that practice makes perfect. As long as you make unremitting efforts, you will make progress in oral English by leaps and bounds.

Editor

Beijing, early summer of 2011

# 前　言

随着中国在世界上经济地位的提升，越来越多的外国人开始走进中国，了解中国。中外间的经济合作与文化交流也变得日益频繁。因而，英语的重要性进一步提高了，更多的国人渴望提高自己的英语水平来进行有效的文化交流。

为了满足广大英语学习爱好者练习口语的要求，本书提供了关于社会文化方面的丰富话题，并将其编写成独立的对话，内容新颖而实用，其中包括：传媒天地、文学与电影、文体娱乐、爱情与家庭、文化与社会等等。

本书采用了中英文对照的形式，每个话题都有相关背景知识的介绍，便于读者学习；其中对于重要表达方式单独列出，读者可以作为句型记忆；每篇对话中的生词和短语都给予了注释，便于读者对词汇进行积累。此外，本书还配有由北京外国语大学专家配音录制的 MP3 光盘，读者在学习的时候可以模仿朗读，对口语和听力的提高都有很大帮助。

本书的每个话题都独立成篇，不需要按章节依次学习。读者可以根据自己的兴趣爱好灵活选择。您可以独立自学，一人扮演两个角色；您也可以选择一个语伴，两人进行交流，互动练习，最终达到相互促进、共同进步的目的。本书还可以作为小班制口语教学的教材，师生共同参与，探讨中西方文化差异，有助于增长知识，开拓眼界。

为了增加本书的权威性并使本书语言标准地道，我们还特别邀请了北京外国语大学美国语言专家 Nellie Connolly 、Logan West 和 Graham Paterson 参与了本书的编写和审校工作。他们也为本书的创作付出了艰辛的劳动，在此，表示衷心地感谢！

希望本书能让您在感受地道英语口语的同时，学习中外文化知识，激发您学习英语的兴趣，培养良好的语速和语感！我们相信“熟能生巧”，只要您坚持不懈，您的英语口语一定会有突飞猛进的提高。

编者

2011 年初夏于北京

# 目录 Contents

## Media 传媒天地



## Literature and Films 文学与电影

## Music and Arts 音乐与艺术



## Food and Party 中外饮食



## Sports and Games 文体娱乐

## Life as Art 生活即艺术

## Love and Family 爱情与家庭



## Culture and Society 文化与社会

## Bits and Pieces 点点滴滴

# Media 传媒天地

# 1. What's Your Favorite TV Series

## 最爱美剧

### 知识链接 拓展视野，掌握背景知识

“美剧”是中国人对美国电视剧的简称。20世纪80年代，《大西洋底来的人》、《加里森敢死队》等热播。《成长的烦恼》让我们走进美国家庭，体验了代际沟通的现象及其背后的美国式幽默。凡此种种，都已成为那个年代的文化切片。“季”是指各大电视网播出新作品的季节，一般从每年的9月中旬开始到次年4月下旬结束，时长约30周。此外，美剧又分肥皂剧(Soap Opera)、情景喜剧(Sitcom)、情节系列剧(Drama)等。

### 难点点拨 知识难点看一看，情景实战热热身

1．present 出品，制作

It is by now the most successful sitcom in America, presented by Warner Bros and initially broadcast on NBC.

这是美国迄今为止最成功的情景喜剧，最初由华纳兄弟公司制作，美国全国广播公司播出。

2．be caring and helpful 互相照顾，互相帮助

They fight like brothers, always caring and helpful toward each other, even In the hardest times.

他们像兄弟一样并肩作战，即便再苦再难也总是互相扶持，互相帮助。

3．make a great success 获得巨大成功

It is hard to change an actor's initial image in the audience's hearts once he has made a great success in a certain play.

演员一成了名，就很难摆脱观众对他的第一印象。

4．be based on 根据，建立在

The TV series *Band of Brothers* is actually based on a book of the same name by a historian Stephen Ambrose.

《兄弟连》实际上是根据一本同名书改编的，这本书是一位叫史蒂芬·安布洛斯的历史学家写的。

## 情景实战 跟着老外听一听，读一读，练一练

**会话 1**

Kelly: Do you like American TV series?

Liz: Of course. I often spend a whole day watching and it is good for my English listening and speaking.

K: So which series do you like most?

L: Hard to say. They belong to different types—I mean, some are humorous, and some are exciting.

K: For me, I like *Friends* most, it always makes me laugh. It is by now the most successful sitcom in America, presented by Warner Bros and initially broadcast on NBC. Besides, it is enormously long—ten seasons, you can imagine, from 1994 to 2004.

L: I appreciate the love affair between Ross and Rachel most. It is so moving and exciting.

K: Yes, and boys are always stupidly cute, especially Joey.

L: Yes, boys are boys.

K: Now I am watching another series *Gossip Girl*, which is very interesting and enthralling. I highly recommend it to you.

L: In fact I am watching it now and it really enthralls me. Besides, I can also learn a lot about American English and the American culture from this story.

K: That's true, you can learn a lot through entertainment.

L: Next time you find some good new series, please let me know.

凯利：你喜欢看美剧吗？

利兹：当然了。我经常一看就是一天。这对英语听力和口语都有好处。

K：那么你最喜欢哪部美剧？

L：很难说。这些美剧各不相同，有的幽默，有的刺激。

K：我个人最喜欢《老友记》了。我一看就笑。这是美国迄今为止最成功的情景喜剧，最初由华纳兄弟公司制作，美国全国广播公司播出。而且这剧也非常长，一共有 10 季，你想一下，从 1994 年一直演到 2004 年。

L：我觉得罗斯和瑞秋的爱情故事最好了，既感人，又有趣。

K：是啊。男孩儿都蠢得可爱，特别是乔伊。

L：嗯，年纪再大也是孩子。

K：现在我在看另一部新剧《绯闻女孩》呢，它既精彩又有趣。我推荐你看。

L：实际上我也在看呢，确实吸引人。而且我能从中学到不少有关美式英语和美国文化方面的知识。

K：是啊，寓教于乐嘛。

L：下次你要是发现好看的新剧了，跟我也说说。

### 核心词汇记一记

**Words Storm**

| | | |
|---|---|---|
| sitcom | ['sitkɔm] *n.* | 情景喜剧 |
| enormously | [i'nɔːməsli] *ad.* | 非常地 |
| appreciate | [ə'priːʃieit] *v.* | 感激，感谢，欣赏 |
| enthralling | [in'θrɔːliŋ] *a.* | 扣人心弦的 |
| recommend | [ˌrekə'mend] *v.* | 推荐，介绍 |
| entertainment | [ˌentə'teinmənt] *n.* | 娱乐 |

**Phrases**

| | |
|---|---|
| love affair | 风流韵事 |
| boys are boys | （男人）年纪再大，也是孩子 |

## 会话 2

Loren: Have you watched *Band of Brothers*?

Matthew: Of course I have. It is a must for me as I am especially interested in military things. The display of warfare is fabulous and shocking—when the combat begins, you can really smell the smoke of gunpowder and experience the cruelty of war.

L: And the friendship between members of the Easy Company?

M: Yes, they are really a good team. They fight like brothers, always caring and helpful toward each other, even in the hardest times.

L: And a funny thing—the instructor at the very beginning of the story is played by David Schwimmer, who has also played Ross in *Friends*.

M: The moment I saw him as a peevish drill instructor in the army, I burst into laughter—only to see his face makes me laugh.

L: It is hard to change an actor's initial image in the audience's hearts once he has made a great success in a certain play. I mean, Schwimmer will always be "Ross" in our hearts because we have already been deeply impressed by that image.

M: That's right. The TV series *Band of Brothers* is actually based on a book of the same name by historian Stephen Ambrose.

L: Therefore it is historically faithful.

M: Correct.

劳伦：你看过《兄弟连》吗？

马修：当然了。对我这种军事迷来说，这个是必须要看的。战争场面非常壮观，震撼人心——每次战斗打响，你都能真切地闻到硝烟的味道，体会到战争的残酷。

L：而且 E 连战友的兄弟之情也很深，对吧？

M：是啊，真是个好队伍。他们像兄弟一样并肩作战，即便再苦再难也总是互相扶持，互相帮助。

L：有件特有趣的事儿——故事开头的教官是大卫·施维默扮演的，他在《老友记》里演过罗斯。

M：我一看他扮演这么一个坏脾气的教官，当场就笑喷了——一看他的脸我就想笑。

L：演员一成了名，就很难摆脱观众对他的第一印象。我的意思是，施维默对大家来说永远都是那个罗斯，因为我们早就已经被这个形象打动了。

M：是啊。《兄弟连》实际上是根据一本同名书改编的，这本书是一位叫史蒂芬·安布洛斯的历史学家写的。

L：所以剧情都是真实可信的。

M：是这样的。

### 核心词汇记一记

#### Words Storm

must [mʌst] *n.* 必须做的事

display [ˌdis'plei] *n.* 展示，表现

warfare ['wɔːfɛə] *n.* 战争，冲突

fabulous ['fæbjuləs] *a.* 难以置信的，极好的

historian [his'tɔːriən] *n.* 历史学家

#### Phrases

burst into 突然爆发

# 2. Is News Unbiased

## 新闻可靠吗

### 知识链接 拓展视野，掌握背景知识

现代媒体的新闻报道，原则上应当是真实可靠、客观公正的。这一方面要求新闻工作者要有一定的自由和勇气，敢于为公众报道真相；另一方面要求他们有社会责任感，不能掺杂私假，不能以自己的观点为绝对真理强加给公众。西方各大媒体一直宣称自己是恪守这些基本原则讲实话的，但是某些时刻依然存在违背客观公正原则的新闻报道。当然，西方媒体的某些批评也是有一定道理的。

### 难点点拨 知识难点看一看，情景实战热热身

1. add sth. in sth. 向某物里添加进某成分

   Sometimes those who report the news will add their own opinions in it, thus making the news full of pride and prejudice.

   有时候新闻工作者会添加一些他们自己的主观意见，这样新闻就会带有傲慢和偏见了。

2. hold back sth. from sb. 向某人隐瞒某事

   Some news reporters will hold back negative information from the public, in order not to irritate them or make a stir.

   一些记者会刻意向公众隐瞒一些负面消息，以免引起民愤，或是招惹是非。

3. make a false accusation against 诬告，诋毁

   Sometimes they intentionally make a false accusation against their enemies.

   有时候他们也会故意造谣诋毁对手。

4. impose on 强加

   Sometimes the western media exaggerates the superiority of western value, and wants to impose this value on other nations.

   有时候西方媒体夸大了西方价值观的优越性，想把这种价值观强加给其他国家。

5. be universally applicable to 普遍适用于

   There are some principles universally applicable to all human beings.

   有一些原则是适用于全人类的。

## 情景实战 跟着老外听一听，读一读，练一练

**会话 1**

Robin: Do you believe what you see in TV news or newspaper?

Maria: Not exactly. Sometimes those who report the news will add their own opinions in it, thus making the news full of pride and prejudice.

R: Really? I have never thought of this point before.

M: Some news reporters will hold back negative information from the public, in order not to irritate them or make a stir. Therefore, what we can see in the news is only a part of the whole situation, and the public opinion on the reported affair might be misled.

R: Sometimes ugly things are not suitable for publicity, so reporters may keep reticent.

M: Sometimes they intentionally make a false accusation against their enemies. They make up stories and false evidence. As a result, their enemies may feel great pressure.

R: So media is a weapon indeed, and it can be used for political purposes. The pen is far mightier than the sword.

罗宾：你相信电视或者报纸上的新闻吗？

玛丽亚：不全信。有时候新闻工作者会添加一些他们自己的主观意见，这样新闻就会带有傲慢和偏见色彩了。

R：真的吗？我还从没想到过这问题呢。

M：一些记者会刻意向公众隐瞒一些负面消息，以免引起民愤，或是招惹是非。所以我们看到的新闻只是事件的一个方面而已，公众对于报道事件的意见可能就被新闻误导了。

R：是的，也许一些丑事不适合公开，记者也就保持缄默了。

M：有时候他们也会故意造谣诋毁对手，编造一些故事和伪证。这样他们的对手就会感到压力很大。

R：所以媒体确实也是武器，可以用在政治斗争上。笔杆子有时候比枪杆子还厉害呢。

### 核心词汇记一记

**Words Storm**

prejudice ['predʒudis] *n.* 偏见
irritate ['iriteit] *v.* 激怒
reticent ['retisnt] *a.* 缄默的
intentionally [in'tenʃənəli] *ad.* 故意地
accusation [ækju:'zeiʃən] *n.* 谴责

**Phrases**

make a stir 引起骚动
public opinion 公众意见
make up 编造

**会话 2**

Kevin: Sometimes I find the news reported by some western news agencies irritating.

Judith: Why is that? because they always report bad news, such as disasters.

K: Nope. It is hard to put it clear. An example—when there is a conflict in some Middle East or African country, the western reporters always show an air of arrogance and prejudice in their reports. They think they are much superior to the local people in the conflict, and often accuse them of inhumanity and insanity. These reporters regard the western people as saviors and the local people as savages, but they never see the inner reason for such a conflict.

J: Yes, sometimes the western media exaggerates the superiority of western value, and wants to impose this value on other nations. This is destined to fail.

K: To me, everything has a deep underlying reason. If we want to know it completely, we should dig out the reason and have a serious study of it. Besides, different cultures have different ways of thinking. We should not interfere with other people's business.

J: However, there are still some principles universally applicable to all human beings, such as friendship, love, peace, and democracy. Sometimes the criticism from westerners is reasonable.

K: Well, it depends.

凯文：有时候我觉得西方的新闻机构报道的一些新闻很讨厌。

朱迪思：为什么？因为他们总是报道坏消息，比如灾难什么的。

K：不是的。很难说清原因。举个例子吧，如果中东或者非洲的某国有冲突事件，西方记者报道的时候，总是表现出一种傲气和偏见。他们觉得自己比深陷冲突中的当地人更聪明、更厉害，总是谴责当地人，说他们没人性，说他们疯了。这些记者认为，西方人就是救世主，而当地人就是野蛮人，但是他们从来不去考虑冲突背后的深层次原因。

J：是的，有时候西方媒体夸大了西方价值观的优越性，想把这种价值观强加给其他国家。这肯定是不行的。

K：依我看，每件事都有某种深层次原因。如果我们想充分了解这个事件，就得究其根源，严肃认真地研究。况且不同文化背景下的人思考问题的方式也不同。我们最好不要干涉别人的私事。

J：可是总归有一些原则是适用于全人类的，比如友谊、关爱、和平和民主。有时候西方的批评也有道理。

K：嗯，这得看情况而定。

**核心词汇记一记**

**Words Storm**

| | | |
|---|---|---|
| conflict | ['kɔnflikt] | *n.* 冲突 |
| savior | ['seivjə] | *n.* 救世主 |
| savage | ['sævidʒ] | *n.* 野蛮人 |
| exaggerate | [ig'zædʒəreit] | *v.* 夸大 |

**Phrases**

| | |
|---|---|
| news agency | 通讯社，新闻机构 |
| be superior to | 比……更强 |
| western value | 西方价值观 |

# 3. Interesting Sidelights

## 花边新闻

### 知识链接 拓展视野，掌握背景知识

*西方的媒体非常注重挖掘一些明星的小道消息、绯闻趣事，在这点上，中外几乎没有差别。狗仔队会想尽办法跟踪明星，监视他们的一举一动，找出各种值得作为谈资的小事，从而吸引读者和观众。而正因为如此，一方面公众对明星的私生活越来越感兴趣，明星的一切都会成为街头巷尾的谈资；另一方面，许多明星越来越不喜欢自己的隐私被曝光。当然，有些人还是会想尽一切办法做出各种雷人的事情来，这样做无非就是为了引起公众的注意，增加知名度。*

### 难点点拨 知识难点看一看，情景实战热热身

1. make a stir 引起大众骚动、议论

   Mrs. Obama wore shorts on her visit to the Grand Canyon, which made a stir.

   奥巴马夫人去大峡谷旅游的时候穿了短裤，这就出了问题。

2. spy on 监视

   The paparazzi always spy on famous people.

   狗仔队总是监视这些名人。

3. be exposed to 暴露在……下

   Their daily life will be exposed to the limelight.

   他们的日常生活坦露在公众目光下。

4. raise one's attention 引人注意

   They do all kinds of crazy things, just to raise the public attention.

   他们做很多疯狂的事情，就是为了引起公众注意。

## 情景实战 跟着老外听一听，读一读，练一练

**会话 1**

Monica: Come, come. I'm reading something interesting from a webpage.

Alicia: What are you reading? You seem so engrossed.

M: Some gossips about stars. You see, Paris Hilton once flirted with Beckham, praising him for his good shape. This irritated Victoria Beckham so much that she warned Paris to 'stay away from David'.

A: Haha! You have a special interest in these gossip things.

M: Don't you think it funny? It is just like what happens in a film. Er… Another thing. Diane Kruger, the actress who has played Helen in the film *Troy*, admits that she is happy to be maltreated and beat up by Brad Pitt in the film *Inglorious Bastards*, because Pitt is so handsome and manly.

A: I just cannot understand why you are so interested in these things.

M: It is funny, isn't it? You see the life of these stars, and you feel their happiness and sorrow—you experience another life, a life totally different from yours. It is just like reading a novel or watching a film.

莫妮卡：过来，过来。我在上网看到一些好玩的东西。

艾莉西亚：都是些什么啊？这么感兴趣。

M：明星的一些花边新闻。你看，帕丽斯·希尔顿有一次跟贝克汉姆调情，夸他身材棒。维多利亚就生气了，并警告帕丽斯“离我丈夫远些”。

A：哈哈！你特别喜欢这类花边新闻吧。

M：你不觉得这些事儿好玩吗？就跟演电影似的。哦，还有一条。黛安·克鲁格，就是在《特洛伊》里演海伦的那个，说她喜欢在电影《无耻混蛋》里被布拉德·皮特虐待毒打，因为皮特太帅太有男人味了。

A：我就是不明白你为什么对这些事情感兴趣。

M：这很好玩，不是吗？你看到这些明星的生活，能感受他们的喜怒哀乐——你简直就是在经历一种完全不一样的人生。就跟读小说看电影是一样的。

### 核心词汇记一记

**Words Storm**

engrossed [in'grəust] *a.* 全神贯注
gossip ['gɔsip] *n.* 闲话，流言蜚语
maltreat [ˌmæl'triːt] *v.* 虐待
manly ['mænli] *a.* 有男人味的
sorrow ['sɔrəu] *n.* 悲伤

**Phrases**

flirt with sb. 与某人调情
praise sb. for sth. 称赞
good shape 好身材

**会话 2**

Mary: Mrs. Obama wore shorts on her visit to the Grand Canyon, which made a stir. Many Americans think it inappropriate for the First Lady to dress so casually.

Jane: I think it is OK. She is our first lady, but first of all she is an ordinary person. She feels hot in such a season and should keep comfortable.

M: Right, I think so. To be public figures sometimes means to suffer a lot. Their daily life will be exposed to the limelight, and nearly everything can become the topic of the whole nation.

J: This is indeed an overt violation of privacy. The paparazzi always spy on famous people. Even when they want to dine out with their friends, they have to pay attention to everything. It seems that if you are the First Lady you are not supposed to wear shorts, no matter how hot the weather is.

M: Yes, it is nearly inhumane. I cannot understand why there are so many people interested in talking about trivial daily things of stars and politicians.

J: Some public figures don't want to always stay in limelight, but others will die for publicity. They do all kinds of crazy things, just to raise the public attention. For them, paparazzi are always good.

M: Life will be tiring then.

玛丽：奥巴马夫人去大峡谷旅游的时候穿了短裤，这就出了问题。很多美国人认为第一夫人穿着这么随便是不得体的。

简：我倒是觉得挺好。她是第一夫人，可首先也是个普通人啊。她在这个季节也觉得热，也想凉快一下。

M：对啊，我也这么想。可成为一个公众人物有时就意味着在很多方面都受到限制。他们的日常生活坦露在公众目光下，每件事都能成为全国上下热议的话题。

J：这实在是对个人隐私的公开侵犯。狗仔队总是监视这些名人，他们想跟朋友出去吃个饭都得考虑各种因素。如果你是第一夫人，你就不能穿短裤，天儿多热也不行。

M：是啊，这简直是惨无人道的。我不能理解为什么这么多人都喜欢讨论明星和政客的生活琐事。

J：确实是有一些公众人物不喜欢总是受众人注目。可是还有一些人渴望引人注目。他们做很多疯狂的事情，就是为了引起公众注意。对他们来说，狗仔队总是好的。

M：那样生活就太累了。

### 核心词汇记一记

**Words Storm**

inappropriate [ˌinəˈprəupriət] *a.* 不合适的

privacy [ˈpraivəsi] *n.* 隐私

paparazzi [pɑːpəˈrɑːtsi] *n.* 狗仔队（复数）

limelight [ˈlaimlait] *n.* 聚光灯

publicity [pʌbˈlisiti] *n.* 曝光，知名度

**Phrases**

the Grand Canyon 科罗拉多大峡谷

be supposed to do 应该做

die for 追求，渴望

# 4. Amusing Advertisements

## 创意广告

### 知识链接 拓展视野，掌握背景知识

广告创意简单来说就是通过大胆新奇的手法来制造与众不同的视听效果，最大限度地吸引消费者，从而达到产品营销的目的。当今西方企业纷纷打出各种创意广告来吸引顾客，而某些大型跨国公司更是把广告做成一种艺术品，达到让观众喜闻乐见的效果。同时，广告也是文化与文明的一个切片，西方的许多广告都反映了西方文化的各个侧面。欣赏广告，也是我们学习语言、了解世界的便利途径。

### 难点点拨 知识难点看一看，情景实战热热身

1．be accompanied with 伴随着，配合着

Every one of her gesture is accompanied with CG effect which is so well-made that it seems the girl has some magic power.

每个动作都配合上电脑动画，动画配得很好，看起来就像是女孩会魔法一样。

2．be delighted with 欣赏，满意

I am greatly delighted with HP's idea.

我很欣赏惠普的创意。

3．the sale of ……的销售

A good advertisement can forcefully improve the sale of the product.

好的广告能有力地促进产品销售。

4．cram... into... 把……塞进……

These advertisements cram images of their products into your mind by force, quite savagely.

这些广告把产品的形象强行灌输到你的脑海里，非常粗俗。

## 情景实战 跟着老外听一听，读一读，练一练

**会话 1**

Richard: Have you seen the famous advertisement for HP laptops?

Seth: Which one? There are many good advertisements for HP electronic products.

R: A girl is standing there talking about her life and making different gestures, meanwhile every gesture is accompanied with CG effect which is so well-made that it seems the girl has some magic power. With the help of CG effect she keeps conjuring up many interesting images, such as a small ship floating on the waves and an album of beautiful photos.

S: Yes, I am greatly delighted with HP's idea. What fabulous advertisements!

R: I am deeply impressed. Now I'm using an HP laptop, because I like its design—its design of advertisements as well as laptops.

S: A good advertisement can forcefully improve the sale of the product. And a bad advertisement gives a bad impression of the product to the audience, and is suicidal.

R: All in all, a good idea is the key. Many big companies have their amusing advertisements.

理查德：你看过惠普笔记本做的那个有名的广告吗？

赛斯：哪一个？惠普电子产品有许多广告都很棒。

R: 一个女孩站着，一边向我们介绍她的生活，一边做着各种手势动作，同时每个动作都配合上电脑动画，动画配得很好，看起来就像是女孩会魔法一样。她在电脑动画的配合下不断变出许多有趣的图像，比如浮在海浪上的一艘小船，或者一本漂亮的相册。

S: 嗯，我看过，其实这广告有多个版本。我很欣赏惠普的创意。广告做得真棒！

R: 我对这广告印象可深了。现在我就用着一台惠普笔记本，因为我喜欢它的设计——广告的设计和笔记本的设计，我都喜欢。

S: 好的广告能有力地促进产品销售。差的广告则会使受众对产品产生坏印象，这是在自取灭亡。

R: 总之，好的创意是关键。许多大企业都有有创意的广告。

### 核心词汇记一记

#### Words Storm

| | |
|---|---|
| laptop | ['læptɔp] *n.* 笔记本电脑 |
| accompany | [ə'kʌmpəni] *v.* 伴随 |
| conjure | ['kʌndʒə] *v.* 变戏法 |
| float | [fləut] *v.* 漂浮 |
| album | ['ælbəm] *n.* 相册 |
| fabulous | ['fæbjuləs] *a.* 好得难以置信的 |

#### Phrases

| | |
|---|---|
| electronic products | 电子产品 |
| all in all | 总之 |

**会话 2**

Ryan: What makes a good advertisement?

Derek: That's really a question. In my opinion, to design a good ad, you have to grab the public attention first. Then it's important not to make your ad too vulgar or offensive, so that others will not detest it.

R: I have seen many advertisements in China, which are so unpleasant—they cram images of their products into your mind by force, quite savagely. They don't even think about the artistry of advertising. What they do is just shout the names of their products loudly and repeatedly on TV.

D: That's too bad. Maybe it's effective, but it will never give a good impression to customers. Good ads must be artistic. It should be a pleasure to enjoy them. If you are unwilling to read or watch an ad, it is because the ad itself is not good enough.

R: An ad for BMW tells a story of how a spy gets out of his enemies' pursuit and survives through quite a lot of obstacles with his car. It is just like a short Hollywood movie. If all ads could be as good as this, we would give up those soap operas and fall in love with advertisements.

瑞恩：怎样才能做好广告呢？

德里克：这真是个难题。我觉得要做好广告，你得首先吸引大众的注意。然后不能做得太粗俗或惹人厌烦，这样大家就不会对这广告反感了。

R：我看过中国的很多差广告，这些广告把产品的形象强行灌输到你的脑海里，非常粗俗。他们根本不考虑广告的艺术效果，就只会在电视上大声地反复喊产品的名字。

D：太差劲了。也许这广告有效果，但绝不能给观众带来好印象。好广告必须要有艺术性，要让观众看了高兴。如果你不喜欢看广告，那肯定是广告本身不够好。

R：有个宝马轿车广告就讲了一个间谍如何驾车越过艰难险阻逃脱敌人的追捕而幸存下来的故事。这简直就是短版的好莱坞大片。如果所有的广告都能做得这么好，我们也不用看肥皂剧了，肯定会爱上这些广告的。

**核心词汇记一记**

**Words Storm**

detest [di'test] *v.* 讨厌

artistry ['ɑːtistri] *n.* 艺术性

impression [im'preʃən] *n.* 印象

obstacle ['ɔbstəkl] *n.* 妨碍，障碍

**Phrases**

soap opera 肥皂剧

# 5. Charm of the Newspaper

## 报纸的魅力

### 知识链接 拓展视野，掌握背景知识

*英国是一个报纸王国，报纸的历史可以追溯到 200 年之前。英国报纸种类繁多，目前发行的主要报纸是：独立报（The Independent），卫报（The Guardian），每日电讯报（Daily Telegraph），泰晤士报（The Times），金融时报（Financial Times），每日快报（Daily Express），每日邮报（Daily Mail），标准晚报（Evening Standard），都市报（Metro），太阳报（The Sun），每日镜报（Daily Mirror）等。无论在火车上还是地铁里我们都可以发现很多乘客手拿一份报纸，这是一个渡过上下班旅程的好办法，既消除了旅程中沉闷拥挤的烦恼，又获得了当天的必要信息，而且反映了英国人不喜欢与陌生人搭讪的性格特征。*

### 难点点拨 知识难点看一看，情景实战热热身

1．serve as... 作为……用

One is directly managed by government's publicity sectors, and serves as voices of the government.

一种是由政府宣传机构直接经营的作为政府传声筒的报纸。

2．much to one's surprise 出乎某人意料

Much to my surprise, he replied me very kindly.

出乎我意料的是他居然很热心地回复了我。

3．busy doing sth 忙着做某事

He is quite busy doing all kinds of things all day.

他成天忙于处理各种各样的事情。

4．cause a stir 引起轩然大波

You cannot make a mistake, or else you'll cause a stir among your readers or you'll be admonished by the public.

你不能犯错误，不然就会在读者群里引起骚动，甚至你会遭到公众的批评。

## 情景实战 跟着老外听一听，读一读，练一练

**会话 1**

Bordes: Can you tell me something about newspaper in your country?

Carter: Yes. British people love newspapers. While traveling by train or by underground, many people read newspaper. Reading educates them, informs them, and entertains them.

B: In China we also love newspapers. There are two kinds of newspapers—one is directly managed by government's publicity sectors, and serves as voices of the government, such as the *China Daily* and the *People's Daily*. Another kind is not so official, and provides readers with information of all kinds as well as entertainment, such as the *Southern Weekend*.

C: In Britain we also have two kinds of newspaper—broadsheets and tabloids. Broadsheets refer to the newspapers that are more serious, specifically for gentlemen who are well educated and who enjoy a good social position. Broadsheets cater to their fine tastes with articles discussing serious issues such as the world economy and political topics. For example, *The Guardian* and *The Times* are important broadsheets.

B: And what about the tabloids?

C: Tabloids are newspapers for everyone. They contain quite a lot of interesting things, such as gossips and interesting sidelights. Almost everyone likes to read tabloids because they are such entertainment. *The Daily Mirror* is the tabloid I like most.

博尔特：你能谈一谈你们国家报刊的情况吗？

卡特：可以啊。英国人很爱读报。不管是在火车上还是地铁上，你可以看到很多人都在读报。人们通过读报接受教育、获得信息和娱乐。

B：中国人也很爱看报纸。在中国有两大类报纸：一种是由政府宣传机构直接经营的作为政府传声筒的报纸，如《中国日报》和《人民日报》。另一种是非官方报纸，向读者提供信息和各种各样的娱乐，如《南方周末》。

C：在英国我们也有两种报纸——大报和小报。大报指的是那种严肃的报纸，面向的是受过良好教育的有地位的绅士。大报上的文章都是讨论有关世界政治经济等严肃事件的，这正好符合他们的品位。如《卫报》和《泰晤士报》就是英国重要的大报。

B：那什么是小报呢？

C：小报是面向所有人的。这种报纸上的内容非常有趣，如八卦和杂闻轶事。几乎每个人都喜欢读小报，因为从中能得到很多娱乐。《镜报》是我最喜欢的小报。

### 核心词汇记一记

**Words Storm**

| | |
|---|---|
| underground | ['ʌndəgraund] *n.* 地铁 |
| entertain | [entə'tein] *v.* 娱乐 |
| publicity | [pʌb'lisiti] *n.* 宣传 |
| broadsheets | ['brɔːdʃiːts] *n.* 大报 |
| tabloid | ['tæblɔid] *n.* 小报 |
| sidelight | ['saidlait] *n.* 杂闻 |

**Phrases**

| | |
|---|---|
| refer to | 涉及，指的是 |
| cater to | 满足 |

**会话 2**

Julie: Do you like reading newspaper?

Veronica: Of course. Some columnists express very good ideas. You read them to get enlightenment.

J: So which column do you like?

V: Many. I like the fashion column, the motoring column and the financial column, for example.

J: Do you always agree with those columnists?

V: No. Sometimes I will disagree with them. Once I even wrote to a famous columnist complaining about one of his articles. Much to my surprise, he replied me very kindly.

J: I have a friend who is now working in a local newspaper office as an editor. He is quite busy doing all kinds of things all day. Editing is a tiring job. And there are also many journalists working for the newspaper. They always run from one place to another, busy interviewing all kinds of people, to get bits and pieces of information for their news.

V: Yes, journalism is quite demanding. You cannot make a mistake, or else you'll cause a stir among your readers or you'll be admonished by the public. Every word you write must be examined carefully.

J: But I dream of being an editor. I like writing and editing.

茱莉：你喜欢读报吗？

维罗妮卡：当然了。一些专栏作家的观点十分不错。读了以后让人觉得很受启发。

J：那你喜欢哪种专栏呢？

V：很多，比如时尚专栏、汽车专栏、财经专栏。

J：你总是赞同这些专栏作家的观点吗？

V：不是的。有时我也不赞同他们。有一次我甚至给一位专栏作家写信抱怨他的一篇文章。出乎我意料的是他居然很热心地回复了我。

J：我有个朋友，现在在当地一家报社做编辑。他成天忙于处理各种各样的事情。编辑是一件很累的工作。一家报社需要很多记者，他们总是从一个地方跑到另一个地方，忙着采访各种各样的人以采集写新闻需要的琐碎信息。

V：是呀，新闻是专业素养要求很高的行业。你不能犯错误，不然就会在读者群里引起骚动，甚至你会遭到公众的批评。你写的每一个字都必须经过认真的核查。

J：但是我还是梦想能成为一名编辑。我喜欢写作和编辑。

### 核心词汇记一记

**Words Storm**

| | |
|---|---|
| columnist | ['kɔləmnist] *n.* 专栏作家 |
| enlightenment | [in'laitnmənt] *n.* 启迪 |
| financial | [fai'nænʃəl] *a.* 财政的 |
| complain | [kəm'plein] *v.* 抱怨 |
| journalist | ['dʒəːnəlist] *n.* 记者 |
| interview | ['intəvjuː] *v.* 采访 |

**Phrases**

| | |
|---|---|
| fashion column | 时尚专栏 |
| make a mistake | 犯错误 |

# 6. Media Online

## 网络媒体

### 知识链接 拓展视野，掌握背景知识

跟中国一样，西方也有各种网络媒体，而且在这方面西方显然比中国还要发达。据统计，西方主流网站有 Myspace，Facebook，Yahoo!，Google，MSN，Twitter，Youtube 等等。在新闻报道方面，网络媒体一般比传统媒体更自由，也更能给大众提供选择的机会。

### 难点点拨 知识难点看一看，情景实战热热身

1. get online 上网

   You can get online with your mobile phone.

   你可以用手机上网。

2. release 发布

   Youtube allows you to release video clips onto the Internet for millions of people to watch.

   你可以通过 Youtube 把视频短片发布到网上，供几十万人观看。

3. grow rampant（坏事物）猖獗

   Governments should pay much attention not to let them grow rampant, or else our children would be misled.

   这应该引起政府的重视，不能让这些网站太猖獗，否则我们的孩子就给带坏了。

## 情景实战 跟着老外听一听，读一读，练一练

**会话 1**

Michael: Have you read newspaper today?

Joey: No, but I've read news online.

M: Which site do you like most?

J: Yahoo, of course. I can get all kinds of information from it. Sometimes I go to MSN. Microsoft has designed a new search engine, named "Bing". When I cannot find what I want from Google, I turn to Bing to try my luck. I find the online media more helpful and informative. It's hard for me to get what I really want from newspaper, but with a computer and Bing—you just get it!

M: If you are taking a bus or walking outside you cannot use it whereas you can take a newspaper with you, but not a computer.

J: Hey, don't you know you can get online with your mobile phone? I always use my mobile to check emails and read things I like.

M: I know that, but I'm afraid it is far too complex for a computer idiot like me. I can only make phone calls and send messages with my phone.

J: It's not difficult at all. It's easy. Give me your phone and I'll show you how to do it.

M: Great, thanks. Here you are.

迈克尔：今天你读报纸了吗？

乔伊：没呢，可是我上网看新闻了。

M：你最喜欢上什么网站？

J：当然是雅虎了。我能从雅虎上了解到各种消息。有时候我会上 MSN。微软研发了一个新的搜索引擎，叫“必应”。我要是从谷歌上找不到想找的东西，我就去“必应”上碰碰运气。我发现网络媒体真是好用，信息量大。从报纸上很难找到我想要的消息，可是用电脑“必应”一下就找到了。

M：如果你坐公交车或者在外面走路，你就不能上网了。你可以随手带份报纸，可是不能扛个电脑。

J：嘿，你不知道用手机可以上网吗？我整天用手机收发邮件，读想读的东西。

M：我知道。可是我怕对于我这种电脑白痴来说这太复杂了。我只会用手机打电话发短信。

J：这根本就不难，很简单的。给我手机，我教你。

M：好的，谢谢。给你。

### 核心词汇记一记

**Words Storm**

informative [in'fɔːmətiv] *a.* 提供知识的

complex ['kɔmpleks] *a.* 复杂的

**Phrases**

try one's luck 碰运气

make phone calls 打电话

send messages 发短信

**会话 2**

Michelle: Nowadays you can see almost everything online.

Daniel: Yes. Online media has many forms. For example, everyone can use Facebook and Twitter to show his life to his friends, and strangers as well. Youtube allows you to release video clips onto the Internet for millions of people to watch. You can buy and sell on eBay—and e-commerce is developing very fast by the way. Besides that there are regular web portals, such as Yahoo and MSN.

M: I know. You don't need to tell me all this. But there are some websites showing bad things such as sex and violence?

D: I have never visited those sites.

M: But they do exist. Some sites show you porn pictures and novels. Some give you photographs of bloody violence. They contaminate one's soul, and degrade you.

D: Yes, it is a serious problem. At least these sites have to be checked. Governments should pay attention not to let them grow rampant, or else our children would be misled. In my view, we should ban them all, and punish those website developers severely.

M: But in some countries, pornography is allowed for adults.

蜜雪儿: 在今天，你能在网上看到各种东西。

丹尼尔: 是啊，网络媒体有多种形式。比如，谁都可以用 Facebook 和 Twitter 来向朋友或是陌生人展示他的生活。你也可以通过 Youtube 把视频短片发布到网上，供几十万人观看。你还能上 eBay 买东西——顺便说一下，电子商务发展得很快。除此之外，还有些门户网站，比如雅虎和 MSN。

M: 我知道。你根本不用跟我说这些。可有一些网站会发布不良信息，比如色情和暴力的内容。

D: 我个人可从没上过这些网站。

M: 可是确实有这种网站。有些网站上发布淫秽图片和小说，有些展示血腥的图片。这些网站污染大家的心灵，使人堕落。

D: 是啊，这可是个严重的问题。至少该控制这些网站的发展。这应该引起政府的重视，不能让这些网站太猖獗，否则我们的孩子就给带坏了。依我看，我们该取缔所有不良网站，严惩那些做网站的人。

M: 可是在某些国家，色情产品是可以发布给成人的。

**核心词汇记一记**

**Words Storm**

release [ri'li:s] *v.* 发布，散发
e-commerce [i'kɔmə:s] *n.* 电子商务
contaminate [kən'tæmineit] *v.* 污染
rampant ['ræmpənt] *a.* 猖獗的
pornography [pɔ:'nɔgrəfi] *n.* 色情产品

**Phrases**

video clip 视频短片
web portal 门户网站

# 7. Radio Broadcast

# 动听电台

## 知识链接 拓展视野，掌握背景知识

在 1906 年圣诞节前夜，美国的费森登和亚历山德逊在纽约附近设立了一个广播站，并进行了有史以来的第一次广播。广播的内容是两段笑话、一支歌曲和一支小提琴独奏曲。这一广播节目被当时四处分散的持有接收机的人们清晰地收听到了。此后，广播节目逐渐发展起来，得到大家的喜爱。

## 难点点拨 知识难点看一看，情景实战热热身

1．listen to 听

Do you like listening to the radio?

你喜欢听广播吗？

2．means 意味着，表示着

Online broadcast often means better quality, because the signal is not lost in transmission.

在线广播的音质更好，因为信号在传输中不会丢失。

3．talk show 脱口秀

I don't like talk shows and news report on the radio.

我不喜欢谈话类节目，也不喜欢听新闻。

4．as much as 尽量多

I used to take the radio everywhere with me and listen as much English as I could.

我经常走到哪里都随身带着收音机，能听多少英语就听多少。

5．very often 经常

Very often I can only get the main idea of the program.

通常我只能听懂节目的大意。

## 情景实战 跟着老外听一听，读一读，练一练

**会话 1**

Josh: Do you like listening to the radio?

Maria: Yes and no. Years ago I used to listen to the radio a lot, but now I have a computer.

J: So you don't use the radio any longer?

M: Not often, I can download almost everything with my computer. I believe it's a better entertainment.

J: But sometimes you cannot use your computer. For example, when you drive a car the best thing to do is listen to the radio.

M: Yes. You don't need to put your eyes and hands on it. You do just listen.

J: Now we have online broadcast. You can listen to the radio with your computer.

M: An online broadcast often means better quality, because the signal is not lost in transmission.

J: Which programs do you like best?

M: I prefer music! I don't like talk shows and news report on the radio. Music is better. It refreshes me a lot.

J: I still remember when I was young my father gave me a radio as my birthday gift. I was so happy and listened to it every day, but it seems that the age of the radio broadcast is coming to an end. Fewer and fewer people listen to the radio now.

乔希：你喜欢听广播吗？

玛利亚：可以说喜欢也可以说不喜欢。几年以前我经常听很多广播，可是现在我有电脑了。

J：所以你就不再用收音机了？

M：是的。我可以用电脑下载各种资料，我觉得从网络上可以获得更好的娱乐。

J：但是有时候你不能用电脑。比如，你要是开车的话，最好的就是听收音机了。

M：是的。听收音机的时候不需要用眼，也不用手。你只需要听就好了。

J：现在我们有在线广播了。你也可以用电脑听广播。

M：在线广播的音质更好，因为信号在传输中不会丢失。

J：你喜欢什么节目？

M：我最喜欢音乐了。我不喜欢谈话类节目，也不喜欢听新闻。音乐好得多，能给我提神。

J：我还记得我小时候父亲送给我一台收音机作为生日礼物。我当时太高兴了，整天听。但是现在好像用收音机听广播的时代要结束了。现在听收音机的人越来越少了。

### 核心词汇记一记

**Words Storm**

entertainment [ˌentəˈteinmənt] *n.* 娱乐
signal [ˈsignl] *n.* 信号
transmission [trænsˈmiʃən] *n.* 传输
refresh [riˈfreʃ] *v.* 提神

**Phrases**

online broadcast 在线广播
birthday gift 生日礼物

## 会话 2

Bruce: What program are you listening to?

Parry: The BBC news broadcast. I keep myself updated everyday by listening to BBC.

B: Why don't you just get online and read some web-pages instead?

P: I want to practice my listening ability. I'm learning English.

B: It reminds me of my experience when learning English. I used to take the radio everywhere with me and listen to as much English as I could. In this way I would submerge myself into this language.

P: Some programs are interesting. For example, once there was an interview of a Chinese writer about social development of China. I'm particularly interested in how westerners see China and the Chinese people.

B: Do you understand every word of it?

P: Not all, very often I can only get the main idea of the program. But never mind, I'm still getting better and better at understanding what they are talking about.

B: Any interesting news today?

P: Not interesting, but horrifying. A slaughter has begun somewhere in Africa. If you listen to the BBC you'll know there are always tragedies happening everywhere in the world—famine, war, flood, earthquake... We should really thank God for our happy, peaceful life.

布鲁斯：你在听什么节目呢？

派利：BBC 新闻。我坚持每天听 BBC 新闻。

B：为什么不上网从网页上直接看新闻呢？

P：我想锻炼自己的听力。我在学英语呢。

B：这倒叫我想起来我学英语的经历了。我经常走到哪里都随身带着收音机，能听多少英语就听多少。这样我就把自己完全融入到英语中了。

P：有些节目很有趣，比如有一次采访一位中国作家探讨关于中国社会发展的问题。我对西方怎么看中国、怎么看中国人特别感兴趣。

B：你经常能听懂每个词的意思吗？

P：不是的。通常我只能听懂节目的大意。但是没关系，我现在理解得越来越好了。

B：今天有什么有趣的新闻吗？

P：没有有趣的，只有可怕的消息。在非洲一个地方有一场屠杀。如果你听 BBC 你就会知道，世界上总是有各种各样的悲剧——饥荒、战争、洪水、地震……我们真该感谢上帝，现在我们还过着幸福、祥和的生活。

### 核心词汇记一记

#### Words Storm

update [ʌp'deit] *v.* 更新
particularly [pə'tikjuləli] *ad.* 特别
horrify ['hɔrifai] *v.* 使害怕
earthquake ['əːθkweik] *n.* 地震

#### Phrases

remind of 提醒
never mind 没关系

# Literature and Films 文学与电影

# 8. Classic Works

## 经典作品

### 知识链接 拓展视野，掌握背景知识

西方文学现今在世界文学领域占据绝对的优势，各种西方经典作品备受推崇，不仅成为西方文化的重要部分，也渗入到了东方文化中，比如俄裔美国作家纳博科夫（Vladimir Nabokov）的《洛丽塔》，就衍生出一系列的"萝莉"等流行词汇和流行文化。当然，阅读西方经典作品有助于我们更深层次地了解西方文化的精髓。

### 难点点拨 知识难点看一看，情景实战热热身

1．enthrall 吸引，使感兴趣

A good book should enthrall readers and give them reading pleasure.

好书必须吸引读者，给读者带来乐趣。

2．grip 抓住，握住

I was gripped by it.

我完全被吸引住了。

3．not only... but also 不仅……而且

Reading is not only for entertainment, but also for education and enlightenment.

阅读不只是为了消遣，还应当有所收获，有所启发。

4．seemingly 后接形容词，表示"看上去"

They use various theories to explain every novel, and try to find underlying meanings from some seemingly unimportant details.

他们用许多理论来解读小说，试图从一些貌似无关紧要的细节中寻找潜在的意义。

## 情景实战 跟着老外听一听，读一读，练一练

**会话 1**

Warren: What are you reading?

Erik: Mark Twain's *The Adventures of Huckleberry Finn*, it's very amusing, a story about a boy's wandering. It gives us a picture of the early American settlement when the Negros were slaves.

W: Why do you like it? What kind of book, in your opinion, is a good book?

E: I've been considering this question for a long time. For me, a good book must have two qualities—entertainment and significance. First of all, a good book should enthrall readers and give them reading pleasure. If you start reading a boring one you'll lose interest in it very quickly and quit soon enough. If you get into a really good story you'll forget about all peripheral things and just go on reading.

W: Right. I can still remember when I first read Hemingway's *A Farewell to Arms*. I was gripped by it. I imagined myself as Henry the hero in the war, and I fell in love with Catherine the heroine. I was moved to tears.

E: Yes, a good book brings you into its story. It confuses you, making you unclear about whom you really are—you are not yourself, but become the protagonist of the story, and everything that happens to the hero seems as though it is happening to you.

沃伦：你在读什么书？

埃里克：马克·吐温的《哈克贝利费恩历险记》，非常有趣，讲的是一个男孩流浪的故事。这本书描绘了一幅早期美国的图画，那时候黑人还是奴隶。

W：为什么喜欢呢？你觉得什么样的书能算好书？

E：我思考这个问题很久了。在我看来，一本好书必须有两个特点——娱乐性和重要性。首先，好书必须吸引读者，给读者带来乐趣。如果你碰见一本无聊的书，你很快就会厌恶了，不读了。如果你碰到有趣的故事呢，你就会忘记一切琐事，一直读下去。

W：是啊，我还记得我读海明威的《永别了，武器》。我完全被它吸引住了。我觉得我自己就是战争里的主角亨利，我爱上了女主角凯瑟琳。我感动得哭了。

E：是啊，一本好书就能把你带进故事里，让你迷惑，搞不清自己究竟是谁——你好像不是你了，你成了故事的主角，切身感受到故事里的一切。

### 核心词汇记一记

**Words Storm**

| | | |
|---|---|---|
| enthrall | [in'θrɔ:l] | v. 迷住 |
| peripheral | [pə'rifərəl] | a. 次要的 |
| grip | [grip] | v. 抓住 |
| hero | ['hiərəu] | n. 男英雄，男主角 |
| heroine | ['herouin] | n. 女英雄，女主角 |
| protagonist | [prəu'tægənist] | n. 主角 |

**Phrases**

| | |
|---|---|
| in one's opinion | 据某人看来 |
| fall in love with | 爱上，迷恋 |
| bring into | 带进 |
| as though | 好象，仿佛 |

## 会话 2

Summer: Do you think that a good book should "improve" a reader?

Wendy: Of course. Reading is not only for entertainment, but also for education and enlightenment. If you read a novel and find it not enlightening for your soul, then that novel is not worth reading. To read books, is to elevate and purify the soul, to bring us a better understanding of the world and ourselves. We learn how to face our lives more courageously.

S: And this is why some books can become classics, while others fade away into the mists of time.

W: You are right. Many newly-written novels only provide superficial entertainment, but not the depth and education of a classic. This is the reason why they will never hold that timeless appeal to the reader, by contrast, many old books are forever popular. They will be eternally alive in the hearts of readers.

S: So we should have literary criticism to analyze all these classics.

W: Yes. You know, I'm studying English literature. By now all important novels have already been carefully studied by those literary critics. They use various theories to explain every novel, and try to find underlying meanings from some seemingly unimportant details—they endeavor to reveal the authors' heart fully to us, that way we can better understand their works.

莎玛：好书应该使读者进步，对吗？

温蒂：当然了。阅读不只是为了消遣，还应当有所收获，有所启发。如果你读了一本小说，发现读后对你心灵成长没什么用，这书就根本不值得读了。我们读书，应当能让自己的心灵得到净化和提升，让自己更能看清这个世界，认识自己，更有勇气去面对生活。

S：这也是为什么有些书能成为经典的原因吧。其他的书就只能是随着时间而消失了。

W：是啊。很多新出的书都只供肤浅的消遣，不能像经典作品一样有深度，来教育读者，因此这些书不会长久吸引读者。相比之下，许多老书永远都畅销，他们永远都活在我们读者心里。

S：所以我们要用文学批评的态度去分析这些经典作品。

W：是啊。你知道，我现在学的就是英语文学。到现在为止，所有重要的小说都被文学批评家仔细研究过了。他们用许多理论来解读小说，试图从一些貌似无关紧要的细节中寻找潜在的意义——他们把作者真正的意图呈现给读者，这样我们也就能更好地理解作品了。

### 核心词汇记一记

#### Words Storm

| | | |
|---|---|---|
| elevate | ['eliveit] | *v.* 提升 |
| purify | ['pjuərifai] | *v.* 净化 |
| eternal | [i'tə:nl] | *a.* 永恒的 |
| analyze | ['ænəlaiz] | *v.* 分析 |

#### Phrases

| | |
|---|---|
| English literature | 英语文学 |
| literary critic | 文学批评家 |

# 9. Shakespeare

## 莎士比亚

### 知识链接 拓展视野，掌握背景知识

莎士比亚是英语文学中公认的最伟大的作家。他 1564 年出生在位于艾汶河畔的斯特拉特福德镇，1616 年去世。在世时就已经是成功的剧作家了。他的戏剧作品很多，著名的有四大悲剧和四大喜剧。另外他也是伟大的诗人，把十四行诗发扬光大，创作了不少脍炙人口的诗作。多年以来，他的剧作一直被反复演出，也有许多版本的电影改编于他的剧本。

### 难点点拨 知识难点看一看，情景实战热热身

1．adapt 改编

There are many performances in theatres, and you can also enjoy different versions of films adapted from this play.

剧院里有很多演出，你也可以欣赏到改编于这个剧本的不同版本的电影。

2．cheat sb. into doing sth. 欺骗某人做某事

He is cheated by the villain, Iago, into killing his own faithful wife Desdemona in a temper, thinking her unchaste.

他被恶人埃古欺骗了，以为妻子黛斯德莫娜对自己不忠，一怒之下把她错杀了。

3．advise sb. to do 建议某人做某事

More than one hundred sonnets were for a mysterious "Fair Lord", advising him to choose a girl and have children, pleasing him by saying that although time flies, my friend—your image will be forever preserved in my eternal poetry.

一百多首十四行是为一位神秘的年轻人写的，嘱咐他赶紧娶妻生子，又取悦他说，虽然时间飞逝，你的形象却因为在我的诗中而得以不朽。

## 情景实战 跟着老外听一听，读一读，练一练

**会话 1**

Nancy: Have you ever read Shakespeare?

Emma: Of course. It's a must for me. You know I'm studying literature.

N: So which play do you like?

E: I like *King Lear*. It's one of his "great tragedies", telling a story of a willful king and his daughters.

N: Yes. It's a play of renowned reputation. There are many performances in theatres, and you can also enjoy different versions of films adapted from this play. And the other three "great tragedies" are... let me see, *Othello*, *Macbeth*, and...

E: And *Hamlet*, which is even more famous than *King Lear*. It tells a story of a Danish prince Hamlet, whose father, the old king, is murdered and has his throne usurped by the father's brother, Claudius. Hamlet then seeks chances to take revenge.

N: Ah...What about *Othello* and *Macbeth*?

E: Othello is Moorish. He is a Venetian general in the army, quite honest and brave. But he is cheated by the villain, Iago, into killing his own faithful wife Desdemona in a temper, thinking her unchaste. Macbeth is also a general of great military feats. He murders the king and usurps the throne, and finally receives his punishment. Shakespeare is a genius. He has a keen mind, always ready to reveal the dark side of the world, and to show us the ugliness of human nature.

南希：你读过莎士比亚的作品吗？

爱玛：当然，我必须读啊。你知道的，我就是学文学的。

N：那么你喜欢哪个剧本？

E：我喜欢《李尔王》。这是"伟大悲剧"之一，讲的是一个任性的国王和他女儿的故事。

N：是啊。这可是出了名的剧。剧院里有很多演出，你也可以欣赏到改编于这个剧本的不同版本的电影。其他三部悲剧是……我想想，《奥赛罗》、《麦克白》，还有……

E：还有《哈姆雷特》，比《李尔王》还要出名，讲的是一个丹麦王子哈姆雷特的故事。他的父亲，也就是老国王，被其弟克劳迪斯杀害，并且克劳迪斯篡夺了王位。哈姆雷特就找机会为父亲报仇。

N：哦……那《奥赛罗》和《麦克白》呢？

E：奥赛罗是摩尔人。他在威尼斯带兵，是个特别勇敢的人。但是他却被恶人埃古欺骗了，以为妻子黛斯德莫娜对自己不忠，一怒之下把她错杀了。麦克白也是战功赫赫的将军。他谋害了国王篡了位，最后受到了惩罚。莎士比亚是个天才，他很有智慧，总是能揭露这个世界的黑暗面，向我们展示人性的丑恶。

### 核心词汇记一记

**Words Storm**

| | |
|---|---|
| willful | ['wilful] *a.* 任性的 |
| reputation | ['repju:'teiʃən] *n.* 名誉 |
| throne | ['θrəun] *n.* 王位 |
| usurp | [ju:'zə:p] *v.* 篡夺 |
| villain | ['vilən] *n.* 坏蛋 |
| unchaste | [ʌn'tʃeist] *a.* 不贞洁的 |
| ugliness | ['ʌglinis] *n.* 丑恶 |

**Phrases**

| | |
|---|---|
| take revenge | 复仇 |
| in a temper | 发脾气 |
| human nature | 人性 |

## 会话 2

Roger: Have you some knowledge about Shakespeare the playwright?

Nick: Yes. He was born in 1564 in Stratford. At the age of 18, Shakespeare married the 26-year-old Anne Hathaway. After the marriage he disappeared for quite a few years. Then he reappeared in London and became a great playwright. He was popular at that time, loved by the general public. When he became old, he retired and lived in the country.

R: Good. And can you tell me something about his sonnets?

N: All right. He wrote 154 poems. More than one hundred were for a mysterious "Fair Lord", advising him to choose a girl and have children, pleasing him by saying that although time flies, my friend—your image will be forever preserved in my eternal poetry.

R: I remember there is a "Dark Lady" then.

N: Yes. Scores of his sonnets were for the dark lady. It seems that Shakespeare once fell in love with the lady, but his love was not returned. He feels depressed.

R: Which sonnet do you like most?

N: Sonnet 18, of course, *Shall I Compare Thee to a Summer's Day*.

罗杰：你了解戏剧家莎士比亚吗？

尼克：了解。他 1564 年出生在英国中部的斯特拉福德镇。18 岁的时候娶了 26 岁的安妮·哈瑟维。结婚之后他消失了几年。后来重返伦敦，成了伟大的戏剧家。那个时候他很受大家欢迎。暮年之时便隐退田园。

R：不错。你能介绍一下他的十四行诗吗？

N：好的。他一共写了 154 首十四行诗。其中有 100 多首是为一位神秘的年轻贵族写的，嘱咐他赶紧娶妻生子，又取悦他说“虽然时间飞逝，我的朋友，你的形象却因为在我的诗中而得以不朽。”

R：我记得还有一个“黑夫人”什么的。

N：是的。有几十首是为这位女子写的。好像莎士比亚曾经爱上了她，可只是一厢情愿。他觉得很郁闷。

R：你最喜欢他的哪首诗呢？

N：当然是第 18 首——《我能否把你比作夏天》。

### 核心词汇记一记

**Words Storm**

playwright ['pleirait] *n.* 剧作家
sonnet ['sɔnit] *n.* 十四行诗
poetry ['pəuitri] *n.* 诗歌

**Phrases**

scores of 几十

# 10. What Makes a Bestseller

## 畅销书的秘密

### 知识链接 拓展视野，掌握背景知识

*1895 年美国出版业期刊《书商》首次每月统计并刊出 6 本在各书店销路最好的图书排名表，称为“6 本畅销书”。1910 年，美国期刊《每月图书》也根据对全国各地 100 家书店销售情况的调查，每月刊登畅销书排名表。被调查的图书既包括小说，也包括其他文学作品。下面就让我们来探求一下畅销书的秘密。*

### 难点点拨 知识难点看一看，情景实战热热身

1．bestseller 畅销书

It's a bestseller of this year.

这是今年的一本畅销书。

2．millions of 几百万

Millions of copies have been sold and you can find it in every bookstore.

已经卖出几百万册了，在所有书店的架子上都能找到这本书。

3．I wish I could 表示“希望”

I wish I could publish it and become a famous novelist.

我希望能够出版它并且成为一个著名的小说家。

4．join the army 参军

A boy joins the army to serve his country.

一个男孩去参军，想要报效他的祖国。

5．be angry about 对……感到愤怒

Readers at first will feel angry about the girl's betrayal, but then begin to worry about her life.

读者们一开始会对女孩的背叛感到很生气，然后便开始担心她的命运了。

## 情景实战 跟着老外听一听，读一读，练一练

**会话 1**

Teresa: What are you reading?

Paul: A novel, *Twilight*, quite popular. There are talks about it everywhere. So I just bought one and look what's new in it.

T: Interesting?

P: Of course. It's a bestseller of this year. Millions of copies have been sold and you can find it in every bookstore.

T: Why are there some books so popular? Have you thought about it?

P: I don't know. But every year, or even every month, there are many new books coming out, and some of them will be bestsellers. The whole world then will talk about these books for some time, and then dump them and never see them again.

T: In my opinion, a book can become a bestseller because the author sees something other people cannot see. For example, a novelist travels through the whole Africa, and sees many strange things there, and then he can write all these things into his books. Others haven't gone through adventures like this, so they feel the book thrilling—it shows a new world for them. However, after they have seen all these, they get bored again and will never read the book twice.

特丽莎：你正在读什么书？

保罗：一本小说《暮光之城》，现在非常流行。到处都在谈论它。所以我也买了本，看看内容究竟怎么样。

T：有意思吗？

P：当然了。这是今年的一本畅销书。已经卖出几百万册了，在所有书店的架子上都能找到这本书。

T：为什么有些书这么畅销呢？你想过为什么吗？

P：我不知道，但是每一年，甚至每个月都有很多新书出来，只有一部分能够成为畅销书。然后一段时间里整个世界都会谈论这本书，然后抛弃它们，再也不会看一眼。

T：在我看来，一本书之所以能成为畅销书是因为作者看到了一些旁人无法观察到的事情。比如一个小说家穿越了整个非洲，并且在那儿看到了很多奇怪的事情，然后他把所有的事情都写进书里。而其他人并不曾亲身经历过这些冒险，所以他们觉得这本书很刺激——它为他们展现了一个新世界。但是，等他们看完之后，他们就又觉得无聊了，绝对不会再读第二遍。

### 核心词汇记一记

**Words Storm**

bookstore ['bukstɔː] *n.* 书店
dump [dʌmp] *v.* 丢弃
adventure [əd'ventʃə] *v.* 冒险
thrilling ['θriliŋ] *a.* 兴奋的

**Phrases**

go through 经历
get bored 厌烦

**会话 2**

Dan: I'm writing a novel now. I wish I could publish it and become a famous novelist.

Bob: What an ambitious dream! Can you tell me something about your story?

D: Of course. A boy joins the army to serve his country. And then he goes abroad for a war. His girlfriend betrays him when he is absent. The boy comes back from the war as a hero, but he feels angry about the girl's betrayal, and wants to torture and kill her in a horrible way. The girl escapes finally, and kills the boy.

B: Great. So what do you want to express in the novel?

D: Nothing but emotion. For a bestseller the emotion is important, you have to let your readers feel what the hero feels. Readers at first will feel angry about the girl's betrayal, but then begin to worry about her life. The pursuit will be sensational—explosions, car crashes... and the boy will finally prove a man of cold blood. Quite like a Hollywood movie, isn't it?

B: Yes. But I think you should put more things into it, to add something philosophical into it, so that it can be educational.

D: I'll think about it.

丹：我现在正在写一本小说。我希望能够出版并且成为一个著名的小说家。

鲍勃：多么富有创意的梦想呀！你能告诉我你要写的故事吗？

D：当然。一个男孩去参军，想要报效他的祖国。然后他被派往了海外战场。当他不在的时候，他的女朋友背叛了他。男孩从战场回来后成了一个英雄，但是他仍然对女友的背叛感到生气，想要用一种恐怖的方法折磨和杀死这个女孩。最后这个女孩逃跑了，并且杀死了这个男孩。

B：挺棒的，那么你想通过小说表达什么呢？

D：除了情感，别无他物。对于畅销小说来说，情感是最重要的。你要让你的读者和这个英雄感同身受。读者们一开始会对女孩的背叛感到很生气，然后便开始担心她的命运了。追击的过程将十分惊悚——爆炸、车祸等等。男孩最终变得冷酷无情。是不是很像好莱坞电影？

B：是的，但是我觉得你应该再多加点东西进去，加点哲学元素，使它具有教育意义。

D：我会考虑的。

### 核心词汇记一记

**Words Storm**

| | | |
|---|---|---|
| ambitious | [æm'biʃəs] | *a.* 有野心的 |
| betray | [bi'trei] | *v.* 背叛 |
| absent | ['æbsənt] | *a.* 缺席的，不在的 |
| sensational | [sen'seiʃənl] | *a.* 耸人听闻的 |

**Phrases**

| | |
|---|---|
| car crash | 车祸 |
| cold blood | 冷血 |

# 11. Poetry and Poets

## 诗人诗语

### 知识链接 拓展视野，掌握背景知识

*西方的诗歌源远流长，从古希腊时期我们就有荷马和萨福，后来我们有但丁、波特拉克、乔叟、莎士比亚等等。直到现在，诗歌一直都敲击着人类心灵最脆弱、最敏感的地方。而诗人则是“世界之光”，照亮了黑暗，给读者一丝启迪、一丝感动。从这方面说，诗人的功劳不可谓不大。若有机会背上一些英文诗歌，不仅对英语学习大有裨益，也能增加对文学以及人生的认识。*

### 难点点拨 知识难点看一看，情景实战热热身

1. hear of 听说

   Have you ever heard of Imagism?

   你听说过意象派吗？

2. overflow of sth. 流溢，流散

   Poetry is the "spontaneous overflow of powerful feelings."

   诗歌应当是“强烈感情的自发流溢”。

3. more or less 差不多

   Other Romantic poets are more or less the same on this point.

   其他的浪漫主义诗人也或多或少在这点上相同。

4. from... to... 从……到……

   The poem is a brief personal history of the poet, from innocence to maturity.

   这首诗是诗人的个人简史，诉说了他从幼年到成年的心路历程。

## 情景实战 跟着老外听一听，读一读，练一练

**会话 1**

Nicolas: I'm trying to recite Tennyson's *Break Break Break*. I find it enchanting.

Tony: "Break, break, break, On thy cold gray stones, O Sea! And I would that my tongue could utter The thoughts that arise in me."

N: Gorgeous! You can recite it.

T: Yes, I like Tennyson's poetry very much. He was a poet laureate in the Victorian Age.

N: For me, I love poetic images. A poem must have images—elegant images. It cannot just talk about some abstract things like a person's thoughts. Romantic and Victorian poetry cannot give me enough pleasure. I like modern American poetry better. Have you ever heard of Imagism?

T: Yes. It's a movement launched by the American poet Ezra Pound in the early twentieth century. Pound asserted that a good poem should be full of beautiful images instead of abstract ideas.

N: Right. One of his famous poem is *In a Station of the Metro*, quite short but impressive. "The apparition of these faces in the crowd; Petals on a wet, black bough."

T: The Imagist movement was supported by many literary giants. For example, T.S. Eliot's theories are very close to it.

尼古拉斯：我在背丁尼生的《海浪喧哗》。我觉得这诗很迷人。

托尼："哗啦，哗啦，哗啦，冲上阴冷的礁石，啊海浪！愿我的语言能够表达埋藏心底的惆怅。"

N：不错嘛！你能背了。

T：是的。我非常喜欢丁尼生的诗。他是维多利亚时期的桂冠诗人。

N：我喜欢诗化的意象。一首诗必须有意象——优雅的意象。诗歌不能单纯讨论抽象的东西，比如一个人的思想。浪漫派和维多利亚诗歌不能给我足够的美感。我更喜欢现代美国诗歌。你听说过意象派吗？

T：听说过。意象派运动是在 20 世纪早期由埃兹拉·庞德发起的。庞德宣称，一首好诗应当满是漂亮的意象，而不是抽象的思想。

N：是的。他的最著名的一首诗是《在地铁站》，非常短，可是给人印象很深。"人群中这些面孔幽灵般浮现；湿漉漉的黑色枝条上的花瓣。"

T：许多文学大家都支持意象派运动。比如，T.S. 艾略特的理论就与之非常相近。

### 核心词汇记一记

**Words Storm**

recite [ri'sait] *v.* 背诵
abstract ['æbstrækt] *a.* 抽象的
apparition [ˌæpə'riʃən] *n.* 显现，幽灵

**Phrases**

poet laureate 桂冠诗人
literary giant 文学大家

**会话 2**

Kevin: Do you like Wordsworth and his Romantic poetry?

Nigel: Of course. In his opinion, poetry is the "spontaneous overflow of powerful feelings." When you submerge yourself into nature, and enjoy the beauty and purity of it, you feel poetry and you can just write it down. It's a natural thing.

K: Yes, you just show your feeling in your poem. The emotion of the common people is most precious. What about other Romantic poets?

N: Other Romantic poets are more or less the same on this point. For example, Coleridge wrote *Kubla Khan*, implying that a poet should dive into his own subconscious to acquire the inspiration of poetry; Byron and Shelley wrote poetry with great passion, and Keats' style is elegant and aesthetic.

K: Of these poems, which do you like most?

N: Wordsworth's *Tintern Abbey*. It is a brief personal history of the poet, from innocence to maturity. It also portrays the poet's intimate relationship with nature. It's quite enchanting and enlightening. I think we can learn a lot from it.

凯文：你喜欢华兹华斯和他的浪漫主义诗歌吗？

奈杰尔：当然了。在他看来，诗歌应当是"强烈感情的自发流溢"。当你陷入自然之中，享受自然的美丽和纯净，你就能感觉到诗意，你就会写下诗句。这是油然而生的。

K：是的，诗歌应当就是表现人的情感的。普通人的感情是最宝贵的。其他的浪漫主义诗人怎么样？

N：其他的浪漫主义诗人也或多或少在这点上相同。比如，柯勒律治写了《忽必烈汗》，指出一个诗人必须深入到自己的潜意识之中来获取诗歌的灵感；拜伦和雪莱也是用满腔激情写诗，而济慈的风格是优雅而唯美的。

K：你最喜欢哪首诗？

N：华兹华斯的《丁登寺》。这首诗是诗人的个人简史，诉说了他从幼年到成年的心路历程。这首诗也描述了诗人跟自然之间的亲密关系，令人陶醉，也很有启发性。我觉得我们能从中获益不少。

### 核心词汇记一记

#### Words Storm

spontaneous [spɔn'teiniəs] *a.* 自发的
overflow [ˌəuvə'fləu] *v.* 流露
inspiration [ˌinspə'reiʃən] *n.* 灵感
elegant ['eligənt] *a.* 优雅的
innocence ['inəsəns] *n.* 纯真，天真

#### Phrases

a matter of course 理所当然的事
submerge into 浸入
dive into 潜入

# 12. Worst-sellers

## 糟糕烂书

### 知识链接 拓展视野，掌握背景知识

*当今出版业到了非常混乱的时期，许多人随意写些东西就能够出书发表，原因是商业利益的驱使。在这种情况下，分辨好书和坏书的任务就落到了各位读者身上。首先，看不懂的甚至没意思的不一定是坏书，许多经典著作，比如乔伊斯的《尤利西斯》(Ulysses)就以晦涩难懂著称。常读此类经典，有助于思想和人生观的成熟。*

### 难点点拨 知识难点看一看，情景实战热热身

1. find+ 名词 + 形容词，感觉某件事物如何

   I found this book extremely terrible to read.

   我觉得这书不好看。

2. a matter of ……的问题

   It's just a matter of translation.

   只是翻译的问题。

3. make a great effort to do 用心、努力做某事

   Sometimes a good book will be very difficult to read and you have to make a great effort to understand the author's real intention.

   有时候一本好书也会很难读的，你必须花功夫来理解作者的真正意图。

4. make up 编造

   Everyone can make up a shoddy story and publish it.

   每个人都能编造一个粗制滥造的故事来发表。

## 情景实战 跟着老外听一听，读一读，练一练

**会话 1**

Gary: Yesterday I bought a book, the Chinese version of a novel called *Lord of the Flies*, but I found it extremely terrible to read.

Sony: Why? It's one of the best literary works on earth.

G: Really? I don't get that. What I could see are unnatural words and sentences.

S: Wait, are you talking about the Chinese version? Maybe it's just a matter of the translation. I suggest you go back to the original one, since you can read English.

G: Good... By the way, I found Faulkner's *The Sound and the Fury* also hard to read. Why can it be so reputable? I always wonder why there are so many famous works I dislike.

S: You mean Faulkner? He's difficult, but philosophically profound. If you cannot understand those classics, you'd better think about whether it's your own problem. What's your ideal good book?

G: First of all, I have to understand it easily and without difficulty. It should make me comfortable while reading.

S: That's the problem. Sometimes a good book will be very difficult to read and you have to make a great effort to understand the author's real intention. This is somewhat like physical training. Easy reading may slow down your mind and slacken your intelligence.

盖瑞：昨天我买了一本书，是中文版的小说《蝇王》。可是我觉得这书不好看。

索尼：为什么这么说啊？这可是全球最经典的书之一。

G：真的吗？我不明白。我觉得词句都太造作了。

S：等等。你是说中文版的吧？也许只是翻译的问题。我建议你读英文原版。

G：好吧。顺便说一下，我发现福克纳的《喧哗与骚动》也很没劲。为什么这书那么有名呢？我就奇怪了，为什么这么多有名的书我都不喜欢。

S：你说福克纳？他的书很难读，但是很有哲学深度。如果你不能理解那些经典的话，你最好就想想是不是你自己的问题了。你觉得什么样的书才算好书？

G：首先，这书必须得易读，不能太难懂。应当让我读起来很舒服。

S：这就是问题所在了。有时候一本好书也会很难读的，你必须花功夫来理解作者的真正意图。这就跟体育锻炼一样，太简单的书使你的脑筋转得越来越慢，思维越来越迟钝。

### 核心词汇记一记

**Words Storm**

| | | |
|---|---|---|
| unnatural | [ˌʌn'nætʃərəl] | *a.* 造作的 |
| reputable | ['repjutəbl] | *a.* 有名的 |
| intention | [in'tenʃən] | *n.* 意图 |
| slacken | ['slækən] | *v.* 使松弛 |

**Phrases**

slow down 使变慢

**会话 2**

Nancy: This is the worst book that I've ever read. I'll drop it.

Emma: Why? I find the cover beautifully painted.

N: The story it tells is self-contradictory and inconsistent.

E: Maybe it's a special technique or something. Who knows?

N: Definitely not. It's obviously a huge defect and the motive for the protagonist's deeds is not justifiable. It seems that the writer wrote the story for the story's own sake, and he was never clever enough to put anything good in it.

E: There are so many people writing so many books now. Everyone can make up a shoddy story and publish it. This is a real problem for our culture nowadays.

N: Several decades ago only the most knowledgeable and talented people could write and publish. At that time a book was always considered as sacred, and a writer, respectable.

E: Let's go back to good old classics.

南希：这是我读过的最烂的书了。我没法继续读了。

爱玛：为什么？封面很漂亮啊。

N: 书里的故事自相矛盾，破绽百出。

E: 也许是作者的特殊技巧什么的呢，谁知道呢？

N: 肯定不是。这肯定是大的瑕疵。主角的行为动机根本说不过去。就好像作者是单纯为了写故事而写故事，根本就没思考往故事里添加什么好思想。

E: 现在太多的人写了太多的书。每个人都能编造一个粗制滥造的故事来发表。这真是我们当今文化的问题所在。

N: 是的。几十年前，只有最有知识和才华的人才能写东西发表。那个时候，大家总觉得书就是神圣的，而作者总是受人尊重。

E: 让我们回头看看昔日的经典吧。

**核心词汇记一记**

**Words Storm**

| | | |
|---|---|---|
| cover | ['kʌvə] | *n.* 封面 |
| unreadable | ['ʌn'riːdəbl] | *a.* 不能读的 |
| inconsistent | [ˌinkən'sistənt] | *a.* 不一致 |
| credulous | ['kredjuləs] | *a.* 轻信的 |
| defect | [di'fekt] | *n.* 缺陷 |
| protagonist | [prəu'tægənist] | *n.* 主角 |
| justifiable | ['dʒʌstifaiəbl] | *a.* 说得通的 |

**Phrases**

| | |
|---|---|
| self-contradictory | 自相矛盾 |
| shoddy story | 粗制滥造的故事 |

# 13. Classic Films

# 经典老片

## 知识链接 拓展视野，掌握背景知识

百看不厌的还是经典老片。在影像的世界中，我们感受亲情、爱情、友情，感受爱，感受恨。我们可以想象自己拥有丰富多彩的、激动人心的生活；想象自己是一个帅哥、一个猛男、一个绅士、一个富豪、一个特工、一个罪犯；想象自己拥有完美的爱情、亲密的友情、成功的事业、幸福的家庭、大把的钞票、优质的睡眠、光明的未来、社会的尊重、人民的爱戴以及历史的记载。穿越时光隧道，我们听到岁月悠长的叹息瞬间凝结成永恒。

## 难点点拨 知识难点看一看，情景实战热热身

1. star（动词）主演

   Who stars it?

   哪些明星演的？

2. class 阶级，阶层

   the working class 工人阶级，the middle class 中产阶级

   They belong to different classes.

   他们是不同阶层的人。

3. good old days 过去的美好时光

   Watching it, you can feel the nostalgia of the good old days.

   看了这部电影，你就会对那逝去的美好时光产生深深的怀念。

4. recommend sth. to sb. 推荐

   I highly recommend them to you.

   我强烈向你推荐。

5. black and white 黑白的

   a black and white film

   黑白电影

## 情景实战 跟着老外听一听，读一读，练一练

**会话 1**

Sara: What are you watching?

Joey: *Roman Holiday*. A classic, black and white, but still very nice.

S: Who stars in it?

J: Audrey Hepburn and Gregory Peck.

S: Famous. I've heard of it, but I haven't watched it. What's it about?

J: Hepburn is a princess of a certain European kingdom. She goes to Rome and has a love affair with Peck, a poor journalist. But they finally part, because they belong to different classes—a princess and a journalist cannot be together. They played very well—Hepburn is so beautiful and charming that I cannot help falling into an imaginary love affair with her.

S: So it's a tragic love story, somewhat like *Waterloo Bridge*.

J: Yes. But it is more amusing and light-hearted, and not so many twists and turns. Watching it, you can feel the nostalgia of the good old days, the care-free holiday in the beautiful city of Rome.

S: Who is the director?

J: I have no idea. But if you like, sit down and watch with me. You'll find it interesting.

S: It seems that you have already watched it before. You're so familiar with it.

J: It's the second time I have watched it, and I still like it so much.

S: Well then, I must sit and watch.

萨拉：你看什么电影呢？

乔伊：《罗马假日》，是一部经典的黑白电影，非常好看。

S：哪些明星演的？

J：奥黛丽·赫本和格里高利·派克。

S：他们都很有名啊，但是我还没有看过这部电影，电影的内容怎么样啊？

J：赫本是欧洲某个王国的公主，她去了罗马，并且和一个穷记者派克产生了爱情。但是最终他们还是分开了，因为他们是不同阶层的人——一个公主和一个穷记者是无法在一起的。他们演得非常好，赫本是如此的美丽动人，她的魅力让我禁不住在想象中跟她陷入了爱河。

S：看来这个爱情故事是个悲剧啊。有点像《魂断蓝桥》。

J：是啊，但是这部电影更加有意思和轻松诙谐，没有那么多的曲折。看了这部电影，你就会对那逝去的美好时光产生深深的怀念，怀念在美丽的罗马城那无忧无虑的假期。

S：导演是谁呀？

J：这我就不知道了。如果你喜欢的话，坐下来跟我一起看吧，你会感到很有趣的。

S：你以前好像看过这部电影了，因为你对它好熟悉啊。

J：这是我第二次看了，还是那么喜欢。

S：那我可得坐下来看一看了。

### 核心词汇记一记

**Words Storm**

| | |
|---|---|
| princess | ['prinsis] *n.* 公主 |
| kingdom | ['kiŋdəm] *n.* 王国 |
| imaginary | [i'mædʒinəri] *a.* 想象的 |
| amusing | [ə'mju:ziŋ] *a.* 有趣的 |
| nostalgia | [nɔ'stældʒiə] *n.* 怀旧 |

**Phrases**

| | |
|---|---|
| have a love affair with | 与……陷入爱河 |
| belong to | 属于 |

**会话 2**

Charlie: What's your favorite movie?

Serena: Let me think about it... *The Last Emperor*, and *Homo Sapiens*.

C: I've seen *The Last Emperor*. It's artistically beautiful, telling me quite a lot about the history of China, as well as man's sadness and helplessness in a stark political environment. What is *Homo Sapiens*? It's not English, obviously.

S: It's a French film. The name "Homo Sapiens" is Latin, meaning "intelligent human kind", and actually refers to modern human kind. The film shows us a brief history of human evolution with many amusing stories, an easy introduction to anthropology. What about your favorite movie?

C: *Wild Strawberries*, it tells the story of an old doctor's life and his inner struggle. *Les Quatre Cents Coups*—*Four Hundred Blows*, is a film about a lonely boy's miserable life. I love these films are real classics.

S: Are they quite old? I've never heard of them.

C: Yes, quite old, all black and white. I highly recommend them to you.

查　理：你最喜欢的电影是什么？

塞雷娜：让我想想……应该是《末代皇帝》和 *Homo Sapiens* 吧。

C：我看过《末代皇帝》，它在艺术上非常美。这部电影使我了解了很多关于中国的历史，还有在严酷的政治环境里人的悲哀和无助。"*Homo Sapiens*"是什么意思？显然这不是英语。

S：这是一部法国电影。它的名字是拉丁语，意思是"智人"，实际上指的是现代人类。这部电影用很多有趣的小故事向我们展示了关于人类进化的一个简要历史概括，是关于人类学的一个简单介绍。你最喜欢的电影是什么呢？

C：《野草莓》，它讲述了一个医生的生活和他内心挣扎的故事。还有"*Les Quatre Cents Coups*"——《四百击》，这部电影讲的是一个孤独男孩的悲惨生活。我喜欢这样的电影，他们是真正的经典。

S：这些电影很老了吗？我怎么都没听说过呢。

C：是呀，很老了，都是黑白片。我强烈向你推荐。

**核心词汇记一记**

**Words Storm**

| | |
|---|---|
| stark | [stɑːk] *a.* 严酷的 |
| Latin | ['lætin] *n.* 拉丁语 |
| intelligent | [in'telidʒənt] *a.* 智力的 |
| evolution | [ˌiːvə'luːʃən] *n.* 进化 |
| anthropology | [ænθrə'pɔlədʒi] *n.* 人类学 |

**Phrases**

| | |
|---|---|
| refer to | 指的是 |
| a brief history of | 关于……的简短历史 |

# 14. Blockbusters

## 震撼大片

### 知识链接　拓展视野，掌握背景知识

顾名思义，大片就是由大导演、大腕、大制作、大投入、大场面、大阵容、大回报等打造的“大”级别的电影作品。比如大家比较熟悉的《泰坦尼克号》，导演是詹姆斯·卡梅隆，演员有莱昂纳多·迪卡普里奥、凯特·温丝莱特、凯茜·贝茨、格罗丽亚·斯图尔特等，获得了第69届奥斯卡最佳影片、最佳导演、最佳音效、最佳摄影等11项大奖。《泰坦尼克号》在全球的票房收入为18亿美元，其中北美地区收入为6亿美元，是目前电影史上票房记录最高的影片。

### 难点点拨　知识难点看一看，情景实战热热身

1. so...that... 如此……以至于……

   Human technology has developed so well that we now can make those fantastic scenes like real.

   人类技术发展如此迅猛，以至于我们做出的那些精彩的电影场景都跟真的一样。

2. grip 抓住

   As a blockbuster, it must grip the audience tightly, and shock them.

   作为一部大片，它必须要能够紧紧地抓住观众的心并且使他们感到震撼。

3. be based on 根据，建立在……之上

   It is based on a true incident in Somalia.

   这是根据索马里的真实事件改编的。

4. get out of the plight 脱离困境

   Bullets are everywhere that a soldier cannot get out of the plight.

   子弹横飞，士兵们根本无处可躲。

5. sacrifice sth. for sb. 为某人牺牲某物

   Soldiers sacrifice their lives for each other.

   士兵们为彼此牺牲自己的生命。

## 情景实战 跟着老外听一听，读一读，练一练

**会话 1**

Ramon: Have you heard about the movie *The Transformers*?

Marlon: Of course. When I was young I loved that cartoon very much—war between Autobot and Decepticon, Optimus Prime, Megatron, Humblebee, Jazz, Ironhide, and Starscream. It is so cool!

R: *The Transformers* have already become an important part of our culture. We'll never forget those handsome machines who can transform from the human shape into a car, a helicopter or a fighter plane. But we've already had a movie before. In 2007, screen director Michael Bay gave us the first transformer movie.

M: A blockbuster.

R: Of course. Its box office earnings have reached 700 million dollars.

M: Now I think we have another transformer movie.

R: Yes, *Transformers 2: Revenge of the Fallen*. There are so many special effects. Human technology has developed so well that we now can make those fantastic scenes like real.

M: So many explosions, so many beautiful weapons, so many handsome guys and sexy girls.

R: As a blockbuster it must grip the audience tightly and shock them. They invest a lot of money to achieve fantastic effects. For example, the 1997 version of *Titanic* cost 200 million dollars, and the director James Cameron decided to rebuild a large model ship as big as the real Titanic.

雷蒙：你听说过电影《变形金刚》吗？

马龙：当然了。我小时候特别喜欢那部动画片，关于汽车人和霸天虎之间的战争。有擎天柱、威震天、大黄蜂、爵士、铁皮、红蜘蛛等，很酷。

R：《变形金刚》已经成为我们文化很重要的一个组成部分了。我们永远都难以忘记这些能从人变成小汽车、直升飞机或者战斗机的机器人。我们现在已经有电影版了。2007 年，导演迈克尔・贝向我们呈现了第一部电影版《变形金刚》。

M：是一部大片。

R：当然了。票房收入达到 7 亿美元。

M：现在我们又有了另外一部变形金刚的电影。

R：是的，《变形金刚 2：堕落金刚的复仇》。里面有很多特技。人类技术发展如此迅猛，我们做出的那些精彩的电影场景都跟真的一样。

M：其中有很多的爆炸场面，很多华丽的武器，还有帅哥美女。

R：作为一部大片，它必须要能够紧紧地抓住观众的心并且使他们感到震撼。于是他们花费巨资以获得特效。比如，1997 年的《泰坦尼克号》花了近 2 亿美元，导演詹姆斯・卡梅隆决定重新建造一个跟泰坦尼克号一样大的模型船。

### 核心词汇记一记

**Words Storm**

| | | |
|---|---|---|
| transformer | [træns'fɔːmə] *n.* | 变形金刚 |
| helicopter | ['helikɔptə] *n.* | 直升飞机 |
| blockbuster | ['blɔkbʌstə] *n.* | 大片 |
| explosion | [ik'spləuʒən] *n.* | 爆炸 |
| invest | [in'vest] *v.* | 投资 |

**Phrases**

| | |
|---|---|
| fighter plane | 战斗机 |
| box office | 票房 |
| special effects | 特技 |

### 会话 2

Sue: I'd like to see some films now. Can you recommend some to me?

Fidel: Do you like war film? Have you seen *Black Hawk Down*? It is based on a true incident in Somalia. American troops—Delta Force and Ranger, invaded a hostile area in Mogadishu. They met strong resistance and took heavy casualties.

S: I've watched that before. The scenes are so cruel. War is so terrible. Bullets are everywhere that a soldier cannot get out of the plight, and what awaits him is only death.

F: But the brotherhood is to be admired. Soldiers sacrifice their lives for each other. I was moved to tears when I saw two soldiers land in the crash site in the hope of saving the pilot, only to get killed in action. I would highly recommend another movie to you—*Saving Private Ryan*.

S: Is it about the Second World War?

F: Yes, about the Normandy Invasion. In this action, numerous soldiers lost their lives. A special task force was sent to cross the enemy line to save a particular soldier, a private Ryan.

S: Who is Ryan? Why should they save him?

F: He is just a common soldier. But his brothers got killed in action, so he became the only child of the family. The US government decided to bring him home.

苏：我现在想看电影。你能给我推荐些吗？

菲德尔：你喜欢看战争片吗？你看过《黑鹰坠落》吗？这是根据索马里的真实事件改编的。美国陆军三角洲部队和游骑兵部队受命深入敌人后方摩加迪沙地区，他们遭到了顽强的抵抗，伤亡惨重。

S：这个我以前看过。那些场景看起来很残忍。战争真地好恐怖。子弹横飞，士兵们根本无处可躲，只能等死。

F：但是他们的兄弟情很值得称赞。士兵们为彼此牺牲自己的生命。当我看到两名士兵降到出事地点，希望能救出飞行员却搭上了自己的性命，我感动得流泪了。我还要向你强烈推荐另一部电影《拯救大兵瑞恩》。

S：是关于二战的吗？

F：是的，是关于诺曼底登陆的。在这次行动中，有无数的士兵失去了宝贵的生命。一个特种部队被派遣穿过敌人的封锁线拯救瑞恩。

S：谁是瑞恩？为什么要救他呢？

F：他只是个普通的士兵。但是他的兄弟们在另一次行动中都牺牲了，所以他成了他们家唯一的孩子。美国政府决定带他回家。

#### 核心词汇记一记

**Words Storm**

| | | |
|---|---|---|
| incident | ['insidənt] | *n.* 事件 |
| hostile | ['hɔstail] | *a.* 敌方的 |
| resistance | [ri'zistəns] | *n.* 反抗 |
| casualty | ['kæʒjuəlti] | *n.* 伤亡 |
| plight | [plait] | *n.* 困境 |
| brotherhood | ['brʌðəhud] | *n.* 兄弟情 |

**Phrases**

| | |
|---|---|
| be moved to tears | 感动落泪 |
| Normandy Invasion | 诺曼底登陆 |

# 15. Humorous Cartoons

## 爆笑卡通

### 知识链接　拓展视野，掌握背景知识

*曾几何时，我们还抱有这样的观点：卡通是小孩子的专利，大人看卡通就太好笑了。但随着现代社会的发展，尤其是80后一代逐渐走向社会、走向婚姻和家庭生活，他们未泯的童心极大地推动了卡通产业的发展。从日本的宫崎骏系列、《蜡笔小新》、《海贼王》到美国的《怪物史莱克》、《汽车总动员》、《玩具总动员》、《飞屋环游记》再到前段时间红遍大江南北的国产动画片《喜羊羊与灰太狼》，里面栩栩如生的卡通形象得到了大人小孩的一致好评，小孩子们喜欢喜羊羊的玩偶，小白领们则宣称“嫁人就嫁灰太狼”。*

### 难点点拨　知识难点看一看，情景实战热热身

1．at the very beginning 最初，一开始

At the very beginning, “cartoon” referred only to caricatures and comic strips.

在最开始的时候，“卡通”指的仅仅是讽刺画和连环画。

2．come to one’s rescue 营救某人

When there is an emergency, they come to our rescue.

只要有紧急情况发生，他们就会赶去援救。

3．individualism 在此是褒义词，指个人的自信和自我价值

Individualism has already deeply grown into the mind of every person.

个人主义已经深深地植入了每个人的脑海里。

4．value 崇尚

We value “collectivism”, and despise individualism

我们崇尚集体主义，鄙夷个人主义。

5．an act of... 一种……的行为

Asking for personal interest is an act of selfishness.

追求个人利益是自私的表现。

## 情景实战 跟着老外听一听，读一读，练一练

**会话 1**

William: Can you tell me something about American cartoons?

Victor: Of course, it has a long history you know. At the very beginning, "cartoon" referred only to caricatures and comic strips, because at that time the cartoon movie was not available. Then the cartoon movies came out, American cartoons have already become part and parcel of the American culture.

W: There are many famous cartoon characters.

V: There sure are. The most famous cartoon-maker is Disney—Mickey Mouse, Donald Duck, Minnie, Goofy, Pluto, Snow White, Winnie the Pooh, and King Lion. It also produced many new cartoons—*Toy Story*, *Mulan*, *Finding Nimo*, *The Incredibles*, *Cars*, *WALL-E* and so on.

W: Are there any other film companies that produce good cartoons?

V: Pixar Animation Studios once was independent, but now it has become a part of the Walt Disney Company. It has produced many good cartoons. Dreamworks is a company led by Steven Spielberg. It is quite prolific—*Chicken Run*, *Shrek*, *Madagascar*, *Kung Fu Panda*, and so on.

W: What's the most important element in American cartoons?

V: I think it is the humor. I admire the wit of those cartoon makers. By the way, the humor shown in American cartoons can often be seen in the life of American people—it is a humorous nation.

威廉：你能跟我说说美国卡通片吗？

维克多：当然可以。美式卡通有很长的历史了。在最开始的时候，“卡通”指的仅仅是讽刺画和连环画，因为卡通电影那时还没出现。后来卡通电影才出来。美式卡通已经成为美国文化中必不可少的一部分了。

V：里面有很多著名的卡通人物。

W：是呀，最富盛名的卡通制作商就是迪士尼公司了，它创造了米老鼠、唐老鸭、米妮、高菲、布鲁图、白雪公主、小熊维尼，还有狮子王等一系列卡通人物。迪士尼还制作了很多新式卡通片，如《玩具总动员》、《花木兰》、《海底总动员》、《超人特工队》、《汽车总动员》、《机器人总动员》等等。

V：还有没有其他电影公司拍的卡通片呢？

W：皮克斯动画公司以前是独立经营，但是现在已经成为沃特迪士尼公司的一员了。这个公司也出品了很多好的卡通片。梦工厂是斯蒂芬·斯皮尔伯格旗下的电影公司，这个公司制作了很多动画片，其中有《小鸡快跑》、《怪物史莱克》、《马达加斯加》、《功夫熊猫》等。

W：美国卡通片中最重要的元素是什么呢？

V：我认为是幽默。我很佩服卡通制作人员的智慧。顺便说一下，美国卡通里面的幽默在美国人的生活中很常见的，这是一个很幽默的国家。

### 核心词汇记一记

**Words Storm**

cartoon [kɑː'tuːn] *n.* 卡通
caricature ['kærikətʃə] *n.* 讽刺画
independent [indi'pendənt] *a.* 独立的
prolific [prəu'lifik] *a.* 多产的
element ['elimənt] *n.* 元素
humorous ['hjuːmərəs] *a.* 幽默的

**Phrases**

comic strips 连环画
cartoon movie 卡通电影

**会话 2**

Eric: Have you heard of a phenomenon? There are so many superheroes in American cartoons.

Alex: Yes, of course. Superman, Spiderman, Batman… They are saviors of the whole world, when there is an emergency, they come to our rescue.

E: But have you ever thought about the cause of this phenomenon?

A: Not really, I guess American people love superheroes and their superpower, maybe that's it.

E: You know, in the American culture individuals are highly valued. Individualism has already grown strongly into the mind of every person. It praises the power of a single man and values the personal interest, hence there superheroes as powerful singular individuals.

A: Yes, it makes sense.

E: In China however we put more emphasis on "the whole". We value "collectivism", and downplay individualism, thinking that we can identify as part of the group, and that asking for personal interest is an act of selfishness. The Americans live for themselves, but we Chinese live for others.

艾瑞克：你有没有观察到一种现象，美国卡通片里有好多超级英雄啊？

阿历克斯：是的，当然。超人、蝙蝠侠、蜘蛛侠……他们是全世界的救世主呢。只要有紧急情况发生，他们就会赶去援救。

E：但是你考虑过这种现象背后的原因吗？

A：没有。大概是美国人民喜欢超级英雄和他们的超能力吧。

E：你知道吗，在美国文化里，人们崇尚的是个人主义。这种思想已经深深地植入了每个人的脑海里。他们鼓吹个人的力量，提倡个人的兴趣爱好，因此他们才崇尚那些有着超能力的超人个体。

A：有道理。

E：但是我们中国人凡事都喜欢强调“整体”。我们崇尚集体主义，鄙夷个人主义。我们大家都生活在一个集体里，因此追求个人利益是一种自私的表现。美国人为自己而活，中国人则为别人而活。

**核心词汇记一记**

**Words Storm**

phenomenon [fi'nɔminən] *n.* 现象
emergency [i'məːdʒənsi] *n.* 紧急事件
individualism [ˌindi'vidʒuəlizəm] *n.* 个人主义
collectivism [kə'lektivizəm] *n.* 集体主义

**Phrases**

make sense 有道理
put emphasis on 把重点放在……

# 16. Movie Stars

# 星光大道

## 知识链接 拓展视野，掌握背景知识

好莱坞星光大道（Hollywood Walk of Fame）是条沿着美国好莱坞星光大道与藤街伸展的人行道，上面有2000多颗镶有好莱坞商会追敬名人姓名的星形奖章，以纪念他们对娱乐事业的贡献。第一颗星于1960年2月9日颁赠予琼安·伍德沃德（Joanne Woodward）。到2006年4月20日凡娜·怀特（Vanna White）得到该荣誉时，上面共有2309颗星。每颗星皆由一颗水磨石制成，将其制成粉色五角星形并镶上青铜，然后嵌入深灰色的方块中。粉色星形内是刻在青铜上的授奖者名字，在此下面则为一环状标志，代表受奖人领取星星的领域。

## 难点点拨 知识难点看一看，情景实战热热身

1. portray 饰演，扮演

   Among so many Hollywood stars, who can portray so many different figures?

   众多好莱坞影星中，谁可以演绎如此多而迥异的角色？

2. do the dubbing 配音

   He has also done the dubbing in several animations.

   他还为几部动画片配过音。

3. the Oscar ceremony 奥斯卡颁奖典礼

   He is a good host and he has hosted many programs, including the Oscar ceremony.

   他是个很不错的主持人，主持过包括奥斯卡颁奖典礼在内的很多节目。

4. make contribution to 为……做巨大贡献

   Only actors who have made great contribution to the film industry can have their names printed there.

   只有那些为电影事业做出了重大贡献的演员才有资格把名字印在那儿。

5. cartoon movie 动画片，等于 animation

   There are names of some famous characters in cartoon movies.

   还有一些卡通电影里面的著名角色。

## 情景实战 跟着老外听一听，读一读，练一练

**会话 1**

Louis: Which movie star do you like best?

Phillip: Tom Hanks of course. Among so many Hollywood stars, who can portray so many different figures—from a gay lawyer to a boy of deficient intelligence, and from an astronaut to a GI Joe? Only Hanks.

L: Tell me some of his movies.

P: So many. *Sleepless in Seattle*, *Philadelphia*, *Forrest Gump*, *Apollo 13*, *Saving Private Ryan*, *The Terminal*... He has also done the dubbing in several animations, such as *Toy Story* and *Polar Express*. Besides, he was the producer of *Band of Brothers*.

L: Er... Great, but why is he so great? I mean, there are so many people, but why him?

P: I don't know, but you see, he is versatile—he is fond of music, for example, and he even writes many songs for his movies. He is a good host and he has hosted many programs, including the Oscar ceremony.

L: He has to work very hard to get all this.

P: Yes. To be a movie star, what you need is not only good luck. You have to make great efforts to show your best side to the audience, to let them know you and love you.

路易斯: 你最喜欢的影星是谁?

菲利普: 当然是汤姆·汉克斯了。在众多好莱坞影星中，只有汉克斯可以演绎如此多而迥异的角色——从同性恋律师到智力有缺陷的男孩，从宇航员到特种兵。

L: 跟我说说他的电影吧。

P: 太多了。如《西雅图不眠夜》、《费城风云》、《阿甘正传》、《阿波罗 13 号》、《拯救大兵瑞恩》、《幸福终点站》等。他还为几部动画片配过音，如《玩具总动员》和《北极特快车》。除此之外，他还是美剧《兄弟连》的制片人。

L: 呵，太棒了，但是为什么他这么棒呢? 我是说，(好莱坞) 有这么多人，为什么偏偏他这么棒呢?

P: 我也不清楚，但是你看，他是个多才多艺的人——比如他热爱音乐，又曾经为他的电影写过很多歌。他还是个很不错的主持人，主持过包括奥斯卡颁奖典礼在内的很多节目。

L: 他必须非常努力地工作才能取得这样的成就。

P: 是的。要成为一个电影明星，光靠好运气是不够的。你还必须尽最大努力向观众展示你最好的一面，让他们来了解你，喜欢你。

### 核心词汇记一记

**Words Storm**

| | | |
|---|---|---|
| portray | [pɔːˈtrei] | *v.* 描绘，饰演 |
| deficient | [diˈfiʃənt] | *a.* 有缺陷的 |
| astronaut | [ˈæstrənɔːt] | *n.* 宇航员 |
| dub | [dʌb] | *v.* (电影) 配音 |
| animation | [ˌæniˈmeiʃən] | *n.* 动画片 |
| versatile | [ˈvəːsətail] | *a.* 多才多艺的 |

**Phrases**

| | |
|---|---|
| be fond of | 喜欢，爱好 |
| make efforts | 努力 |

**会话 2**

Chris: Do you know the Hollywood Walk of Fame?

Paul: No, is it related to famous actors?

C: Yes, it is a sidewalk of the Hollywood Boulevard. There are names of many famous movie stars on the walk—2309 of them to be exact. Only actors who have made great contribution to the film industry can have their names printed there.

P: Are there names of Chinese stars?

C: Yes. Jet Li, Jackie Chan, John Woo… All actors, actresses and directors have their signatures, handprints and footprints on it.

P: Lovely.

C: Also there are names of some famous characters in cartoon movies—Mickey Mouse, Donald Duck, Winnie the Pooh…

P: Cute.

C: During the Oscar ceremony this year, there was red carpet on the walk. All famous movie stars walked on it to the hall where the ceremony was held.

P: They always wear flamboyant clothes, usually the latest and most expensive fashions, and journalists take photos like crazy.

C: Yes, it's an interesting topic of the whole world. We are usually very interested in their styles at that moment.

P: And many people will copy them—they will follow those stars' styles, and a new fashion then comes into being.

C: So movie stars are quite influential.

查尔斯：你知道好莱坞的星光大道吗？

保罗：不知道，是和著名的演员有关吗？

C：是的。它是好莱坞林荫大道上的一条人行道。上面有很多著名影星的名字，总共有 2309 个。只有那些为电影事业做出了重大贡献的演员才有资格把名字印在那儿。

V：有中国影星的名字吗？

C：有。如李连杰，成龙，吴宇森等。所有（被选中）的男女演员还有导演都要把他们的签名、手掌印以及脚印留在这条路上。

P：真可爱。

C：而且还有一些卡通电影里面的著名角色，像米老鼠、唐老鸭，还有小熊维尼等。

P：太可爱了。

C：今年举行奥斯卡颁奖典礼时，这条路铺上了红地毯。所有的著名影星都走过红地毯进入大厅。

P：他们穿着光鲜亮丽的时髦服装，记者们就会狂拍照片。

C：是的，全世界都会谈论这个有趣的话题。我们通常会对明星们此时的着装风格很感兴趣。

P：很多人会学这些明星们的着装风格，然后就会引发新一轮的流行时尚。

C：所以说电影明星是很有影响力的。

**核心词汇记一记**

**Words Storm**

| | | |
|---|---|---|
| sidewalk | ['saidwɔːk] | *n.* 人行道 |
| contribution | [ˌkɔntri'bjuːʃən] | *n.* 贡献 |
| signature | ['signətʃə] | *n.* 签名 |
| handprint | [hændprint] | *n.* 手印 |
| flamboyant | [flæm'bɔiənt] | *a.* 华丽的 |

**Phrases**

Hollywood Walk of Fame　好莱坞星光大道

# 17. Oscar and Hollywood

# 奥斯卡和好莱坞

## 知识链接　拓展视野，掌握背景知识

奥斯卡从诞生之日起就与好莱坞有着千丝万缕的联系，第一届颁奖典礼就是在一个好莱坞的私人聚会上举办的，其观众还不足250人次。自2002年起，奥斯卡颁奖典礼才开始在著名的柯达剧院举办。奥斯卡金像奖的正式名称是“电影艺术与科学学院奖”，它是由电影界知名人士在好莱坞发起的一个“非赢利组织”。1931年后，“学院奖”逐渐被其通俗叫法“奥斯卡金像奖”所取代，关于这个名称的来历有好几个故事，但比较可信的版本如下。1931年电影艺术与科学学院图书馆的女管理员玛格丽特·赫里奇在仔细端详了金像奖之后，惊呼道：“啊！他看上去真像我的叔叔奥斯卡！”隔壁的新闻记者听后写道：“艺术与科学学院的工作人员深情地称呼他们的金塑像为‘奥斯卡’”。从此，这一别名不胫而走。

## 难点点拨　知识难点看一看，情景实战热热身

1. lead the trend 引领潮流

   It is always leading the trend of the film industry.

   它一直引领着电影业的潮流趋势。

2. come into vogue 开始流行

   In the 1940s, detective movies and musicals came into vogue.

   20世纪40年代侦探电影和音乐片成为流行时尚。

3. witness 见证了，证明了

   The next decade witnessed the development of western films.

   下一个10年见证了西方电影的发展历程。

4. aim at doing 目的在于

   Horror movies aim at frightening the audience.

   恐怖片的目的在于让观众受到惊吓。

5. broaden one’s horizon 拓宽视野

   Science fictions broaden our horizon and challenge our imagination.

   科幻片拓宽了我们的视野，冲击着我们的想象力。

## 情景实战 跟着老外听一听，读一读，练一练

**会话 1**

Daniel: Can you tell me something about Hollywood?

Peter: Okay! It is the movie capital of the world, located in the northwest of Los Angeles, famous for its film industry. Many film companies have settled there—Metro Goldwyn Mayer, Paramount Pictures, 20th Century Fox, Warner Brothers, Columbia Pictures...

D: It has a long history?

P: Of course. Nearly one hundred years. It is always leading the trend of the film industry. In the 1930s many gangster movies were produced there, to show the violent lives of criminals to the public. Then comedies prospered. In the 1940s, detective movies and musicals came into vogue. The next decade witnessed the development of western films—cowboys, Indians and early settlers.

D: Great! You know so much. Go on then.

P: After that, horror movies, documentaries, science fiction all came into our cinemas. Horror movies aim at frightening the audience—and strangely enough, the more you frighten them, the happier they feel. Documentaries are sometimes a serious study of a social problem. Science fiction, such as *Star Wars* and *2001: A Space Odyssey*, broaden our horizon and challenge our imagination.

丹尼尔：你能告诉我一些关于好莱坞的事情吗？

彼得：可以。它是世界电影之都，位于洛杉矶的西北部，以电影业而闻名天下。很多电影公司都落户在那儿，如米高梅、派拉蒙、20世纪福克斯、华纳兄弟、哥伦比亚电影公司等。

D：它的历史很长吗？

P：当然了，接近100年呢。它一直引领着电影业的潮流趋势。在20世纪30年代的时候，警匪片大批产生，向公众展示了罪犯的暴力生活。接着喜剧片繁荣起来。20世纪40年代侦探电影和音乐片成为流行时尚。下一个10年见证了西部片的发展历程——牛仔、印第安人还有早期定居者。

D：太棒了！你知道的真多。继续讲吧。

P：再后来，恐怖片、纪录片、科幻片都进了电影院。恐怖片的目的在于让观众受到惊吓，但奇怪的是，你越吓他们，他们越觉得开心。纪录片研究的是严肃的社会问题。像《星球大战》和《2001：星际漫游》之类的科幻片则拓宽了我们的视野，冲击着我们的想象力。

### 核心词汇记一记

**Words Storm**

gangster ['gæŋstə] *n.* 歹徒，强盗
criminal ['kriminəl] *n.* 罪犯
comedy ['kɔmidi] *n.* 喜剧
detective [di'tektiv] *n.* 侦探
decade ['dekeid] *n.* 十年
frighten ['fraitn] *v.* 惊吓

**Phrases**

be located in 坐落于
film industry 电影工业
horror movie 恐怖片
science fiction 科幻片

**会话 2**

Jeremy: I'm watching the Oscar ceremony. It's so interesting.

Randy: "The academy award now goes to…"When I hear this, I am always excited.

J: Yes, it is a big event, a great honor for those actors and directors. They get their awards, and go to the stage to say thanks to their friends and relatives. Very often they have so many people to thank, but so little time to name all of them.

R: The cup itself is interesting. It is a gilded statue of a man.

J: But how do they decide who should get this award?

R: To get an award, the film should be artistic, and be able to earn money as well. Some films are great in artistry, but their box office earnings are not good. The audience doesn't love them, so they cannot get this award.

J: Winning an 'Oscar' is of great importance?

R: Absolutely! It is influential not only to America, but also to the whole globe. If a film is awarded, it will definitely become a classic, and earn more money. We Chinese also pay much attention to this award.

杰瑞米：我正在看奥斯卡颁奖典礼，非常好看。

兰迪："奥斯卡金像奖得主是……" 每当我听到这句话，心里就异常激动。

J：是的，这是一次盛事，对演员和导演来说是一个莫大的荣誉。他们得奖后就会走上舞台去向他们的朋友和亲人致谢。情况经常是他们有很多人要感谢，但是时间太少了，无法一一提及他们的名字。

R：这个奖杯本身就挺有趣的，是个小金人雕像。

J：他们怎么判断谁应该得奖呢？

R：要得到奥斯卡奖，电影必须要有艺术性，并且还能赚钱。有些电影艺术性非常强，但是票房收入却不那么尽人意。观众不喜欢，所以也不能拿到奖项。

J：赢得奥斯卡那么重要吗？

R：是的。它不仅在美国很有影响力，在全球范围内都有很大影响。若一个电影得了奥斯卡奖，它肯定会成为一部经典电影，并且会带来更多的票房收入。我们中国人也很重视这个奖项。

**核心词汇记一记**

**Words Storm**

gild [gild] *v.* 镀金
statue ['stætju] *n.* 雕像
artistic [ɑː'tistik] *a.* 艺术的
influential [ˌinfu'enʃəl] *a.* 有影响力的

**Phrases**

big event 盛事
box office 票房
pay attention to 注意

# 18. Magic and Fantasy

## 魔幻故事

### 知识链接 拓展视野，掌握背景知识

魔幻故事在当今文学和电影中占有很大的比重，无论是中国的《聊斋志异》式的鬼故事，还是西方充满宗教色彩的神魔故事，都对我们有着强烈的吸引力。如《百年孤独》这类拉美的魔幻现实主义，以及19世纪初英国的哥特小说，都给西方文化添上了浓墨重彩的一笔。

### 难点点拨 知识难点看一看，情景实战热热身

1．be based on 建立在，由……而来

The Lord of the Ring is loosely based on the novel of the same name by Tolkien.

《指环王》大致上改编于托尔金的同名小说。

2．grand background 宏大的场景

It's really an epic, with a grand background and highly complicated narrative threads.

这简直就是史诗，背景壮阔，叙事复杂。

3．a system of 一个关于……的系统

The ancient Greece has an epic system of gods and heroes.

古希腊有一个关于神和英雄的庞大的体系。

4．no wonder 难怪，怪不得

No wonder he is so skillful and strong in the combat.

怪不得他作战这么厉害，有勇有谋。

## 情景实战 跟着老外听一听，读一读，练一练

**会话 1**

Peter: It's too noisy, so much strange sound... What are you watching?

Justin: *The Lord of the Rings*. It's loosely based on the novel of the same name, written by an English linguist and writer—J.R.R. Tolkien, and has been awarded the academy award. It is a trilogy—*The Fellowship of the Ring*, *The Two Towers*, and *The Return of the King*.

P: I'd like to know more about it.

J: It's really an epic, with a grand background and highly complicated narrative threads. The scenes are shockingly huge, with so many monsters and elves locked in combat against each other. The spirit of it—bravery, responsibility and love of honor, really moves my heart.

P: I think I should sit and watch with you. Do you know another fantasy—*The Chronicles of Narnia*? I've watched that movie the day before yesterday.

J: Yes, of course. It is also adapted from a novel. The author C.S. Lewis is quite famous in literary circles. He's also a good friend of Tolkien.

P: It's a small world.

J: In *The Lord of the Rings*, Tolkien as a linguist has invented various languages for elves and other nations. It's miraculous.

彼 得：太吵了，这么多奇怪的声音。你在看什么？

贾斯汀：《指环王》，它大致上改编于英国语言学家及作家托尔金的同名小说。该电影获得了奥斯卡奖，是三部曲——《护戒使者》、《双塔奇兵》以及《王者归来》。

P：你再多给我介绍点吧。

J：这简直就是史诗，背景壮阔，情节复杂，场面宏大，各种怪物和精灵征战不休。其中的精神——勇敢、责任和对荣誉的追求，让我感动不已。

P：我得坐下来跟着你看看了。你知道另一部魔幻电影《纳尼亚传奇》吗？前天我刚看了那部电影。

J：当然知道了，那也是改编自小说的。作者 C.S. 路易斯是文学界泰斗，也是托尔金的好朋友。

P：这个世界真小啊。

J：在《指环王》里，托尔金这个语言学家为精灵和其他种族发明了各自的语言，真不可思议。

### 核心词汇记一记

#### Words Storm

| | |
|---|---|
| loosely | ['lu:sli] *ad.* 松散地 |
| linguist | [liŋ'gwist] *n.* 语言学家 |
| trilogy | ['trilədʒi] *n.* 三部曲 |
| epic | ['epik] *n.* 史诗 |
| shockingly | ['ʃɔkiŋli] *ad.* 令人震惊地 |
| monster | ['mɔnstə] *n.* 怪物 |
| elf | [elf] *n.* 精灵 |

#### Phrases

| | |
|---|---|
| narrative threads | 叙事线索 |
| be adapted from | 改编自 |

**会话 2**

Mark: I'm really addicted to *Harry Potter*.

Daisy: Yes. J.K. Rowling is the author of the original novels. I highly suggest you go back to the books to learn more about Harry Potter. By the way, do you know why the western people like to tell stories full of magic power and supernatural heroes?

M: I've no idea about that.

D: We should go back to the Greek mythology. The ancient Greeks had an epic system of gods and heroes. It's a polytheistic nation, believing in a family of gods—Zeus the god of the sky and thunder, Poseidon the god of the sea, Hades the god of the underground, Hera, Athena, Apollo, Aphrodite, Hermes, Dionysus... They all live on Mount Olympus.

M: Yes, and there are many heroes.

D: Some heroes are pure human kind, but some are semi-god. In Homer's great epics *Iliad* and *Odyssey*, there are many heroes who can do supernatural things. Have you ever seen the film *Troy*? It's a good adaptation of *Iliad*. In it, the hero Achilles is the son of a god and a human.

M: No wonder he is so skillful and strong in combat.

马克：我真地喜欢上了《哈利波特》。

黛西：是啊。J.K. 罗琳是原小说的作者。我强烈建议你回头看看书，这样才能更加了解哈利波特。顺便说一下，你知道为什么西方人喜欢创作带有魔幻色彩以及神话人物的故事吗？

M：我不知道。

M：让我们回顾一下希腊神话吧。古希腊有一个关于神和英雄的庞大的体系。古希腊人是信奉神的——天与雷之神宙斯、海神波塞冬、冥王哈德斯、赫拉、雅典娜、阿波罗、赫尔墨斯、迪奥尼索斯……他们都住在奥林匹斯山上。

M：是啊，还有许多英雄呢。

M：有些英雄是纯人类，可是有些是半人半神。在荷马史诗《伊里亚特》和《奥德赛》中就有许多有神奇能力的英雄。你看过电影《特洛伊》吗？那是根据《伊里亚特》改编的，其中阿喀琉斯就是凡人和神共生的儿子。

M：怪不得他作战这么厉害，有勇有谋。

### 核心词汇记一记

**Words Storm**

supernatural [sju:pə'nætʃərəl] *a.* 超自然的

mythology [mi'θɔlədʒi] *n.* 神话

polytheistic [pɔliθi:'istik] *a.* 多神的

**Phrases**

semi-god 半神

# Music and Arts 音乐与艺术

# 19. Rock and Roll

## 摇摇滚滚

### 知识链接 拓展视野，掌握背景知识

究竟什么是摇滚呢？ 长头发、皮夹克、有破洞的牛仔裤……也是，也不是；吉他、贝司、鼓……也是，也不是；Elvis Presley、The Beatles、Bob Dylan、Nirvana……也是，也不是；年轻的自由、荷尔蒙的冲动、离经叛道……也是，也不是；节奏、歌词、旋律、梦想、真实、感觉、狂野、信仰、力量、愤怒……也是，也不是。 其实这些相关的联想只是一些表象，对于真正的摇滚文化，对于掩藏在这些"皮相"之下的"核"，你是否有兴趣去了解呢？摇滚不仅是一种音乐形态，实际上它是一种"人生的态度和哲学"，也正因为如此，摇滚乐才有别于一般流行音乐(Pop Music)。真正的摇滚文化至少可以提炼出这样一个缩微的全貌：嬉皮文化、艺术摇滚、朋克乐、先锋音乐、重金属等。

### 难点点拨 知识难点看一看，情景实战热热身

1．above the average 高于常人

I know your voice—it is above the average, but not exceedingly great.

我知道你的声音，比一般水平高一些，但不是特别出众。

2．cooperate with sb. 与某人合作

You need to learn a lot about how to sing professionally and how to cooperate well with your teammates.

你还需要学习如何唱得专业一些，以及如何与你的队友好好合作。

3．There is a long way for you to go.

你还有很长的路要走呢。

## 情景实战 跟着老外听一听，读一读，练一练

**会话 1**

Ray: Hey, I wanna build a rock band. What do you think?

Leo: You get the right people?

R: No. I can be the lead singer because my voice is sweet. I'll try to get others who can play musical instrument for me.

L: Can you play the guitar?

R: No, but I look really cool even without a guitar.

L: Can you read the score?

R: No, but I know how to sing the melody.

L: Can you write lyrics then?

R: No, but my autograph is beautiful.

L: I feel that you really have to rethink all this. I know your voice—is above average, but not exceedingly great and to build a good band, you must have people who can play the guitar, the bass, the keyboard and drums very well. You need to learn a lot about how to sing professionally and how to cooperate well with your teammates. There is a long way for you to go in order to do this.

R: So you don't believe I'm a good singer?

L: That's not the point.

R: I'll become very popular, and I'll be loved by those beautiful girls, but you just don't believe this!

L: To be a great singer, you need to make great efforts.

瑞：嘿，我想组建一支摇滚乐队，你觉得怎样？

雷欧：你找到人了吗？

R：还没有。我可以担任主唱，因为我的声音很甜。我还得找一些会弹乐器的人来。

L：你会弹吉他吗？

R：不会，但是我不弹吉他看起来也很酷。

L：你识谱吗？

R：不识。但是我知道如何哼唱旋律。

L：那你能写歌词吗？

R：不能，但是我的签名很好看。

L：我认为你真地需要再好好考虑一下。我知道你的声音比一般水平高一些，但不是特别出众。要建立一个好的乐队，还必须有吉他手、贝斯手、键盘手和鼓手。你还需要学习如何唱得专业一些，如何与你的队友好好合作。你还有很长的路要走呢。

R：你不相信我是个好歌手？

L：这不是重点。

R：我会很出名的，而且会被那些漂亮女生喜欢的。但是你就是不相信这一点。

L：要成为一位出色的歌手，你必须要付出很大的努力。

### 核心词汇记一记

**Words Storm**

autograph ['ɔːtəugrɑːf] *n.* 签名
rethink [riː'θiŋk] *v.* 再考虑
exceedingly [ik'siːdiŋli] *ad.* 极其
bass [bæs] *n.* 贝斯
keyboard ['kiːbɔːd] *n.* 键盘
teammate ['tiːmmeit] *n.* 队友

**Phrases**

rock band 摇滚乐队
musical instrument 乐器

**会话 2**

Paul: Which rock band do you like most?

Steve: The Beatles. They were without doubt the miracle group of the world—they made great changes to the culture of the whole globe. John Lennon was a legendary singer who loved peace, equality, and freedom, and they put all their thoughts into their songs, to enchant and educate us. What about your favorite band?

P: Guns N' Roses, and the Sex Pistols. I love Punk music—I believe the world is chaotic and dirty… violence, betrayal, deception, despair, and death… I hate all these, and I want to break away from all tyrannous powers.

S: Terrible indeed. Have you been hurt by someone before?

P: More to the point, I'm now being hurt by an imperfect world.

S: So cynical. You guys who love these bands are always rebellious.

P: In the mid-20th century there was the "beat generation", and then hippies came. They were against all established rules. They protested against the modern value in strange ways. I admire them.

S: So you will follow them and get dressed up like a mad thing? You will paint your hair green and have earrings and tattoos?

P: No. I dare not.

保罗：你最喜欢哪支摇滚乐队？

斯蒂夫：披头士。它是全世界的奇迹，因为它极大地改变了整个世界的文化。约翰是一位传奇歌手。他热爱和平、平等和自由。他们把所有的思想都倾注到歌里面，使我们为之着迷，受到教化。你最喜欢的乐队是哪个？

P：“枪和玫瑰”，还有“性手枪”乐队。我喜欢朋克音乐，我相信这个世界是混乱和肮脏的。暴力、背叛、欺骗、绝望、死亡……我厌恶所有这一切，我想挣脱这暴虐的权力。

S：太恐怖了，你以前被别人伤害过？

P：更确切地说，我现在正在被这个不完美的世界所伤害。

S：太愤世嫉俗了。像你们这种热爱这种乐队的人都很叛逆。

P：在 20 世纪中期有“垮掉的一代”，然后嬉皮士就出现了。他们反对一切既定的规则，他们用奇怪的方式反对现代价值观。我很羡慕他们。

S：所以你要步他们的后尘，穿得像疯子一样？还要把头发染成绿色并且打耳洞、文身？

P：不，我还不敢。

### 核心词汇记一记

**Words Storm**

| | |
|---|---|
| legendary | ['ledʒəndəri] *a.* 传奇般的 |
| enchant | [in'tʃænt] *v.* 使迷惑 |
| pistol | ['pistl] *n.* 手枪 |
| chaotic | [kei'ɔtik] *a.* 混乱的 |
| deception | [di'sepʃən] *n.* 欺骗 |
| tyrannous | ['tirənəs] *a.* 暴虐的 |
| cynical | ['sinikəl] *a.* 愤世嫉俗的 |
| rebellious | [ri'beljəs] *a.* 反叛的 |
| tattoo | [tə'tuː] *n.* 文身 |

**Phrases**

| | |
|---|---|
| break away from | 脱离 |
| beat generation | 垮掉的一代 |

# 20. Pop Music

## 流行音乐

### 知识链接 拓展视野，掌握背景知识

流行音乐植根于大众生活的丰厚土壤之中，起源于美国的爵士音乐。20世纪初，美国出现了一种由多民族文化汇集而成的爵士音乐。这种新兴音乐，以它独特的演奏（演唱）方式，刷新了听众的耳目，轰动了全美国，又很快传遍西欧各国。流行音乐中器乐作品的特点是：节奏鲜明，轻松活泼或抒情优美，演奏方法多种多样，音响多变，乐队规模不大，现代作品多使用电声乐器。

### 难点点拨 知识难点看一看，情景实战热热身

1. I never thought I would/could... 我没想到竟然……
   I never thought I could meet you here!
   没想到在这儿碰到你了！
2. a bit of 一点
   In Jay's music you can always taste a bit of Chinese flavor.
   在杰伦的音乐里你总是能品到中国风的味道。
3. devoid of 缺乏，缺少
   They try their best to copy the westerners, only to make their music devoid of personality.
   他们竭尽所能地效仿西方音乐，没想到反而使得他们的音乐缺少个性。
4. a moment ago 刚才，刚刚
   A moment ago I listened to a song by a Middle East singer, but I can find American elements everywhere in it.
   刚才我在听一个中东歌手的歌，但是我却发现了无处不在的美国元素。
5. smooth over 消解，消除
   The difference between nations is being smoothed over.
   国家间的差异正在被消除。

## 情景实战 跟着老外听一听，读一读，练一练

**会话 1**

Rose: Hey, I never thought I would meet you here. Are you fond of music?

Jennifer: Of course. Which CD do you want?

R: I heard that Jay Chou has a new CD, so I just came around to see whether I could get one here. I'm a big fan of him.

J: Why him?

R: His songs are always artistic—they are not just music, but also beautiful poems. You may feel other singers' songs vulgar and simple, but his song will always refresh you. You will never get tired of his voice.

J: But I don't love Chinese pop music. You should try some western music and we'll see which one is better.

R: This is just what I want to talk about. In Jay's music you can always appreciate the Chinese flavor. He puts Chinese elements into his music to make it distinctive from the western music. I really appreciate it.

J: Most other Chinese pop singers, by contrast, don't care about "the Chinese feature". They try their best to copy the westerners, only to make their music devoid of personality. It's a poor imitation indeed.

罗斯：嘿，没想到在这儿碰到你了。你也喜欢音乐？

詹妮弗：当然了，你想要哪张 CD？

R：我听说周杰伦出了张新 CD，所以我就过来看看能不能买到一张。我可是他的超级粉丝。

J：为什么呢？

R：因为他的歌总是很有艺术性，不只是音乐，更是优美的诗篇。你会觉得其他歌手的歌都庸俗且简单，但周的歌总是能让你耳目一新，让你永远都听不厌他的声音。

J：但是我不喜欢中国流行音乐。你可以试着听些西方音乐，然后比较一下哪个更好。

R：这正是我想讨论的。在杰伦的音乐里你总是能品到中国风的味道，他在音乐里加入了中国元素，使得它有特色且不同于西方音乐。我真地很喜欢。

J：与之不同的是，大部分的中国流行歌手都不注意“中国特色”，他们竭尽所能地效仿西方音乐，没想到反而使得他们的音乐缺少个性，着实是很差的模仿。

### 核心词汇记一记

**Words Storm**

vulgar ['vʌlgə] *a.* 庸俗的

refresh [ri'freʃ] *v.* 使精神振作

element ['elimənt] *n.* 元素

devoid [di'vɔid] *a.* 缺乏的

**Phrases**

pop music 流行音乐

by contrast 形成对比

**会话 2**

Amy: I have found an interesting phenomenon to discuss with you.

Julia: Tell me then.

A: As the whole world is becoming smaller and smaller, pop songs of different countries are getting more or less uniform in style.

J: What do you mean? The Chinese pop music and the American one are getting similar to each other?

A: Right. A moment ago I listened to a song by a Middle Eastern singer, but I can find American elements everywhere in it—Hip-Hop, country music, jazz… You can find all of them in a single song.

J: Yes, the whole globe is being Americanized. We sing as the Americans sing; we dance as they dance; we eat as they eat; we write and read as they do… The world is in trouble—the difference between nations is being smoothed over.

A: I feel terrible about this. You see, before, we have different styles, but now we have only one style—the American one. Pop music is Americanized music—all American melodies and lyrics.

艾米：我发现了一个有趣的现象，想跟你讨论一下。

茱莉亚：跟我说说呗！

A：随着整个世界变得越来越小，不同国家的流行歌曲在形式上也变得差不多统一了。

J：什么意思？你是说中国流行乐和美国流行乐变得越来越相似了？

A：是的。刚才我在听一个中东歌手的歌，但是我却发现了无处不在的美国元素——Hip-Hop、乡村音乐、爵士乐等。居然在一首歌里发现如此多的美国元素！

J：是呀，全球都在变得美国化。我们像美国人那样唱歌，像美国人那样跳舞，像美国人那样吃饭、写作和阅读。这是个世界性问题，国家间的差异止在被消除。

A：对此我觉得挺可怕的。你看，我们以前是不同的风格，但是现在我们却只有同一种风格，那就是美国风。流行音乐就是美国化的音乐——美国的旋律和歌词。

### 核心词汇记一记

**Words Storm**

phenomenon [fi'nɔminən] *n.* 现象
uniform ['juːnifɔːm] *a.* 统一的
Americanize [ə'merikənaiz] *v.* 美国化
melody ['melədi] *n.* 旋律
lyric ['lirik] *n.* 歌词

**Phrases**

more or less 差不多
American elements 美国元素

# 21. Musical Instruments

## 吹拉弹唱

### 知识链接　拓展视野，掌握背景知识

现在随着经济发展，越来越多的人想拥有一些才艺，乐器就成了很好的选择。一般来说，钢琴、电子琴、小提琴和吉他是最近比较热门的乐器，尤其是吉他，由于乐器成本低，而且简单易学，随意唱和，越来越受大家的喜欢。如果有时间，不妨培养一下自己在音乐方面的才艺吧，你会发现，生活随之丰富多彩起来，在朋友面前也有拿手好戏了。

### 难点点拨　知识难点看一看，情景实战热热身

1．a microcosm of ……的缩影

Hand is just a microcosm of the body.

手就是身体的一个缩影。

2．join a team/group 加入队伍，社团

Recently I joined a group to learn guitar.

最近我参加了一个吉他学习班。

3．wear out 磨破

Your finger tips are worn out.

你的指头尖都磨破了。

4．calm down 镇静

Music can always calm you down and purify your soul.

音乐能够净化人心，使人心如止水。

## 情景实战 跟着老外听一听，读一读，练一练

**会话 1**

Olivier: Which musical instrument can you play?

Isabella: None. I don't know anything about music. What about you?

O: I'm good at playing piano. I began to learn it when I was four.

I: Fabulous! Now you can play beautiful music?

O: Sure, I can give you a short show right now.

I: Great. What have you learnt from playing piano, I mean, something physical or spiritual?

O: My fingers are nimbler now. It's just like dancing you see, a dancer can make difficult body movements that others cannot do. Your hand is just a microcosm of the body. Another thing is that now I do needle work with more dexterity.

I: You must also type faster than others.

O: Sure, keyboard is easy for me. As to the spiritual, I should say I have a good sense of art, especially music. I'm sensitive and emotional.

I: So learning to play some musical instrument can be a really good thing. It's a pity that I didn't learn.

O: It's not too late! If you are interested in music, I think I can help you.

I: Good! I hope one day I can play as well as you do.

O: But it's a long-term thing, and you need perseverance.

奥利弗：你会哪种乐器？

伊莎贝拉：哪种也不会。我对音乐一点也不懂。你呢？

O：我擅长弹钢琴。我从 4 岁就开始学钢琴。

I：不错！那你现在可以弹动听的音乐了？

O：是的。我现在就可以给你弹一段小曲。

I：好的。你从弹琴之中学到了什么，我的意思是，有没有一些身体或精神上的收获？

O：我的指头更灵敏了。弹琴就跟跳舞一样。一个舞者能做出常人做不出的高难度动作。手就是身体的一个缩影。现在我做针线活更灵巧了。

I：你肯定打字也比别人快。

O：是的。键盘对我来说很简单。精神方面呢，应该说我对艺术感知力提高了，尤其是对音乐的感知力。我更敏感、更细腻了。

I：学习乐器真是件好事。我没有学真是可惜了。

O：现在还不晚。如果你感兴趣，我可以帮你。

I：好的。我希望有一天我也能像你一样弹得这么好。

O：这可是长久的事情，你得有恒心。

### 核心词汇记一记

**Words Storm**

nimble ['nimbl] *a.* 灵巧的
microcosm ['maikrəukɔzm] *n.* 缩影
dexterity [dek'steriti] *n.* 灵活
sensitive ['sensitiv] *a.* 敏感的

**Phrases**

musical instrument 乐器
needle work 针线活

**会话 2**

Samia: Recently I joined a group to learn guitar.

Patrick: Really? Can you play anything now? Can you give me a show?

S: No way. I'm just learning basic chords at present and my fingers ache. You don't know how difficult it is to touch and press different strings.

P: Let me have a look at your left hand. Oh! Your finger tips are worn out. You should give them a rest.

S: Our teacher says it's a good thing, a proof that I've taken enough pains. What I need is to keep practicing. Practice makes perfect!

P: Your right thumb is broken too.

S: It's really difficult to change from one chord to another with my left hand and strike different strings with my right hand at the same time. But the sound of a guitar is so enchanting.

P: Why are you learning it? You want to be a singer?

S: Just for fun. Maybe someday I can pick up the guitar and sing a song for you. That's good enough. Music can always calm you down and purify your soul. I'd like to be a romantic singer singing about love, life, the good old days and freedom. To just be poetic, like a minstrel.

P: Enjoy the guitar my friend!

撒米亚：最近我参加了一个吉他学习班。

帕特里克：真的？你能弹了吗？给我弹一曲吧。

S：还不行。我才刚学了基本的和弦，我的手指就疼。你不知道，摸到并且按到那些弦有多难。

P：我看看你的左手。哦，指头尖都磨破了。你应该让手指休息一下了。

S：我们老师说这是好事，这证明我用功了。我需要继续练习，熟能生巧嘛。

P：你的右手拇指也磨破了。

S：左手从一个和弦换到另一个，同时右手弹拨不同的弦，真的是很难。可是吉他的声音非常动听。

P：你为什么学吉他？你想做歌手吗？

S：只是娱乐一下。也许有一天我能拿起吉他为你唱首歌。能这样就不错了。音乐能够净化人的心灵，使人心如止水。我真想成为一个浪漫派歌手，歌唱爱、生活、逝去的美好时光，还有自由。很诗意吧，就像吟游诗人一样。

P：哥们，那就享受吉他吧！

**核心词汇记一记**

**Words Storm**

| | | |
|---|---|---|
| proof | [pruːf] *n.* | 证据 |
| thumb | [θʌm] *n.* | 拇指 |
| chord | [kɔːd] *n.* | 和弦 |
| string | [striŋ] *n.* | 弦 |
| minstrel | ['minstrəl] *n.* | 吟游诗人 |

**Phrases**

| | |
|---|---|
| finger tip | 指尖 |
| practice makes perfect | 熟能生巧 |

# 22. Broadway

## 百老汇

### 知识链接 拓展视野，掌握背景知识

百老汇是纽约曼哈顿区一条大街的名称，其历史可追溯至 19 世纪初。当时的百老汇大道就已经成为美国戏剧艺术的活动中心。“百老汇”上演的是比较高雅的音乐剧，以经典剧目为主，黑色、夸张、幽默、风趣、自然、轻松、活泼是百老汇的一贯表演风格。演员们身着缤纷绚丽的服装，在优美动听的音乐中热情奔放、酣畅淋漓地表演着舞蹈，使观众亲身感受到美国的文化和音乐。百老汇上演的剧目，往往一演就是七八年，有的甚至十几年。拿《猫》来说，从 1982 年 10 月开始上演到 2000 年 6 月落幕，上演时间长达 18 年之久。而今百老汇大道是美国现代歌舞艺术以及美国娱乐业的代名词。每年都有数百万的来自世界各地的游客到纽约欣赏百老汇的歌舞剧。

### 难点点拨 知识难点看一看，情景实战热热身

1．have a good time 玩得开心

You must have had a good time in America.

你在美国一定玩得很开心啰！

2．be renowned for 因为……而著名

Broadway is a wide street in Manhattan, renowned for its theaters.

百老汇是曼哈顿的一条很宽的街道，这条街以剧院而驰名天下。

## 情景实战 跟着老外听一听，读一读，练一练

**会话 1**

Baton: Welcome back! You must have had a good time in America.

Daniel: Yes. I travelled around the continent, from the west to the east coast. I went to New York," the Big Apple", and had fun there. I visited Manhattan and Brooklyn and I even saluted the Statue of Liberty. I walked the length of Wall Street and had a picture taken next to the famous bull there. Fifth Avenue and Central Park enchanted me. But there was one place I really loved and that was Broadway.

B: Tell me something about it.

D: Broadway is a wide street in Manhattan, renowned for its theaters. Many famous operas are shown there, including *Cats*, *The Phantom of the Opera*, and *Miss Saigon*.

B: Great. I love Beijing Opera, but I've never seen western opera.

D: They act and sing enchantingly. The stories are quite moving, full of twists and turns. By the way, have you heard about the "Off-Broadway" and the "Off-Off-Broadway"?

B: What's that?

D: They are theaters near Broadway, where the land price is relatively lower. There they stage many avant-garde and low-budget plays. New actors make their debuts there.

巴 顿：欢迎回来！你在美国一定玩得很开心吧！

丹尼尔：是呀，我从西海岸到东海岸，游遍了这个国家。我去了传说中的“大苹果”纽约，玩得挺开心的。我参观了曼哈顿和布鲁克林，瞻仰了自由女神像，在华尔街散了散步，还和华尔街那头著名的公牛合了张影。第五大道和中央公园让我深深为之着迷，但是我最爱的还是百老汇。

B：说点百老汇的事情吧。

D：百老汇是曼哈顿的一条很宽的街道，这条街以剧院而驰名天下。很多著名的歌剧都在这里上演，包括《猫》、《歌剧魅影》和《蝴蝶夫人》。

B：太棒了。我喜欢京剧，但我还从来没看过西方歌剧呢。

D：他们演技超绝，唱功非凡。故事情节非常精彩，充满曲折，荡气回肠。顺便问一下，你听说过“外百老汇”和“外外百老汇”吗？

B：是什么呀？

D：它们是靠近百老汇的一些剧院，这里的地价相对低一些。这些剧院经常上映一些先锋派的并且成本低廉的戏剧。很多新演员在这里初试牛刀。

### 核心词汇记一记

**Words Storm**

| | | |
|---|---|---|
| continent | ['kɔntinənt] *n.* | 大陆 |
| coast | [kəust] *n.* | 海岸 |
| salute | [sə'lu:t] *v.* | 敬礼 |
| bull | [bul] n | 公牛 |
| enchant | [in'tʃɑ:nt] *v.* | 使迷惑 |
| opera | ['ɔpərə] *n.* | 歌剧 |
| relatively | ['relətivli] *ad.* | 相对地 |
| debut | ['deibju:] *n.* | 初次登场 |

**Phrases**

twists and turns 曲折的情节

**会话 2**

Ellis: Do you like classical music?

Gray: Yes. I love Mozart and Beethoven. It is reported that listening to Mozart makes you smarter and helps you concentrate better. I have CDs of many versions of Mozart. Different conductors and orchestras give you different feelings even though they perform the same symphony. But I love opera the most.

E: Really? I love opera too. Which piece do you like best?

G: Many. I think Mozart's are the best. *Don Giovanni, The Marriage of Figaro, Magic Flute* and *Cosi Fan Tutte*…

E: I like the coloratura by the "Queen of the Night" in *The Magic Flute*. Then when the young couple sing their love song merrily in *The Marriage of Figaro*, I feel so delighted and I am carried away with the music.

G: Yes. I have the same feeling. I dream that one day I can go to Broadway and get the opportunity to appreciate operas there, but I don't have enough money now.

E: It's really expensive. I can only afford to buy the CDs, I never go to music halls or theaters.

埃利斯: 你喜欢古典音乐吗?

格 雷: 嗯，我喜欢莫扎特和贝多芬。据说听莫扎特的音乐会让你集中

精力，变得聪敏。我有很多版本的莫扎特的 CD。尽管演奏的是同一首交响曲，但不同的指挥家和乐队会带给你不同的感受。不过我还是最喜欢歌剧。

E: 真的吗? 我也喜欢歌剧。你最喜欢哪一部?

G: 多着呢。莫扎特的最好听，像《唐璜》、《费加罗的婚礼》、《魔笛》，还有《女人心》等。

E: 我喜欢《魔笛》里面“夜女王”的花腔女高音。每当《费加罗的婚礼》里面的年轻夫妇高唱欢乐的爱之歌时，我就感到非常欢欣鼓舞，陶醉在音乐里了。

G: 是的，我也有同样的感觉。我梦想有一天我能去百老汇观赏歌剧，但是我现在还没有足够的钱。

E: 真的很贵。我只能买得起 CD，从来都没去过音乐厅和剧院。

**核心词汇记一记**

**Words Storm**

concentrate ['kɔnsentreit] *v.* 集中
version ['vəːʃən] *n.* 版本
conductor [kən'dʌktə] *n.* 指挥家
orchestra ['ɔːkistrə] *n.* 乐队
symphony ['simfəni] *n.* 交响乐
coloratura [kɔlərə'tuətə] *n.* 花腔女高音
flute [fluːt] *n.* 笛子

**Phrases**

It's reported that 据说
carry away 带走，随……而去

# 23. Peking Opera

## 爱听京戏

### 知识链接 拓展视野，掌握背景知识

京剧又称京戏，是中国戏曲曲种之一。京剧创始于19世纪中期，融合了徽调和汉调的特点，并吸收了秦腔、昆曲、梆子、弋阳腔等艺术的优点，被称为中国国粹。京剧形成后在清朝宫廷内空前繁荣。但京剧的主体在中国文化整体中更偏于民间文化或底层文化，即使它因满清帝后及八旗王公青睐有加而迅速繁荣，也不足以改变美学上的这一特质。当然，恰因基于民间趣味的京剧从清末直到整个20世纪获得了此前所有民间艺术从未有过的地位，它也从艺术本体的层面最大限度地扩展了民间文化与美学的影响，提升了民间趣味在中国文化传统中的地位。

### 难点点拨 知识难点看一看，情景实战热热身

1. originate in/from 源自，发源于

   Peking Opera originated in the late 18th century, a synthesis of music, dance, and acrobatics.

   京剧发源于18世纪末，集音乐、舞蹈和杂技于一体。

2. duc to（等于 because of）因为

   It is remarkable due to its highly stylized music and performing techniques.

   京剧的显著特点就在于高度风格化的音乐和表演技术。

3. bid/say farewell to each other

   In despair, his lover Yuji chooses to commit suicide. So they say farewell to each other.

   他的爱妾虞姬在绝望中选择了自刎，所以他们向对方互道永别。

4. be skilled in 精通某物

   He is robust and very often skilled in Chinese martial arts.

   他精力过人，并且精通中国武术。

5. burst into laughter 哄堂大笑

   He behaves humorously and makes the audience burst into laughter.

   他表现得很滑稽，往往让观众哄堂大笑。

## 情景实战 跟着老外听一听，读一读，练一练

**会话 1**

Asher: You have sat here watching TV for a long time. Is this a new film?

David: No. It's Peking Opera—*The Conqueror Xiang Yu's Farewell to His Lover Yuji*.

A: Amazing. They are colorfully painted and dressed, and they act rather…er, rather pretentiously on the stage.

D: Peking Opera originated in the late 18th century, a synthesis of music, dance, and acrobatics.

A: Therefore it enjoys a long history. Hundreds of years ago those actors and actresses had already begun to act like this?

D: Yes. It is based on traditional Anhui Opera, with the repertoire, music and performing techniques adopted from Kun Opera and Qinqiang Opera. It is remarkable due to its highly stylized music and performing techniques.

A: I'm interested. What's the story of this opera?

D: Its repertoire includes historical plays, comedies, tragedies and farces. What we are seeing is the story about Xiang Yu the conqueror, a famous general who rebelled against the Qin Dynasty and overthrew it. He is cornered by Liu Bang, the leader of another troop. In despair, his lover Yuji chooses to commit suicide. So they say farewell to each other.

阿舍：你已经坐在这儿看了好一会儿电视了，是新电影吗？

大卫：不是，是京剧——《霸王别姬》。

A：真神奇。他们脸上画的很花哨，身上穿的也很花哨，在舞台上表现的……哦，拿腔拿调的。

D：京剧发源于 18 世纪末，集音乐、舞蹈和杂技于一体。

A：因此它已经有很久的历史了。几百年前的男女演员们就已经开始这样表演了吗？

D：是的。京剧建立在传统的徽剧的基础之上，还吸收了昆曲和秦腔的剧目、音乐和表演技巧。京剧的显著特点就在于高度风格化的音乐和表演技术。

A：真有意思。京剧讲的是什么故事？

D：京剧的剧目包括历史剧、喜剧、悲剧和滑稽剧。我们现在正在看的是关于西楚霸王项羽的故事，他是起兵反秦并且推翻了秦朝的一个将军。他被刘邦的部队包围了，爱妾虞姬在绝望中选择了自刎，所以他们向对方互道永别。

### 核心词汇记一记

**Words Storm**

| | | |
|---|---|---|
| conqueror | [ˈkɔŋkərə] | *n.* 征服者 |
| farewell | [ˈfɛəˈwel] | *n.* 永诀 |
| pretentious | [priˈtenʃəs] | *a.* 装腔作势的 |
| repertoire | [ˈrepətwɑː] | *n.* 剧目 |
| stylize | [ˈstailaiz] | *v.* 使风格化 |
| farce | [fɑːs] | *n.* 滑稽剧 |
| overthrow | [ˌəuvəˈθrəu] | *v.* 推翻 |

**Phrases**

| | |
|---|---|
| Peking opera | 京剧 |
| in despair | 在绝望中 |
| commit suicide | 自杀 |

**会话 2**

Stephen: I want to know more about Peking Opera.

John: I'll tell you something about it if you wish. In Peking Opera there are many kinds of characters—Sheng, Dan, Jing, Mo and Chou, for example.

S: What are they? I'm confused. It sounds like some Chinese words.

J: Right. Sheng means male character. He is very often the leading role in the opera. Dan is the female character. Jing is a male whose face is colorfully painted. He is robust and very often skilled in Chinese martial arts. Different Jings have different designs of paintings on their faces to symbolize their different personalities.

S: Formidable. What about Chou?

J: Chou is a male clown. He behaves humorously and makes the audience burst into laughter.

S: Can male actors play female roles?

J: Of course. Mei Lanfang is a famous actor who plays the role of Dan. He sings and acts just like a soft woman. Someone contends that men can do better than women in acting female figures, because only men know where the best side of women lies.

史蒂芬：我想知道更多关于京剧的知识。

约翰：要是你想听，我来告诉你吧。京剧中有很多种角色，如生、旦、净、末、丑。

S：他们都是什么角色啊？我有点不明白。听起来好像是汉语词汇。

J：是的。生指的是男性角色，一般是京剧中的主角。旦是女角，净是脸上被画得花里胡哨的男人，他精力过人，并且精通中国武术。不同的净脸上会画不同的造型来象征不同的性格。

S：真了不起啊。丑呢？

J：丑是男性丑角。他表现得很滑稽，往往让观众哄堂大笑。

S：男演员可以扮演女角吗？

J：当然可以。梅兰芳就是以扮演旦角而蜚声中外的男演员。他的演唱和表演就像一个柔弱的女人。有的人认为男人比女人更适合演女性角色，因为只有男人才知道女人最好的一面在哪里。

**核心词汇记一记**

**Words Storm**

robust [rəu'bʌst] *a.* 精力充沛的
symbolize ['simblaiz] *v.* 象征
personality [,pə:sə'næliti] *n.* 人格
formidable ['fɔ:midəbl] *a.* 强大的
contend [kən'tend] *v.* 主张

**Phrases**

martial arts 武术

# 24. Photography

## 浮光掠影

### 知识链接 拓展视野，掌握背景知识

摄影是一项光与影的艺术，自诞生之日起，就与绘画有着千丝万缕的联系。绘画是摄影的姊妹艺术。绘画的很多基本功，如对明暗的把握、色彩的认识和运用、构图的选择等等，摄影者无不用之。有绘画基础的人进入摄影行业可在很多方面轻车熟路、事半功倍。数码摄影和数码暗房是时代进步、科学发展的产物，让更多的人更快捷地进入了摄影世界，分享着摄影的快乐。

### 难点点拨 知识难点看一看，情景实战热热身

1. think of doing sth. 考虑做某事
   I'm thinking of buying a camera.
   我正考虑买一台照相机呢。
2. 形容词 +in+ 属性，表示“修饰，限定”
   A compact camera is smaller in size, simpler in structure and function.
   傻瓜相机体积比较小，结构和功能也更简单些。
3. take down 记录，记下
   You can take pictures, but a camera always takes down what it meets faithfully.
   你可以拍照，但是相机拍的东西总是忠实于原物的。
4. in terror 恐惧；in despair 绝望
   A photo about the war of some African country shows a boy standing before houses on fire, staring forward in terror and despair.
   有一张关于某个非洲国家战争的照片，展示了一个小男孩站在着火的房子前凝视，眼中充满了恐惧和绝望。
5. I concede that 我承认……
   I concede that we cannot make pictures of Impressionism and Surrealism with a camera.
   我承认我们是不能用相机创造出印象派和超现实主义的画作的。

## 情景实战 跟着老外听一听，读一读，练一练

**会话 1**

Kerry: Can I use your digital camera? Tomorrow I'll go out camping. I will take some fine pictures.

Serena: Sorry. Jack and I just agreed that we would meet tomorrow. You know Jack, don't you? He is a shutterbug and we will try to take some pictures.

K: What a pity. Never mind. I'm thinking of buying a camera. Can you give me some advice?

S: Sure. You want an SLR or a compact one?

K: I don't understand. What is an SLR and what is a compact camera?

S: SLR means single lens reflex camera. It is usually clumsier, more complex and expensive, used by advanced photographers. But you can change lenses freely, and if you want to learn photography seriously, I think you need one.

K: But you said it is clumsier.

S: A compact camera is smaller in size, simpler in structure and function. It is usually automatic. You just point it to the scene and press the button. However, it is a pity that you cannot change its lens, and it is absolutely not professional. If you just want to have one for daily use, I think it's a good choice.

K: All right. I'll get a compact one.

凯莉：可以用一下你的数码相机吗？明天我要出去野营。我想会拍到些不错的照片。

塞丽娜：不好意思，我和杰克刚约好明天出去见面。你知道杰克吧？他是摄影发烧友，我们得拍照。

K：太遗憾了，不过没关系。我正考虑买一台照相机呢。你能给我点建议吗？

S：当然可以了。你想要单反相机还是傻瓜相机？

K：我不懂什么意思。什么是单反相机，什么是傻瓜相机？

S：单反相机就是单镜头反光相机，通常看起来很笨重，很复杂，而且比较贵，是水平高一点的摄影者用的。你可以随意地换镜头，如果你想认真学习摄影的话，还是需要一台的。

K：但是你说它很笨重呀。

S：傻瓜相机体积比较小，结构和功能也更简单些。它通常是自动的。你只需要对着景色按下按钮就可以了。但遗憾的是这种相机不能更换镜头，非常不专业。如果你只是日常用的话，傻瓜相机是个不错的选择。

K：好吧，那就买个傻瓜相机。

### 核心词汇记一记

**Words Storm**

| | | |
|---|---|---|
| shutterbug | ['ʃʌtəbʌg] *n.* | 摄影爱好者 |
| clumsy | ['klʌmzi] *a.* | 笨拙的 |
| lens | [lenz] *n.* | 镜头 |
| absolutely | ['æbsəlu:tli] *ad.* | 完全地，绝对地 |
| professional | [prə'feʃənl] *a.* | 专业的 |

**Phrases**

| | |
|---|---|
| digital camera | 数码相机 |
| SLR | 单反相机 |
| compact camera | 傻瓜相机 |

**会话 2**

Mark: Do you think one day photography will supersede painting?

Ben: No. You can take pictures, but a camera always takes down what it meets faithfully. It cannot create pictures of wild imagination which only exists in an artist's mind before it is painted.

M: But photos are more realistic. Don't you think so? I've seen many photographs about wars and disasters. They really sincerely shocked me! For example, a photo about the war of some African country shows a boy standing before houses on fire, staring forward in terror and despair. If you try to paint this scene, it will lose its authenticity—viewers don't credit it.

B: Yes, I grant you that, but how can you create a picture of *Sunflowers* as Van Gogh has done, with a camera? Nor can you replicate Salvador Dali's *Premonition of Civil War* with your lens?

M: No. I concede that we cannot make pictures of Impressionism and Surrealism with a camera. But if you are putting a picture in a newspaper, to show some reality, you'll need a photo instead of a painting.

B: Yes, you are right and have good reason to say so.

马克：你觉得摄影会不会有一天取代绘画？

本：不可能。你可以拍照，但是相机拍的东西总是忠实于原物的，它不能创造蕴含着丰富想象力的画面，因为这种想象力在未被画出之前只存在于艺术家的脑海中。

M：但是照片更真实。你不觉得吗？我看到过很多关于战争和灾难的照片，深深地触动了我的心。有一张关于某个非洲国家战争的照片，展示了一个小男孩站在着火的房子前凝视，眼中充满了恐惧和绝望。如果你试图画下这一幕的话，就会失去它的真实性，观看者可能不会相信。

B：是的，这点我同意。但是你怎样才能创造出一幅像梵高的《向日葵》那种图片呢？用相机吗？不行吧。也不能用镜头复制出萨尔瓦多·达利的《内战的前兆》吧？

M：不能。好吧，我承认我们是不能用相机来创造出印象派和超现实主义的画作的。但如果你要把一张图片放到报纸上说明一些事实，最好用照片而不是画作。

B：是的，很有道理。

### 核心词汇记一记

#### Words Storm

supersede [ˌsjuːpəˈsiːd] *v.* 代替
realistic [riəˈlistik] *a.* 现实的
replicate [ˈreplikeit] *n.* 复制
premonition [ˌpriːməˈniʃən] *n.* 前兆
impressionism [imˈpreʃənizəm] *n.* 印象派
surrealism [səˈriəlizəm] *n.* 超现实主义

#### Phrases

instead of 代替，而不是

# 25. Modern Arts

## 现代艺术

### 知识链接 拓展视野，掌握背景知识

人们将保罗·塞尚（Paul Cézanne）称为“现代艺术之父”，第一部西方现代艺术史就是从他开始写起的。塞尚与前人的区别就在于他将西方艺术从宗教与政治的束缚中解放出来，不注重“画什么”，而将“怎样画”的课题作为自己创作的主要目的，他追求的是“形式主义”，亦即“为艺术的艺术”。西方现代艺术所追求的精髓就是把人类从工具理性中解放出来，因为世界上很多事情是科学所不能解决的。比如，用科学和逻辑去分析情感问题就是徒劳和荒唐的。

### 难点点拨 知识难点看一看，情景实战热热身

1. an album of 一册（图片、照片）

   I'm seeing an album of pictures.

   我在看一本画册。

2. be accustomed to 习惯于

   I am accustomed to realistic paintings.

   我一直习惯于看写实风格的绘画作品。

3. get a clear view (of sth.) 看清楚某物

   Sometimes you don't have to get a clear view—sometimes the world itself is chaotic disjunctive, and intangible.

   有些时候你并不需要去搞得很清楚，因为有时这个世界本身就是混乱无序、支离破碎的和无法捉摸的。

4. mistake... for... 把……误认为……

   These paintings look so real and three-dimensional that we can mistake them for real things lying on the floor.

   这些画都是三维的，看起来很真实，以致于我们会误认为它们都是真的在地上呢。

## 情景实战 跟着老外听一听，读一读，练一练

**会话 1**

Kate: I'm looking at an album of pictures. Look, there are so many strange things. I've never seen a clock painted in that way, it is as soft as a piece of meat.

Billy: It's Dali! He always paints things like that. It's an album of modern arts.

K: I cannot understand. They look bizarre. I am accustomed to realistic paintings.

B: A distinctive feature of modern arts is that they look unconventional, dramatically out of your life experience. For example, you may see a man screaming with a horrible and distorted face—that's Munch's Expressionism. You may see a village full of twisted human limbs and heads—that's Picasso's Cubism. A urinal can also be taken as a piece of art, if you know Duchamp. Many avant-garde artists created their own highly stylistic works, some of which are quite sensational and difficult for interpretation.

K: I still cannot understand what's good in it. For me, art must be seen to be understood.

B: But sometimes you don't have to get a clear view—sometimes the world itself is chaotic, disjunctive, and intangible. What we can get from these works is only a true feeling of reality. We see them and we find they're true to life, though we don't understand, because life itself sometimes is not understandable.

凯特：我在看一本画册。看，居然有这么多奇怪的东西。我还从来没见过那样画的钟呢，它就像一块肉那么软。

比利：这是达利的作品。他总是画那样的物体。这是一本现代艺术的画册。

K：我不理解，它们看起来都很奇异。我一直习惯于看写实风格的油画。

B：现代艺术最与众不同的风格就在于它们看起来是非传统的，而且游离于你的生活经验之外。比如，你可能看到一个惊声尖叫的男子有一张恐怖和扭曲的脸，这是蒙克的表现主义作品。你还可能看到一个布满扭曲的人的肢体和头颅的村庄，这是毕加索的立体派作品。如果你知道杜尚的话，你会发现小便盆也能成为一件艺术作品。很多前卫的艺术家创作出了一批高度个性化的作品，这其中有些作品非常有冲击力，但是也难于理解。

K：我还是看不出这些作品到底有什么好。我觉得艺术必须要能被人理解。

B：但是有些时候你并不需要去搞得很清楚，因为有时这个世界本身就是混乱无序、支离破碎和无法捉摸的。我们从这些作品中所能获得的仅仅是一种对现实的真实感受。我们可能不理解这些画的意思，但我们看着这些画，发现它们反映了现实生活，因为生活本身有时就是无法理解的。

### 核心词汇记一记

**Words Storm**

| | | |
|---|---|---|
| bizarre | [bi'zɑː] | *a.* 奇异的 |
| accustom | [ə'kʌstəm] | *v.* 使习惯于 |
| distort | [dis'tɔːt] | *v.* 扭曲 |
| expressionism | [iks'preʃənizəm] | *n.* 表现主义 |
| intangible | [in'tændʒəbl] | *a.* 难捉摸的 |

**Phrases**

modern art 现代艺术

**会话 2**

Gary: What's that guy doing over there? He must be mad!

Paul: He dressed himself like a fly, with a pair of ugly wings. Now he is running here and there, just like a huge "flyman". I guess this is a kind of performance art.

G: Strange enough. Once I saw a man cutting himself with a keen knife, and blood gushed out of his arm. It was quite horrible, but he shouted that we should say no to wars because war is even worse than what he was doing.

P: Sometimes they disgust me. I don't sympathize with those performers—they must be lunatics. We need composure and rationality, but I don't see these qualities in their behavior.

G: But some artists can do well. A painter paints all kinds of things directly on the pavement. These paintings look so real and three-dimensional that we can mistake them for real things lying on the floor. Then finally we'll find that we are fooled by the artist and we cannot hold our laughter.

盖瑞：那个家伙在干吗呢？他一定疯了！

保罗：他把自己打扮得像个苍蝇一样，戴着一对丑陋的翅膀。现在他居然在跑来跑去的，简直像个"苍蝇人"。我猜这是一种行为艺术吧。

G：太奇怪了。有次我还看到一个男人用锋利的小刀割自己，血从他的胳膊里流出。太恐怖了。但是他却呼吁我们应该拒绝战争，因为战争比他现在正在做的事情还要糟糕。

P：有时他们会让我觉得恶心，我不同情这些表演者们，我认为他们都是疯子。我认为我们需要的是沉着和理性，但是在他们的行为中我一点都看不到。

G：但是有些艺术家就做得很好。有一个画家在公路上画了各种各样的东西。这些画都是三维的，看起来很真实，以致于我们会误认为它们都是真的在地上呢。最后我们发现，原来我们被艺术家愚弄了，就忍不住笑了起来。

**核心词汇记一记**

**Words Storm**

ugly ['ʌgli] *a.* 丑陋的

lunatic ['luːnətik] *n.* 疯子

composure [kəm'pəuʒə] *n.* 沉着

rationality [ˌræʃə'næliti] *n.* 理性

**Phrases**

performance art 行为艺术

# Food and Party 中外饮食

# 26. Local Special

## 特色菜肴

### 知识链接 拓展视野，掌握背景知识

相传意大利粉是马可波罗看过中国人的拉面之后自行在意大利尝试重做而成的产品，但自从考古学家在意大利中部的一个公元前4世纪的伊特鲁里亚人墓穴里发现了古人制成的意大利粉后，有关传言不攻自破。东西方都有自己的特色菜肴，意粉就是意大利的经典菜肴之一。中国的八大菜系里面，目前最受欢迎的是川菜。因起源于四川一带而得名，以麻、辣、鲜、香为特色，其代表菜有宫保鸡丁、干烧鱼、回锅肉、麻婆豆腐、夫妻肺片、樟茶鸭子、干煸牛肉丝、怪味鸡块、灯影牛肉、鱼香肉丝、水煮牛肉等。

### 难点点拨 知识难点看一看，情景实战热热身

1．have a taste of 尝一尝

I want to have a taste of some Italian food.

我想尝尝意大利菜。

2．be introduced by sb. from... to... 被某人从某地引入某地

Some people even say that pizza was introduced by Macro Polo from China.

有的人甚至说披萨是马可·波罗从中国引进的。

3．be famous for / be distinguished for 因……出名

Sichuan food is famous for its use of hot pepper.

四川菜以用辣椒而出名。

Why is Sichuan food distinguished for its hot pepper?

为什么四川菜以辣椒而出名呢?

4．live on 凭靠……而生活

If you live on the mountain,you depend on the mountain.

靠山吃山。

## 情景实战 跟着老外听一听，读一读，练一练

**会话 1**

Pamela: I want to have a taste of some Italian food. Can you give me some guidance?

Amie: You cannot avoid pizza then and there are pizza restaurants everywhere, but you need the most original ones. Go to some real Italian restaurant and find them.

P: There are lots of Pizza Huts around. Are pizzas there as good as they say?

A: Almost as good, by the way, do you know the history of it?

P: No idea and I don't really care.

A: There are lots of ridiculous talks about it. Some people even say that pizza was introduced by Macro Polo from China. God only knows whether that's true.

P: Have some idea of other good Italian food?

A: Yes, there is spaghetti of course, but that is relatively easy to make. Next time you come to visit me, stay for lunch and I'll introduce you to the taste of it.

P: Thank you. Don't Italians eat something like snails?

A: That's basically French, you got mixed up. It's the French who cook snails. You should try French cuisine some day.

P: What about tomorrow? You decide the restaurant, and it'll be my treat, okay?

A: Really? That's great, but you are a newcomer. I cannot let you pay. Let's go Dutch.

帕梅拉: 我想尝尝意大利菜。你能给我点建议吗?

艾米: 那你一定得尝尝披萨。披萨店到处都有，但是你需要尝一下最原汁原味的披萨。只有到真正的意大利餐馆才可以找得到呢!

P: 附近有很多披萨店，那些披萨真的像他们说的一样美味吗?

A: 大部分都不错。顺便说一下，你知道披萨的历史吗?

P: 不知道，我不太注意这个。

A: 关于披萨有很多好笑的说法呢。有的人甚至说披萨是马可波罗从中国引进的，上帝知道这是不是真的。

P: 还有什么其他好吃的意大利菜吗?

A: 有啊，当然是意大利面条了。但这个相对来说制作简单。下次你来看我的时候，一定要留下来吃中饭，我要让你尝尝意大利面的味道。

P: 谢谢。意大利人是不是吃一种类似蜗牛的东西?

A: 这主要是法国人吃的东西，你搞混了。法国人喜欢做蜗牛吃。你改天应该尝一下法式菜。

P: 明天如何? 你决定去哪个餐馆，我请客，好吗?

A: 真的吗? 可你初来乍到的，我也不能让你付钱呀。那咱们就 AA 吧。

### 核心词汇记一记

**Words Storm**

guidance ['gaidns] *n.* 指导
pizza ['piːtsə] *n.* 披萨
hut [hʌt] *n.* 小屋
spaghetti [spə'geti] *n.* 意大利面条
snail [sneil] *n.* 蜗牛
cuisine [kwiː'ziːn] *n.* 烹调风格

**Phrases**

Italian food 意大利菜
mix up 混淆

**会话 2**

Karen: Hey! Mr. Green. Welcome to Sichuan. Let's go for lunch.

Green: Great. You lead the way and I follow.

K: Do you like Sichuan food? It's famous for its use of hot pepper.

G: I know Chinese food, but what's Sichuan food?

K: There are four cooking styles in China—Shandong Cuisine, Sichuan Cuisine, Jiangsu Cuisine, and Guangdong Cuisine.

G: So every kind has some special courses to offer? Why is Sichuan food distinguished for its hot pepper?

K: Sichuan is in a basin geographically, so it's quite humid. The peppers help people get dry.

G: Therefore food is a way to reflect the living environment of people?

K: Yes, that is so true. There is a Chinese saying goes like this—"If you live on the mountain you depend on the mountain; If you live by the riverside you live on the river." China is so huge that different areas have different situations. People living by the sea get sea food, while we Sichuan people have our own local specials.

G: I really appreciate this. It's unlike America where you can only have the same food wherever you go.

凯琳：嗨！格林先生，欢迎来到四川。咱们去吃午饭吧。

格林：太棒了。你来带路，我跟着你走。

K：你喜欢吃四川菜吗？它因为辣而出名。

G：我知道中国菜，但是四川菜是什么？

K：在中国有四大菜系——鲁菜、川菜、苏菜和粤菜。

G：那么每一种都有特别的菜肴吗？为什么四川菜以辣椒而出名呢？

K：从地理上来说四川处在盆地里，所以气候湿润，而辣椒可以祛湿。

G：所以食物是反映人们生活环境的一种方式啰？

K：是的。中国有句谚语是这么说的——靠山吃山，靠水吃水。中国如此之大，不同的地区有不同的情况。生活在海边的人就吃海鲜，而四川人民也有自己的特色菜肴。

G：这点我很喜欢。不像美国，不管你走到哪儿，吃到的东西都是一样的。

### 核心词汇记一记

**Words Storm**

| | |
|---|---|
| pepper | ['pepə] *n.* 辣椒 |
| distinguished | [dis'tiŋgwiʃt] *a.* 著名的 |
| basin | ['beisn] *n.* 盆地 |
| geographically | [dʒiə'græfikəli] *ad.* 地理上 |
| humid | ['hju:mid] *a.* 潮湿的 |
| reflect | [ri'flekt] *v.* 反映 |
| appreciate | [ə'pri:ʃieit] *v.* 欣赏，感激 |

**Phrases**

| | |
|---|---|
| give a lecture | 作演讲 |
| local specials | 特色菜肴 |

# 27. Western Food

## 西方饮食

### 知识链接 拓展视野，掌握背景知识

西餐包括餐汤、开胃菜、主菜、餐后甜品及饮品。最正式的西餐当属法式西餐。但在亚洲的饮食文化中，如香港的茶餐厅、日本的日式西餐厅、台湾的简餐店等都不会提供全套的食品，故广义的西餐会是一顿包含西式主菜的膳食，咖啡可被一般饮品取代。在香港的茶餐厅和快餐店，餐汤亦可被中式餐汤取代。西方人很重视礼仪，餐桌的礼仪更加复杂，如一道菜一道菜地吃。吃正式的西餐时，不能发出声响，不能吃一半，吐出一半等。吃每一道菜都有不同的餐具，在餐桌上按从外到内顺序排列。

### 难点点拨 知识难点看一看，情景实战热热身

1. What kind of food do you like most?

   你最喜欢吃什么饭？

2. fast food 快餐，速食

   I'm definitely addicted to fast food.

   我的确很爱吃快餐。

3. a portion of 一份

   Next time when I go to a restaurant I will order a portion of medium steak for a try.

   下次我去餐馆的时候，要点一份半熟的牛排试试。

4. feel like doing 想要做某事

   I'm so tired that I don't feel like cooking now.

   我现在太累了，不想做饭。

## 情景实战 跟着老外听一听，读一读，练一练

**会话 1**

Samantha: What types of food do you like most?

Erin: I don't know, but I'm definitely addicted to fast food. I like fried chicken and potato crisps.

S: They are junk food. You have to have a taste of the real western food.

E: So what exactly should I taste?

S: Steak is a good choice. It can be cooked in different ways—rare, medium, and well done.

E: So next time I go to a restaurant I will order a portion of medium steak for a try.

S: Then salad is also a must. Fruit and vegetable can refresh you and you should also try a omelet.

E: I know salad because it's also common in China. We cut different fruits into small dices and mix them together.

S: Caviar is always delicious. It's a little bit expensive, but you will love it.

E: Then I promise I'll try all of them and experience typical western food.

S: My mum is really good at making pudding and apple pie. Next time you come to see me, you can try them.

E: Really? Thank you so much.

瑟曼莎：你最喜欢吃什么饭？

埃林；我不知道，但是我的确很爱吃快餐。我喜欢炸鸡和薯片。

S：但这是垃圾食品。你应该尝尝真正的西餐。

E：那我应该尝点什么呢？

S：牛排是个不错的选择。它有很多种不同的做法——生的，半熟，还有熟透的。

E：所以下次我去餐馆的时候要点一份半熟的牛排试试。

S：当然也必须要尝尝沙拉。水果和蔬菜能够让你觉得清新，你还应该尝尝煎蛋卷。

E：嗯，我知道沙拉，这在中国也很常见。把水果切成小片，并且拌在一起。

S：鱼子酱非常美味。就是有一点贵，但是你一定会喜欢的。

E：我保证一定会尝遍这些美味的。这些可是正宗的西方食品。

S：我妈妈很会做布丁和苹果派。下次你来看我的时候，可以尝尝她的手艺。

E：真的吗？那真是太感谢了！

### 核心词汇记一记

**Words Storm**

| | | |
|---|---|---|
| definitely | ['definitli] | *ad.* 肯定地 |
| junk | [dʒʌŋk] | *n.* 垃圾 |
| steak | [steik] | *n.* 牛排 |
| rare | [rɛə] | *a.* 生的 |
| omelet | ['ɔmlit] | *n.* 煎蛋卷 |
| dice | [dais] | *n.* 块 |
| caviar | ['kæviɑː] | *n.* 鱼子酱 |

**Phrases**

| | |
|---|---|
| fried chicken | 炸鸡 |
| potato crisp | 薯片 |

**会话 2**

Nancy: Darling? Let's dine out this evening. I'm so tired that I don't feel like cooking tonight.

Frank: All right, what do you want to have?

N: Lobster.

F: Impossible! It's too expensive. You'll have to settle for something a little more humble.

N: But I want lobster! You still love me, don't you?

F: Sure I do, but we'll have cheese and mashed potatoes, and then some roast beef.

N: I want lobster…

F: Then some onion soup and finally two glasses of wine will do.

N: I want lobsters…

F: Okay! The small restaurant at the corner of the street will do, but it doesn't offer lobster at all.

N: I want lobster.

F: Don't be silly. Let's go now. I'm starving. I could eat a horse.

N: You don't love me at all. I want a divorce!

F: All right. Calm down my dear, we'll have lobster. Okay?

南希：亲爱的，今天晚上我们出去吃吧。我太累了，不想做饭。

弗兰克：好的，你想吃什么呢？

N: 龙虾。

F: 不可能，太贵了，我们简单吃一顿饭吧。

N: 但是我想吃龙虾。你还爱我对吗？

F: 我们去吃点奶酪和土豆泥吧，然后再来点烤牛肉。

N: 我想吃龙虾。

F: 然后再来点洋葱汤，最后再来两杯酒。

N: 我想吃龙虾。

F: 好吧。就在街角那个餐厅吃吧，那儿没有龙虾。

N: 我想吃龙虾。

F: 别傻了，我们走吧，我都快饿死了，现在能吃下一匹马。

N: 你一点都不爱我，我要离婚！

F: 好了，平静一下亲爱的！我们去吃龙虾，好吗？

**核心词汇记一记**

**Words Storm**

lobster ['lɔbstə] *n.* 龙虾
cheese [tʃi:z] *n.* 奶酪
roast [rəust] *v.* 烘烤
starve [stɑ:v] *v.* 使挨饿
divorce [di'vɔ:s] *n.* 离婚

**Phrases**

mashed potato 土豆泥
calm down 镇静

# 28. Chinese Food

## 中国菜

### 知识链接 拓展视野，掌握背景知识

中国菜与中华饮食在日本和韩国称为中华料理或中国料理，欧美称之为唐餐，是中国文化的组成部分，深远地影响了东亚地区的饮食文化。菜谱来源于中国各个地区和民族。“中国菜”只是一个统称，各个地方差异极大，因为中国是一个多民族的国家，由于地理、气候、物产、文化、信仰等的差异，菜肴风味差别很大，有四大菜系、八大菜系之说。四大菜系，即黄河下游的鲁菜、长江上游的川菜、长江下游的苏菜、珠江流域的粤菜。

### 难点点拨 知识难点看一看，情景实战热热身

1．claim 声称，宣称

They claim that they have invited a very famous Chinese chef who has won many awards for cookery.

他们宣称请了一位非常著名的中国大厨，说他得过很多烹饪的奖项。

2．rich or poor 无论穷富

When the Spring Festival comes, every family, rich or poor, will make dumplings.

过春节的时候，家家户户，不管穷还是富，都要吃饺子。

3．resemble 相像，相似

Their shape resembles that of gold ingots used in ancient China, thus symbolizing good fortune.

它们的形状类似中国古代用的金元宝，因此象征着好运和财富。

4．stuff sth. into 把某物填进去

Dumplings are delicious, and we can stuff different things into them to have different flavors.

饺子很好吃，我们可以包不同的馅儿吃到不同味道的饺子。

## 情景实战 跟着老外听一听，读一读，练一练

**会话 1**

Barry: I like Chinese food so much. Every weekend I go to dinner at the Chinese restaurant on the corner of the street near my apartment.

Tom: That place isn't good enough. The food it provides isn't genuine Chinese.

B: What? They claim that they have invited a very famous Chinese chef who has won many awards for cookery.

T: I've been there once and ordered a course—"shredded pork with garlic sauce", only to find it quite different from what we get in China. They even put cream into it.

B: I have never been to China, so I don't know what real Chinese food is like. Maybe you can help me.

T: Haha. I know what you mean. Do you have time tomorrow? Come to visit me. I'm not a good cook, but I can let you taste some genuine Chinese courses.

B: All right! Ha! I'm so happy to go.

T: Through Chinese food you can taste Chinese culture. I've a bottle of Mao-tai for you to try as well.

巴利：我很喜欢中国菜。我每周末都去中国餐馆吃饭，那家餐馆位于我家公寓附近的街拐角处。

汤姆：那个地方不太好。他们家的中国菜不地道。

B：什么？他们宣称请了一位非常著名的中国大厨，说他得过很多烹饪的奖项。

T：我曾经去过一次，点了一盘鱼香肉丝，发现跟我们中国的做法太不一样了，他们甚至加了奶油进去。

B：我从来没去过中国，所以不知道真正的中国菜是怎样的。也许你能帮帮我。

T：哈哈，我懂你的意思了。你明天有时间吗？来找我吧。我虽不是个好大厨，但是我可以让你尝尝真正的中国菜。

B：好的！哈哈，我很乐意前往。

T：吃吃中国菜，你就品到中国文化的韵味了。我还给你备了瓶茅台呢！

### 核心词汇记一记

**Words Storm**

| | | |
|---|---|---|
| chef | [ʃef] *n.* | 厨师 |
| cookery | ['kukəri] *n.* | 烹饪 |
| course | [kɔːs] *n.* | 一道菜 |
| garlic | ['gɑːlik] *n.* | 大蒜 |
| dumpling | ['dʌmpliŋ] *n.* | 饺子 |
| peanut | ['piːnʌt] *n.* | 花生 |

**Phrases**

put... into 输入，使进入

**会话 2**

Robbie: Why do Chinese people like dumplings?

Monica: Traditionally, Chinese people eat dumplings only once a year. When the Spring Festival comes, every family, rich or poor, will make dumplings. Their shape resembles that of gold ingots used in ancient China, thus symbolizing good fortune.

R: So they eat dumplings partly as a ritual, to pray for good fortune of the next year?

M: Yes. But dumplings are delicious, and we can stuff different things into them to have different flavors.

R: And I know you Chinese people eat noodles very often, especially on birthdays.

M: A noodle is long. So it is symbolic of longevity. We have them also as a ritual, to pray for a long life.

R: So food contains cultural significance. No wonder many scholars are committed to the study of traditional food.

M: In China there is a proverb "Food is as important as heaven to people", which means food is the paramount necessity for the people. We attach great importance to food, because without it a man cannot live.

罗 比：为什么中国人爱吃饺子呢？

莫妮卡：按以前的传统，中国人一年只吃一次饺子。过春节的时候，家家户户，不管穷还是富，都要吃饺子。饺子的形状类似中国古代用的金元宝，因此象征着好运和财富。

R：那他们吃饺子部分是因为祈求来年好运？

M：是的，但是饺子也很好吃，我们可以包不同的馅儿吃到不同味道的饺子。

R：我知道你们中国人经常吃面条，尤其是在生日的时候。

M：一根面条很长，所以象征着长寿。我们吃面条也是为了祈求长寿。

R：因此食物里包含着文化意义。怪不得很多学者投入到传统食品的研究中去呢！

M：中国有句谚语“民以食为天”，意思就是说食物是人们极为重要的必需品。我们很注重食物，因为没有食物我们无法生存。

**核心词汇记一记**

**Words Storm**

| | | |
|---|---|---|
| resemble | [ri'zembl] | *v.* 类似 |
| ritual | ['ritʃuəl] | *n.* 仪式 |
| stuff | [stʌf] | *v.* 填满，塞满 |
| flavor | ['fleivə] | *n.* 口味 |
| longevity | [lɔn'dʒeviti] | *n.* 寿命 |
| proverb | ['prɔvəːb] | *n.* 谚语 |

**Phrases**

| | |
|---|---|
| Spring Festival | 春节 |
| gold ingots | 金元宝 |

# 29. Healthy Diet

## 健康饮食

### 知识链接 拓展视野，掌握背景知识

常言道“五谷为养，五果为助，五畜为益，五菜为充，气味合而服之，以补益精气”。以现在科学的说法称为蛋白质的“互补作用”，意即要获得人体所必需的各种营养素，必须注意食品的合理搭配，切忌吃荤不吃素或吃素不吃荤。科学家发现，由于长期要求自己少食甚至不食荤腥，许多人已不知不觉地成了素食者。但是，长期不沾荤腥会使人体内所需要的一些养分得不到及时的补充，使人体内的某些零部件受到损害，这就需要我们进行合理而健康的饮食。

### 难点点拨 知识难点看一看，情景实战热热身

1．be lacking in 缺乏

They are high-calorie and lacking in protein and dietary fiber.

它们含有很高的卡路里，而且缺少蛋白质和食用纤维。

2．do harm to sb. 对某人有害

Sugar gives you energy, but eating too much will do harm to your health.

糖能供应能量，但是吃得太多却对健康有害。

3．question 质疑，怀疑

Traditionally people think it good, but now many people begin to question it.

传统的观点认为这样做挺好的，但是现在人们开始质疑了。

4．so...that... 太……而……

At noon, I often eat so much that I feel lazy in the afternoon.

中午我经常吃得很多，以至于整个下午都懒洋洋的。

5．whet the appetite 开胃

Have some haws to whet your appetite.

吃点山楂可以开胃。

## 情景实战 跟着老外听一听，读一读，练一练

**会话 1**

Bob: I'm getting fatter and fatter. I must control my diet.

Daisy: What do you often eat?

B: Junk food—hamburgers, ice cream, colas, hot dog, pop corn…

D: Yes, they are junk indeed. They are high-calorie and lacking in protein and dietary fiber.

B: So what kind of food should I have?

D: Food that is low in fat and sugar and high in vitamins and fiber. Sugar gives you energy, but eating too much will harm your health. Fat makes you fat.

B: So can you give me some advice for my diet?

D: You should eat more vegetables and less meat. Avoid sweets and carbonated beverages.

B: But vegetables are not as delicious as meat. I don't like vegetables.

D: You have to get used to it. Look at me. I'm a vegetarian myself and I love all kinds of vegetables—celery, spinach, eggplant, cucumber… They taste good. I'll give you a recipe.

B: Thank you so much.

鲍勃：我变得越来越胖了。我必须控制自己的饮食。

黛茜：你经常吃些什么呢？

B：垃圾食品，像汉堡、冰激凌、可乐、热狗，还有爆米花等。

D：是的，这些确实是垃圾食品，含有很高的卡路里，而且缺少蛋白质和膳食纤维。

B：那我应该吃些什么样的食物呢？

D：低脂低糖但富含维他命和纤维的食物。糖能供应能量，但是吃得太多却对健康有害。脂肪会使你变胖。

B：那你能给我的饮食提点建议吗？

D：你应该多吃蔬菜，少吃肉。戒掉糖果和碳酸饮料。

B：但是菜没有肉好吃。我不喜欢吃蔬菜。

D：你必须要习惯。我是个素食主义者。各种各样的蔬菜我都喜欢——芹菜、菠菜、茄子、黄瓜等，味道还不错。我待会儿给你个食谱。

B：太感谢了。

### 核心词汇记一记

**Words Storm**

protein ['prəutiːin] *n.* 蛋白质
vitamin ['vaitəmin] *n.* 维他命
celery ['seləri] *n.* 芹菜
spinach ['spinitʃ] *n.* 菠菜
eggplant ['egplaːnt] *n.* 茄子
recipe ['resipi] *n.* 食谱

**Phrases**

pop corn 爆米花
carbonated beverages 碳酸饮料

**会话 2**

Arron: I always have a glass of water after I get up in the morning. I don't know if it's a good habit.

Iwa: Hard to say. Traditionally people think it is good, but now many people begin to question it. It depends on you I guess, if you feel good you can continue, but if it ails you, just stop.

A: I don't know. Then I'll have only a little for my breakfast. As a result, I often feel quite hungry before noon.

I: You should take more breakfast. Eat an egg or a rasher of bacon, and a slice of bread. A glass of milk will cheer you up.

A: At noon, I often eat so much that I feel lazy in the afternoon. I cannot control it.

I: Try to balance your diet. I don't have a good appetite, so I eat only a little.

A: Have some haws to whet your appetite, we both have our own problem, perhaps we need to consult a doctor for advice.

I: OK. I'll call Doctor Johnson to fix the time.

艾伦：我总是在早上起床后喝一杯水。我不知道这是不是个好习惯。

伊娃：难说。传统的观点认为这样做挺好的，但是现在人们开始质疑了。这取决于你自己。如果你感觉不错就继续下去，如果你觉得不舒服，就别这样了。

A：我不知道。喝完后我早饭只吃一点，结果我经常在中午之前就会觉得很饿。

I：你应该多吃点早饭。吃一个鸡蛋或者一片培根，再加一片面包。一杯牛奶会让你感到振奋的。

A：中午我经常吃得很多，以至于整个下午都懒洋洋的。我无法控制自己。

I：那就试着去调理一下饮食。我胃口不太好，所以我只吃一点东西。

A：吃点山楂可以让你开胃。我们俩都有各自的问题。我觉得我们需要向医生咨询一下。

I：好的。我给约翰逊医生打个电话约一下时间。

**核心词汇记一记**

**Words Storm**

ail [eil] *v.* 生病
rasher ['ræʃə] *n.* 薄片
slice [slais] *n.* 薄片，切片
appetite [ˌæpitait] *n.* 胃口
consult [kən'sʌlt] *v.* 请教，咨询

**Phrases**

cheer up 使振奋

# 30. Table Manners

## 餐桌礼仪

### 知识链接 拓展视野，掌握背景知识

餐桌礼仪，是指人类社会在进餐时的各种公认礼貌标准。而有些举止行为，在进餐时被认为是无礼，或影响别人食欲的。由于文化差异，餐桌礼仪在各国都有很大的不同。通常死亡、疾病和排泄都是不应该在餐桌上提起的话题。在有些文化中，进餐时要表现出优雅的态度，所以就有些特定的习惯和礼仪。下面我们就来看看中西方不同的餐桌礼仪吧。

### 难点点拨 知识难点看一看，情景实战热热身

1．Long time no see.

好久不见。

2．Don't talk with your mouth full.

嘴巴塞得满满的时候不要说话。

3．take a breath 喘气

He never stops to take a breath, and keeps his head dipped in the food and drink.

他从来都不停下来喘口气，而是一直埋头吃。

4．be occupied (with...) 忙，从事……

I'm occupied with my homework.

我在写作业。

## 情景实战 跟着老外听一听，读一读，练一练

**会话 1**

Rick: Long time no see. What about you?

Eric: Good. Tomorrow I'm going to have dinner with a friend, but you know I'm new around here and I don't know too much about table manners in the States.

R: I can give you some advice if you like.

E: Great, please do. I would sure appreciate it.

R: If your friend is a girl, pull the chair out for her and let her sit first and then you sit down and put the napkin on your lap. Use your knife and fork gently and eat without making any unpleasant noises.

E: All right. I'll follow your instruction.

R: Then don't talk with your mouth full. If you need salt or something out of your reach, you just say "Can you pass me the salt please".

E: I'll bear it in mind.

R: Use your spoon to drink the soup. Eat slowly as a gentleman.

E: I got it.

里克：很久不见，你怎么样？

艾瑞克：挺好的，明晚我要和一个朋友共进晚餐。但你知道我刚来到这边，还不太知道美国的餐桌礼仪。

R：我倒可以给你点建议。

E：太棒了！说吧。我会很感激的。

R：如果你的朋友是个女孩，你要为她拖出椅子，并且让她先坐。然后你才能坐下，并把餐巾放在你的腿上。用刀叉时要绅士些，吃东西时不要发出一些让人不愉快的声音。

E：好的，我会照做的。

R：还有嘴巴塞得满满的时候不要说话。如果你需要盐或者一些你够不到的东西，你只要说一句"你能把盐递给我吗"就行了。

E：我会牢记的。

R：喝汤时要用你的汤匙，要像一个绅士那样慢慢吃。

E：明白了。

### 核心词汇记一记

**Words Storm**

napkin ['næpkin] *n.* 餐巾

lap [læp] *n.* 大腿前部，膝盖

fork [fɔːk] *n.* 叉子

instruction [in'strʌkʃən] *n.* 指示

spoon [spuːn] *n.* 汤匙

**Phrases**

table manners 餐桌礼仪

make noise 发出噪音

bear in mind 记住

**会话 2**

Zack: If you have time this Sunday we can dine out with some friends.

Billy: I'm not occupied. Who will you go with?

Z: Joe, Mary, and Jack. We can have a good time at the restaurant. What do you think?

B: Jack? I don't think it's a good idea. He is always so... er... uncultivated at the table.

Z: What? He may eat fast, but it's his style. I don't think it's bad.

B: It's not "eat fast", it's "devour savagely". He never stops to take a breath, and keeps his head dipped in the food and drink and besides that, he makes loud noises.

Z: Yes, I know it might be a little crude, but we are good friends, and I don't think it is much too inappropriate.

B: The girls cannot endure it. Just ask Mary, she will say the same thing.

Z: Okay, but I think we should give him a last chance to see whether he can change his style.

B: I don't think he can.

扎克：如果你这周日有空我们可以跟一些朋友一起吃饭。

比利：我有空。你想跟谁出去？

Z：乔、玛丽和杰克。我们可以在餐馆度过一段美好时光。你觉得呢？

B：杰克？我认为这可不是个好主意。他在餐桌上总是很……哦……没教养。

Z：什么？他可能吃饭挺快的，但这是他的风格呀。我不觉得这有什么不好。

B：不是“吃得快”，而是“野蛮地狼吞虎咽”。他从来都不停下来喘口气，而是一直埋头吃。此外，他还发出很大的声响。

Z：是，我知道这可能不太礼貌，但是我们是好朋友，我觉得他的行为并没有很不合适。

B：但是女孩子是不能忍受这个的。问问玛丽吧，她可能会说同样的话。

Z：好，但是我们应该给他最后一次机会，看他能不能改正。

B：我觉得他改不掉。

### 核心词汇记一记

**Words Storm**

| | |
|---|---|
| dine | [dain] *v.* 吃饭 |
| occupy | ['ɔkjupai] *v.* 占据 |
| uncultivated | [ˌʌn'kʌltiveitid] *a.* 无教养的 |
| devour | [di'vauə] *v.* 狼吞虎咽 |
| savagely | ['sævidʒli] *ad.* 野蛮地 |
| inappropriate | [ˌinə'prəupriət] *a.* 不相称的 |

**Phrases**

give sb. a chance 给某人一次机会

# 31. In a Bar

## 酒吧时光

### 知识链接 拓展视野，掌握背景知识

酒吧最早起源于美国西部大开发时期。最初，在美国西部，牛仔和强盗很喜欢聚在小酒馆里喝酒。由于他们都是骑马而来，所以酒馆老板就在馆子门前设了一根横木(bar)，用来拴马。后来，汽车取代了马车，骑马的人逐渐减少，这些横木也多被拆除。有一位酒馆老板不愿意扔掉这根已成为酒馆象征的横木，便把它拆下来放在柜台下面，没想到却成了顾客们垫脚的好地方，受到顾客的喜爱。酒吧大约于十几年前进入我国，之后便得到了迅猛的发展，目前都市的夜空已离不开酒吧，都市人更离不开酒吧，人们需要在繁忙中遗忘、沉醉。

### 难点点拨 知识难点看一看，情景实战热热身

1. This is the first time... 这是第一次……
   This is the first time I've been to a bar.
   这是我第一次来酒吧。
2. follow one's advice 照着某人说的做
   I'll just follow your advice.
   我就照着你说的来做。
3. a shot of 少量的，一口
   I want a shot of whiskey.
   我要一小杯威士忌。
4. cannot do without 离不开
   A man cannot do without his spirits—good for the soul!
   没有酒男人是没法过活的——这可是命根子啊！
5. I cannot agree with you more.
   我太同意你的观点了。
6. fool around with 鬼混，厮混
   In some bars boys and girls fool around with each other.
   在一些酒吧里，很多男孩女孩彼此厮混在一起。

## 情景实战 跟着老外听一听，读一读，练一练

**会话 1**

Alice: This is the first time I've been to a bar. Cover me. I don't want to appear like I am stupid.

Harry: No Problem. Follow me and we'll take our seats, then the waiter will come to us.

A: OK. I'll just follow your advice.

H: (get the menu from the waiter) What would you like then? I want a shot of whiskey.

A: Let me have a look. I'll have a dry martini, please.

H: I'm not overly particular about my drinks, so long as they are alcoholic. I always drink what I can get. Brandy, gin, sherry, vermouth, beer… don't care.

A: Likewise for me. A man cannot do without his spirits—good for the soul! If you read Hemingway, you'll find that for a soldier in a war, the most precious thing is neither life nor victory, but alcohol. As long as you got alcohol, you've got everything.

H: Ha! What a wonderful theory.

A: But I still prefer some drinks to others. For example, I love mixed drinks, such as cocktails, but if it's not available, anything will do.

爱丽丝：这是我第一次来酒吧呢，你可得关照我，我可不想表现得很傻。

哈里：没问题，跟我来吧。我们先坐那儿，然后服务员就会过来的。

A：好的，我就按照你说的来做。

H：(从服务员手里接过菜单)你喝点什么？我要一小杯威士忌。

A：我先看看。干马提尼吧。

H：事实上我并不是很在意喝的是什么，只要是酒就行。我总是拿到什么就喝什么，白兰地、杜松子酒、雪利酒、苦艾酒、啤酒……我统统不在乎。

A：我也是。没有酒男人是没法过活的——这可是命根子啊！如果你读过海明威的作品，你就会发现，对于战争中的士兵来说，最宝贵的东西既不是生命也不是胜利，而是酒。只要能有酒喝，就别无所求了。

H：哈，多么精彩的理论呀！

A：但是我还是更加偏爱一些种类的酒，比如我更爱像鸡尾酒那样的混合酒。但是如果没有这种酒，其他的也可以接受。

### 核心词汇记一记

**Words Storm**

| | |
|---|---|
| bar | [bɑː] *n.* 酒吧 |
| whiskey | ['hwiski] *n.* 威士忌 |
| alcoholic | [ˌælkə'hɔlik] *n.* 酒 |
| precious | ['preʃəs] *a.* 宝贵的 |
| cocktail | ['kɔkteil] *n.* 鸡尾酒 |

**Phrases**

| | |
|---|---|
| dry martini | 干马提尼 |
| neither...nor... | 既不是……又不是…… |
| as long as | 只要 |

**会话 2**

Nate: Why do you go to a bar?

Peter: You know bars are different. Some are quiet and elegant and some are noisy and full of sexy girls dancing. My preference is drinking with a few friends at a bar gracefully and peacefully, talking about something philosophical, but a bar is a place for thinking and talking, not for dancing.

N: I cannot agree with you more. In Paris many intellectuals love staying in coffee bars, thinking, talking and writing. Hemingway, Sartre and Camus once frequented the cafés there. The most famous coffee bars are *"Le Café de Flore" and "Les Deux Magots" at "Rive Gauche".*

P: *Bien!* You know a lot about bars.

N: Yes. But in some bars boys and girls fool around with each other.

P: Once I was in a foreign city and I felt tired, so I entered a bar only to see men kissing each other. They are all gays.

N: After all, a bar is a place for people to know and love each other.

内特：你为什么要去酒吧？

彼得：你知道的，酒吧跟酒吧也是不一样的。有的酒吧就比较安静和高雅一些，而有的就充斥着喧嚣和跳热舞的性感女孩。对我来说，我更喜欢跟几个朋友到一个安静雅致的酒吧去喝点东西，聊一聊哲学什么的。酒吧是一个思考的地方，而不是跳舞的地方。

N：我太同意你的观点了。巴黎有很多知识分子都喜欢待在咖啡馆里思考、交谈和写作。海明威、萨特还有加缪就曾经常光顾咖啡馆。最富盛名的咖啡馆有在塞纳河左岸的“花神咖啡馆”和“双偶咖啡馆”。

P：哇塞，你知道好多关于酒吧的知识呀。

N：嗯，但是在一些酒吧里，很多男孩女孩彼此厮混在一起。

P：有次我在国外一个城市里，感到很累，所以就去了一家酒吧，结果看到了男人在互相接吻。去那个酒吧的人都是同性恋。

N：不管怎么说，酒吧是人们彼此了解和产生好感的好去处。

**核心词汇记一记**

**Words Storm**

| | |
|---|---|
| elegant | ['eligənt] *a.* 文雅的，优雅的，高雅的 |
| preference | ['prefərəns] *n.* 偏爱，偏好 |
| philosophical | [ˌfilə'sɔfikəl] *a.* 哲学的 |
| intellectual | [ˌinti'lektjuəl] *n.* 知识分子 |
| gay | [gei] *n.* 男同性恋 |

**Phrases**

| | |
|---|---|
| coffee bar | 咖啡馆 |
| after all | 毕竟，终究，到底 |
| as long as | 只要 |

# 32. Chatting

## 交谈的技巧

### 知识链接 拓展视野，掌握背景知识

*人是群居性动物，也是社会性动物，在衣食住行的各个过程中，不可或缺的就是彼此之间的交流和交往。交往是人生存和生活的需要，更是工作的需要。每个人都有足够的条件成为主管，平步青云，但必须要懂得一些待人处事的技巧。推销人际关系的书也开始不断推向市场，从一个侧面证明如何进行交流在当今社会变得越来越重要。*

### 难点点拨 知识难点看一看，情景实战热热身

1. interact with sb. 与某人交往

   Recently I read a book about how to interact with others.

   最近我读了一本关于如何与人交往的书。

2. be supposed to do 应该做某事

   You are not supposed to laugh aloud while chatting with your friends.

   跟朋友在一起聊天的时候不能放肆大笑。

3. be familiar with 熟悉

   If you are not so familiar with each other you can talk about the weather first.

   如果你们彼此不太熟的话，可以先讨论天气的问题。

4. to/till the end 直到最后

   Listen to him carefully and patiently to the end.

   认真耐心地听他讲完。

5. personal affairs 私人问题

   Never ask him about his personal affairs such as his salary and age.

   一定不要问他诸如薪水和年龄之类的私人问题。

## 情景实战 跟着老外听一听，读一读，练一练

**会话 1**

Betty: I think John is rather arrogant. When you talk to him, he doesn't even look at you.

Summer: Indeed, but he is a good guy. The problem is that he doesn't know how to talk with others. He may not look at you, but every word of yours will be remembered and noticed.

B: So it is a misunderstanding between us. I was quite angry with his seemingly ignorant attitude.

S: Yes. Recently I read a book about how to interact with others.

B: Tell me something about that. I'm interested. You know I usually don't get along well with my roommates.

S: When you speak or your friend speaks, look him in the eyes, and show you care about what he is saying.

B: Yes, of course. But sometimes I stared at my friend so carefully that he would think there was something on his teeth or face and feel quite uneasy. It's so embarrassing.

S: So you have to practice a lot. Then, you have to learn how to interact with others. Smile warmly and naturally.

B: Er… You are not supposed to laugh aloud while chatting with your friends, right?

S: Right. Be light-hearted, but check your laughter.

贝蒂：我认为约翰这个人很自大。你跟他说话的时候，他甚至都不看看你。

莎玛：其实他这个人还不错。问题在于他不知道如何与别人交流。他可能不会看着你，但是你说的每一个字他都能记得。

B：所以我们之间只是一场误会。可是我对他看起来无所谓的态度很恼火。

S：是呀。最近我读了一本关于如何与他人交往的书。

B：说说呗！我挺有兴趣的。你也知道，我平常跟室友处得就不好。

S：当你说话或者你的朋友说话的时候，你要盯着对方眼睛，表示你很在乎他。

B：嗯，当然了。但是有时我盯着朋友很认真地看，他会觉得自己牙齿或者脸上有什么东西，就会很不自然，还挺尴尬的。

S：所以你必须要多加练习。然后你要学习如何与他人交往，微笑要轻盈自然。

B：哦，是不是说跟朋友一起聊天的时候你不能大笑?

S：是的。要表现得轻松，但是要留意自己的笑声。

### 核心词汇记一记

**Words Storm**

interact ['intərækt] *v.* 互动
embarrassing [im'bærəsiŋ] *a.* 尴尬的
light-hearted ['lait'hɑːtid] *a.* 轻松的

**Phrases**

be angry with 生（某人）的气
get along with 与……相处

**会话 2**

Rachel: I feel nervous. What topic should I choose when I talk with Mr. Green?

Ross: He is British. So if you are not so familiar with each other you can talk about the weather first. It's a rainy day today. You just ask him if it rains much in Britain. Then gradually you'll find other topics that are more interesting.

Rachel: Great. Should I stay close to him or should I keep a certain distance away from him during the talk?

Ross: You are not old friends, so I suggest you don't touch him. You'd better not stand too close to each other either.

Rachel: Shall I interrupt him if I disagree with him?

Ross: No. Listen to him carefully and patiently to the end. Then it's your turn to speak.

Rachel: Shall I talk about many personal affairs with him? Shall I ask him some private questions to show that I care about him?

Ross: No. Never ask him about his personal affairs such as his salary and age. It's not your business.

Rachel: Shall I speak very humbly and show respect for him?

Ross: Don't behave too pretentiously—just be yourself.

瑞秋：我感到很紧张。跟格林先生谈话要选择什么话题呢？

罗斯：他是个英国人，所以如果你们对彼此不太熟的话，可以先讨论天气问题。比如，今天下雨，你就问他英国是否多雨，然后你就会发现其他更有趣的话题。

R：太好了。那在我们交谈的时候，我应该离他近一些，还是与他保持点距离呢？

R：你们并不是老朋友，所以我建议你不要有身体接触，最好不要靠对方太近。

R：如果我对他的话有异议可以打断他吗？

R：不行，要耐心认真地听他讲完，然后你再开始说。

R：我可以跟他讨论很多私人问题吗？是不是我问他这种问题可以显示出我很在意他呢？

R：不。一定不要问他诸如薪水和年龄之类的私人问题。这不关你的事儿。

R：我是不是应该表现得很谦逊，以显示我尊敬他呢？

R：不要表现得太做作，表现自然就行了。

### 核心词汇记一记

**Words Storm**

nervous ['nə:vəs] *a.* 紧张的

familiar [fə'miljə] *a.* 熟悉的

humbly ['hʌmbli] *ad.* 谦逊地

pretentiously [pri'tenʃəsli] *ad.* 装腔作势地

**Phrases**

keep a certain distance away from 与……保持一段距离

show respect for 向……表示尊敬

Sports and Games 文体娱乐

# 33. Travel

## 户外野游

### 知识链接 拓展视野，掌握背景知识

二战结束后，户外运动成为西方年轻人的一大爱好。越来越多的人开始登山、攀岩、徒步跋涉，一方面锻炼了身体，缓解了西方工业发达之后造成的现代人茫然无事的生活状态；另一方面也培养了团队合作精神和勇敢坚毅的个人品质。当然，户外运动还要有足够的安全保障，也需要某些工具，一般是有经验的人带领新手成长的过程。具体的运动十分复杂，纸上谈兵却简单有趣，下面大家就来谈论一下流行的户外运动吧。

### 难点点拨 知识难点看一看，情景实战热热身

1．spend sometime (doing sth.) 花时间

We'll stay there for two days, and spend two nights there.

我们在那里待两天两夜。

2．make a fire 生火

We'll collect some fire wood, and when night comes we'll make a campfire.

我们会找些木柴，晚上生篝火。

3．go through 经过，经历

I've gone through a lot of adventures.

我有很多探险经历。

## 情景实战 跟着老外听一听，读一读，练一练

**会话 1**

Sam: Where are you going this weekend?

Adam: To a forest in the suburban area. I've already called two friends to go. Would you like to go too?

S: Of course. How can we get there?

A: A friend of mine, Mike, has a car. He will drive us there this Friday afternoon. Then we'll stay there for two days, and spend two nights there.

S: Terrific! I haven't done that before. I feel so exited! Do we need to take something with us?

A: Yes. You'd better get a big backpack, because the car cannot go deep into the forest, and we have to walk a long distance. Get a flashlight, lighter, compass, knife, lunch box, canteen, sleeping bag, and other useful things you can imagine, and cram all these into your backpack. I'll get a big tent for us.

S: Cool! I think I should take my camera with us, too. I can take a lot of beautiful pictures.

A: Right. In daytime, we'll walk a long distance and see what we can find there. We'll even think about laying snares for rabbits and fishing. Then we'll collect some fire wood, and when night comes we'll make a campfire. I play the guitar, and you sing.

萨姆：这个周末你去哪儿？

亚当：去郊区的森林。我已经叫了两个朋友要一起去了，你也想去吗？

S：当然了。我们怎么去？

A：有个朋友，迈克，他有车。周五下午他开车送我们到那儿。然后我们在那里待两天两夜。

S：太棒了！我以前从没这样玩过呢。真刺激！我们需要带点什么东西吧？

A：是啊。你最好带个大背包，因为车子开不进林地，我们需要步行好长一段路。带上手电筒、打火机、指南针、刀子、饭盒、水壶、睡袋，还有别的你认为有用的东西，都塞进背包里。我为大家带一顶大帐篷。

S：真帅！我想我还该带上相机，这样就可以拍漂亮的照片了。

A：对。白天我们长途跋涉，看林地里有什么好玩的。我们想设陷阱逮兔子和钓鱼。之后我们找些木柴，晚上生篝火。我弹吉他，你们唱歌。

### 核心词汇记一记

**Words Storm**

| | | |
|---|---|---|
| backpack | ['bækpæk] | *n.* 背包 |
| flashlight | ['flæʃlait] | *n.* 手电筒 |
| lighter | ['laitə] | *n.* 打火机 |
| compass | ['kʌmpəs] | *n.* 指南针 |
| canteen | [kæn'tiːn] | *n.* 水壶 |
| snare | [snɛə] | *n.* 陷阱 |

**Phrases**

| | |
|---|---|
| lunch box | 饭盒 |
| lay snares | 设陷阱 |

**会话 2**

Simon: You have a lot of experience about living in the wilderness.

Carl: Yes, yes. I've gone through a lot of adventures. Once I even encountered a grizzly.

S: He wanted to attack you?

C: No. I was scared to death. I tried my best to keep cool, and murmured "good boy, let me go" repeatedly. Then I walked back slowly out of his territory. It seemed that he was not so hostile.

S: So do we need to take some weapons with us?

C: A big knife is enough. It must be keen and handy, because we may use it to cut some firewood. There is a saying, "One knife, one life". A flashlight, if it is bright enough, can also keep those animals away from us. But you have to take your tools wisely. Never do things stupid.

S: You mean, we should not take some other more powerful weapons?

C: No. We're not going into a war. Live, and let live. Sometimes we may try to catch some fish or rabbits, but we never attack animals if unnecessary.

S: But it would be cool if we took a double-barrel with us, isn't it?

C: No.

西蒙：你在野外生活方面很有经验啊。

卡尔：是啊。我有很多探险经历。我还遇到过一只灰熊呢。

S：它想攻击你吗？

C：不。我吓得要命，竭力叫自己镇定下来，不停嘟囔着"好孩子，让我走吧"。然后我就慢慢退出它的领地。看上去它并不是很有敌意。

S：那么我们需要随身带着武器咯？

C：一把大号的折刀就够用了。刀必须锋利且便于携带，因为我们可能得用它砍柴火。有个谚语叫"一把刀能救一条命"。如果有把足够亮的手电，也能驱赶动物。但是一定得适当地使用工具，别干蠢事。

S：你的意思是我们不用带更厉害点的武器了？

C：是的。我们又不是去打仗。自己要生存，也得叫别的物种生存啊。有时候我们可能逮兔子，钓鱼什么的，但如果不是出于必要，我们绝不猎杀动物。

S：可你不觉得带把双筒猎枪很酷吗？

C：不觉得。

**核心词汇记一记**

**Words Storm**

| | |
|---|---|
| encounter | [in'kauntə] v. 遇到 |
| grizzly | ['grizli] n. 灰熊 |
| murmur | ['məːmə] v. 小声说 |
| territory | ['teritəri] n. 领地 |
| hostile | ['hɔstail] a. 敌对的 |

**Phrases**

| | |
|---|---|
| keep cool | 保持冷静 |
| keep away from | 使……避开 |

# 34. Extreme Sports

## 极限运动

### 知识链接 拓展视野，掌握背景知识

极限运动，是结合了一些难度较高，且挑战性较大之组合运动项目的统称，如直排轮、滑板、极限单车、攀岩、雪板、空中冲浪、街道疾降、极限越野、极限滑水等都是极限运动项目。极限运动除了追求竞技体育超越自我生理极限“更高、更快、更强”的精神外，更强调参与和勇敢精神，追求在跨越心理障碍时所获得的愉悦感和成就感，同时，它还体现了人类返璞归真、回归自然、保护环境的美好愿望，因此已被世界各国誉为“未来体育运动”。

### 难点点拨 知识难点看一看，情景实战热热身

1．in mid-air 在半空

Have you ever thought about the possibility that your parachute may fail in mid-air?

你有没有想过你的伞可能在半空中坏掉啊？

2．front line 前线

You'll feel as if you are a soldier landing in enemy territory, far behind the front line.

你会觉得你自己就像一个真正的战士，空降在远离前线的敌人的领土之上。

3．one... and... 一旦有……就……

One mistake and you'll pay severely for your error.

一个差错可能就会使你遭到重创。

4．an outlet of 出口，释放口

Doing extreme sports serves as an outlet of my passion for nature.

做极限运动释放了我对大自然的热爱之情。

5．immerge oneself into 把自己沉浸在

I tackle all obstacles and at the same time immerge myself deep into nature.

我冲破所有的障碍，沉浸在大自然的深处。

## 情景实战 跟着老外听一听，读一读，练一练

**会话 1**

Tom: Hey! What's up?

Steven: I'm preparing my parachute. Tomorrow I'll jump out of an airplane.

T: Goodness me! Are you crazy? Have you done this before? Have you been trained properly for it?

S: Easy, my friend. I've been doing parachuting for three years. I'm a veteran now, well-experienced.

T: Why didn't you ever mention this? Taking that risk is unnecessary. We are not in the war yet.

S: I know. But we have to do something exciting in our lives, life can be boring otherwise. War is not an issue for us. What else could I do offers the exhilaration? Parachuting saves me in one sense, because it fills my life with excitement, it gives me a sense of significance and orientation.

T: But you can get hurt. Have you ever thought about the possibility that your parachute may fail in mid-air?

S: Every time I jump, I make sure of everything beforehand. A good parachutist never worries unnecessarily about things like this.

T: Airborne...? It sounds so interesting, but I don't dare to join you.

S: Come on, try it! You'll feel as if you are a soldier landing in enemy territory, far behind the front line.

汤姆：嘿！干吗呢？

斯蒂文：我正在整理我的降落伞，明天我要跳伞。

T：我的天！你疯了？你以前做过这个吗？你接受过相关训练吗？

S：别着急，哥们。我已经练习跳伞 3 年了。现在是一名经验丰富的老手了。

T：为什么你从来没告诉过我呀！冒那个险是不必要的，我们现在又没战争。

S：我知道。但是生活是无聊的，我们总得做点什么。战争离我们那么遥远，我们能做些别的什么让自己兴奋一点呢？跳伞从某种意义上解救了我，它让我的生活充满了刺激，让我的生命有了意义和方向。

T：但是你可能会受伤呀。你有没有想过你的伞可能在半空中坏掉啊？

S：每次跳伞前，我都会提前做好一切准备。一个好的跳伞员从来都不会做这种无谓的担忧。

T：空降，听起来很有趣的样子，但是我实在不敢加入。

S：来吧，尝试一下。你会觉得你自己就像一个真正的战士，空降在远离前线的敌人的领土之上。

### 核心词汇记一记

**Words Storm**

parachute ['pærəʃuːt] *v.* 跳伞

veteran ['vetərən] *n.* 老手，老兵

unnecessary [ˌʌn'nesəsəri] *a.* 不必要的

significance [sig'nifikəns] *n.* 意义

orientation [ɔːrien'teiʃən] *n.* 方向

**Phrases**

jump out of 从……中跳出来

in the war 在战争中

**会话 2**

Gary: What's your favorite sport?

Vincent: Rock climbing and bungee jumping.

G: I like skateboarding myself. I often choose the more difficult ways to go, to test my skills. Sometimes people will applaud my performance.

V: True, extreme sports require strength, endurance and intelligence. You need to be perceptive enough to make your decision quickly.

G: You have to keep your balance, move fast and smoothly. One mistake and you'll pay severely for your error.

V: It is also a good idea to have some pads for your knees and elbows. These are necessary equipment.

G: Have you thought about why you love these dangerous sports?

V: Every day I just stay indoors and never have a chance to get out. Doing extreme sports serves as an outlet of my passion for nature. I tackle all obstacles and at the same time immerge myself deep into nature. It's invigorating.

G: Besides, you can get acquainted with people who share the same activity with you. It was with skateboarding that I met my girlfriend and fell in love with her. You see, God favors me.

V: You do have all the luck my friend.

加　里: 你最喜欢的运动是什么?

文森特: 攀岩和蹦极。

G: 我喜欢玩滑板。我经常选一些难走的线路，并且会尝试些新技术。有时大家会为我的表演鼓掌呢。

V: 是的，极限运动需要力量、耐性和智慧。你必须要有足够的感知力来迅速做出决定。

G: 你必须要设法保持平衡，快速平稳地移动。一个差错可能就会使你遭到重创。

V: 所以你必须要戴护膝和护腕。这些是必需的装备。

G: 你有没有想过你为什么会爱上这么危险的运动?

V: 我每天都待在室内，没有任何出去的机会。做极限运动释放了我对大自然的热爱之情。我冲破所有的障碍，沉浸在大自然的深处。这令我精神振奋。

G: 除此之外，你还可以交到这个圈子里的朋友，他们也跟你一样喜欢这种活动。我就是通过玩滑板跟我女朋友坠入爱河的。你看，上天还是很眷顾我的。

V: 你确实运气不错。

### 核心词汇记一记

#### Words Storm

skateboard ['skeitbɔːd] *n.* 滑板
endurance [in'djuərəns] *n.* 忍耐
pad [pæd] *n.* 衬垫
outlet ['autlet] *n.* 出口
obstacle ['ɔbstəkl] *n.* 障碍
immerge [i'məːdʒ] *v.* 埋头

#### Phrases

rock climbing 攀岩
bungee jumping 蹦极

# 35. Walking and Jogging

## 跑步散步

### 知识链接 拓展视野，掌握背景知识

*不少古代养生家都提倡散步。散步可改善心脏血管系统，对大脑皮质是一种温和而有节奏的刺激，对中枢神经有着良好的调整作用，且缓解神经肌肉的紧张，达到放松镇静的效果，帮助消除疲劳。跑步是简单的健身运动，也是大量需氧的运动，可防止冠心病的发生。但是跑步必须循序渐进，逐步提高运动量，否则会对身体健康造成负面影响。*

### 难点点拨 知识难点看一看，情景实战热热身

1. go out for a walk 出去散步

   How about going out for a walk this evening?

   今晚出去散散步怎样？

2. run a circle 跑一圈

   Let's go to the playground and run a few circles.

   我们去运动场跑上几圈吧。

3. sweat salt out 出汗把盐排出

   We sweat salt out, and we have to get resupplied.

   我们（跑步时）出汗导致盐分流失，得设法补充点。

4. to begin with 开始的时候

   To begin with, you should get yourself warmed up so that you'll not strain your muscle.

   开始的时候你要先热身，以使你的肌肉不致被拉伤。

5. capable of 能够

   A few months later you'll find yourself capable of covering many circles.

   几个月后你就会发现自己能跑很多圈了。

## 情景实战 跟着老外听一听，读一读，练一练

**会话 1**

Susan: Hey. How about going out for a walk this evening?

Kelly: Walk? I'd rather run. Let's go to the playground and run a few circles.

S: Negative. I'm so full that my stomach refuses running.

K: So we can stroll a little bit, then we come jogging for a while.

S: Sure. Why do you want to jog so much?

K: I'm weighty, you see. I read an article saying jogging is the best way to get rid of fat.

S: Yes. But we'll carry a canteen with us because you don't want to suffer from dehydration, do you?

K: No. Maybe we can put a pinch of salt into it. We sweat salt out of our bodies and we have to get resupplied. This will be good for your body.

S: Yes. Maybe it tastes strange, but it's helpful. We can have a race to see who runs faster, you or me.

K: Great. You can never beat me. I was in the long-distance running team when I was a student.

S: So let's have a short-distance race, say, a one-hundred-meter race.

K: Oh. You really get to me.

苏珊：嗨，今晚出去散散步怎样？

凯莉：散步？我更喜欢跑步。我们去运动场跑上几圈吧。

S：不好。我吃得太饱了，如果跑的话胃要抗议的。

K：那我们可以先走一会儿。然后再慢跑会儿。

S：好呀，你为什么想慢跑呢？

K：你看我挺胖的。我读过一篇文章说慢跑是一项最有利于减肥的运动。

S：是的，但是我们得带个水壶，你总不想脱水吧？

K：不想。我们也可以放点盐进去。我们跑步时出汗会导致盐分的流失，得设法补充点。这对身体好。

S：好的。尝起来可能怪怪的，但是很有用。我们可以来一场比赛，看我们俩谁跑得快。

K：太棒了。你是不会赢我的。我当学生时可是长跑队的。

S：那我们就来个短跑比赛，比如 100 米比赛。

K：哎呀，这你可把我难倒了。

### 核心词汇记一记

**Words Storm**

negative ['negətiv] *n.* 否定

stroll [strəul] *n.* 漫步，闲逛

jogging ['dʒɔgiŋ] *n.* 慢跑

dehydration [ˌdiːhai'dreiʃən] *n.* 脱水

**Phrases**

short-distance race 短跑

**会话 2**

Sam: I want to build up my strength, but I don't know how. I tried doing push-ups and pull-ups, but they only made my arms strong. I need to enhance the muscles on the legs.

Laura: You can try to do some running. It really helps you develop your lung capacity and physical endurance.

S: So how should I begin?

L: To begin with, you should get yourself warmed up so that you'll not strain your muscles. Then, try to run a few circles around the playground. Then add the number of circles slowly as you run everyday. A few months later you'll find yourself capable of covering many circles.

S: And then my strength will be improved? Do you have any more suggestions?

L: Don't overwork yourself with exercise. That will not accelerate your stamina or growth, but just wreck your body. Once I ran too fast and too long, and after that I vomited a lot and fell ill. It'll be wise of you to avoid it.

S: Sure. I need to do this scientifically so that I'll never get hurt.

山姆：我想让自己变得强壮些。但是不知道该怎么办。我试过做俯卧撑和引体向上，但是这只能增强我的臂力，我需要增强腿部肌肉的力量。

劳拉：你可以试着跑跑步。这可以增大你的肺活量，增强体质。

S：那我该怎样开始呢？

L：开始的时候你要先热身，以使你的肌肉不致被拉伤。然后绕着操场跑上几圈。每天加一点圈数。几个月后你就会发现自己能跑很多圈了。

S：这样我的力量就会得到提升了是吗？还有其他建议吗？

L：不要练得太过了。那样不仅不会促进你身体的生长，不会增加体力，还会极大地伤害自己的身体。有一次我跑得又快时间又长，跑完我就吐了，而且生病了。你最好明智些，防止这种事情发生。

S：当然，我要用科学的方式锻炼，不会使自己受伤的。

**核心词汇记一记**

**Words Storm**

| | |
|---|---|
| enhance | [in'hæns] *v.* 增强 |
| strain | [strein] *n.* 扭伤，损伤 |
| accelerate | [ək'seləreit] *v.* 促进 |
| wreck | [rek] *v.* 破坏 |

**Phrases**

| | |
|---|---|
| push-up | 俯卧撑 |
| pull-up | 引体向上 |
| lung capacity | 肺活量 |
| warm up | 热身 |

# 36. Soccer

## 绿茵漫步

### 知识链接 拓展视野，掌握背景知识

足球运动是一项古老的体育活动，源远流长。最早起源于中国古代的一种球类游戏“蹴鞠”，后来经过阿拉伯人传到欧洲，发展成现代足球。现代足球起源于英国，足球运动是世界上最受欢迎的体育运动之一，也是当今世界上开展最广、影响最大的体育项目之一，被称为“世界第一运动”。不少国家将足球定为“国球”。

### 难点点拨 知识难点看一看，情景实战热热身

1. engage oneself in sth. 致力于，投身于

   They are good players who will engage themselves actively in pressing and tackling.

   他们可都是拼抢非常积极的。

2. hurl sth. at/to sth. 扔，抛

   He acts awesomely quick and always hurls himself directly to the ball.

   他反应异常迅速，总是能直接扑到球。

3. succeed in doing 成功，胜利

   He has succeeded in defending a lot of penalty kicks with ease.

   他已经轻松守住过很多点球了。

4. indicate 意味着，意思是

   The referee whistles and indicates that's an offside!

   裁判吹哨了，说球越位了。

5. be in good form 状态很好

   guard against 保卫，守住

   Though the keeper today is in good form, he cannot guard against so sudden an attack.

   虽然今天守门员状态很好，可是他一个人也守不住这种突袭。

## 情景实战 跟着老外听一听，读一读，练一练

**会话 1**

Jeremy: Hey. I've some friends here. We're going to play football. Will you join us? I know you're a good striker.

Randy: Good! We will have two teams to compete against each other. I like the thrill of getting the ball past the enemy defendants and then shooting it into the goal.

J: Don't underestimate my friends. They are good players who will engage themselves actively in pressing and tackling. In midfield, we have a boy nicknamed "roller-coaster", who always plays the ball like dancing and gives long passes accurately. The goalkeeper is quite professional too. He acts awesomely quick and always hurls himself directly to the ball. You have to fight hard.

R: Every time I breakthrough the enemy line into the penalty area, I stare directly and angrily at the goalkeeper and you know what? He becomes nervous and clumsy.

J: But this one is different. He has succeeded in defending a lot of penalty kicks with ease.

R: Watch how I play him.

J: Good. I hope so.

杰瑞米: 嗨，我这儿有些朋友。我们要去踢足球。你要一起去吗？我知道你是个不错的前锋。

兰迪: 太好了！我们会有两个队来对打，我喜欢那种带着球冲破敌人防线后射门的感觉。

J: 不要小瞧我的朋友。他们可都是拼抢非常积极的。在中场，我们有一个外号叫“过山车”的男孩，他踢起球来就像跳舞一样，而且远距离传球十分精准。守门员也十分专业，他反应异常迅速，总是能直接扑到球。你有一场苦仗要打。

R: 每次我突破敌人的防线冲到禁区的时候，我就会直接而愤怒地盯着守门员。你知道吗，他就会紧张起来，动作也变慢了。

J: 但是这个人不一样。他已经轻松守住过很多点球了。

R: 你就看我怎么整他吧。

J: 好啊，我希望你真能做到。

### 核心词汇记一记

**Words Storm**

defendant [di'fendənt] *n.* 后卫
underestimate [ˌʌndə'estimeit] *v.* 轻视，小瞧
tackle ['tækl] *v.* 拼抢
midfield ['midfiːld] *n.* 中场
nickname ['nikneim] *n.* 昵称
goalkeeper ['gəulˌkiːpə] *n.* 守门员

**Phrases**

penalty area 禁区
penalty kick 点球

**会话 2**

Quincy: Look. The striker gives a long pass, and... Great shot! The whole stadium is boiling!

Joseph: Wait... The referee whistles and indicates that's an offside!

Q: Oh no! That could have become the best goal of the year, what a fantastic show!

J: No way now. Look patiently, the goal is near.

Q: That's foul play! They have to give a free kick.

J: No. The referee says it's a penalty! Hold your breath!

Q: Wow! The goal keeper behaves marvelously. He boxed the ball out!

J: Then the corner. What a good pass! Header...Goal!

Q: You see. They made a mistake. The defendants didn't defend that striker well.

J: They are dead meat. Although the keeper today is in good form, he cannot guard against so sudden an attack.

Q: What a fantastic game... They start again. Long pass to the right. Oh, no. The ball goes out the sideline.

J: He throws it badly and the ball belongs to the opponents... I think time is up and our team wins, two-nil.

Q: Wait. There is four-minute injury time.

J: We have won anyway.

昆西：看，前锋来了个长传……好球！整个场馆都沸腾了！

乔瑟夫：等一下，裁判吹哨了，说球越位了。

Q：不！多精彩的一幕呀！本来可以成为本年度最佳进球的！

J：现在不可能了。耐心看，结果快出来了。

Q：是犯规。他们要踢一个任意球了。

J：不，裁判说要罚点球，屏住呼吸！

Q：哇，守门员表现得太出色了，他用拳把球击出去了。

J：角球。这个传球很到位！头球……进了！

Q：你看，他们犯了个大错误。后卫没有防守住那个前锋。

J：他们死定了。虽然今天守门员状态很好，但是他一个人也守不住这种突袭。

Q：多精彩的比赛啊……他们又开始了。右路长传。哦，坏了。球出了边线。

J：他扔得不好，球到了对方球员脚下……我想时间到了。我们队赢了，2∶0。

Q：等等。还有 4 分钟伤停补时呢。

J：反正我们赢定了。

### 核心词汇记一记

**Words Storm**

| | | |
|---|---|---|
| referee | [ˌrefəˈriː] *n.* | 裁判 |
| offside | [ˈɔːfˈsaid] *n.* | 越位 |
| penalty | [ˈpenəlti] *n.* | 点球 |
| box | [bɔks] *v.* | 用拳击出 |
| sideline | [ˈsaidlain] *n.* | 边线 |

**Phrases**

| | |
|---|---|
| long pass | 长传 |
| free kick | 任意球 |
| dead meat | 死定了 |
| injury time | 伤停补时 |

# 37. NBA

## 篮坛风云

### 知识链接　拓展视野，掌握背景知识

篮球比赛的形式多种多样，标准为5对5。对当下最流行的街头三人篮球赛而言，是3对3的比赛，更讲究个人技术。当今世界篮球水平最高的联赛是美国职业篮球联赛（NBA）。篮球在1904年被列入奥运会的表演项目，而到了1936年柏林奥运会，更改成为正式比赛项目。至于女子篮球直到1976年蒙特利尔奥运会才成为正式项目。

### 难点点拨　知识难点看一看，情景实战热热身

1．a sense of 一种感觉，一种精神

You have to have a good sense of cooperation.

你必须要有良好的合作精神。

2．pass the ball 传球

Sometimes you cannot break through, so you have to pass the ball to the right person.

有时你无法攻破的时候，你就要传球给适当的人。

3．concentrate one's mind 集中精神

Playing basketball requires you to concentrate your mind.

打篮球需要你集中精力。

4．as far as I know 据我所知

As far as I know, basketball as a sport was invented by an American professor called James Naismith.

据我所知，篮球作为一项运动，是美国的一个叫做詹姆斯·奈史密斯的教授发明的。

## 情景实战 跟着老外听一听，读一读，练一练

**会话 1**

Michelle: Look and watch! He dribbles the ball so well, like a magician. I love the Lakers and I love Kobe! He is like a burst of flame when breaking through the enemy defense.

Kevin: A good slam dunk! He is adept at driving the lane, in a perfect movement like a whirlwind.

M: He is also a good shooting guard.

K: By the way, do you often play basketball?

M: Yes, of course, I am good at rebounding. You see, I'm tall enough to get what I want and I can jump higher than others.

K: I'm now practicing the cross-leg dribble. I find it hard.

M: We don't often use this skill. You have to have a good sense of cooperation. Sometimes you cannot break through, so you have to pass the ball to the right person.

K: Teamwork is important, but I still want to develop some unique skills to make those girls love me.

M: With your mind on that, the more likely you are to fail. Playing basketball requires you to concentrate your mind.

K: But I love to show off before the audience. They love me. I love them.

米歇尔：看，他运球运得如此之妙，简直就像个魔术师一样。我爱湖人，我爱科比，当他冲破敌人防线的时候，就像一团迸发的火焰。

凯文：好棒的扣篮！他简直就是轻车熟路，动作完美如同一阵旋风。

M：他是一名优秀的后卫。

K：顺便问下，你经常打篮球吗？

M：当然。我篮板球很厉害。你瞧，我的个头高到足够让我抢到篮板。我能比别人跳得高一些。

K：我现在正在练习胯下运球。我觉得很难。

M：我们不是经常用这项技术。你必须要有良好的合作精神。有时你无法突破的时候，你就要传球给适当的人。

K：团队合作是很重要的。但是我仍然想搞出点独家技巧来让女孩子们爱上我。

M：你越这么想，就越可能失败。打篮球需要你集中精力。

K：但是我喜欢在观众面前展示自己。他们爱我，我也爱他们。

### 核心词汇记一记

**Words Storm**

whirlwind ['hwəːlwind] *n.* 旋风
rebound [ri'baund] *v.* 回弹
dribble ['dribl] *n.* 运球
unique [juː'niːk] *a.* 独一无二的
audience ['ɔːdiəns] *n.* 观众

**Phrases**

pass the ball 传球
break through 突破

**会话 2**

Danny: Do you know the history of basketball? I need to write something for it, because it's my assignment in the writing class.

Willy: As far as I know, basketball as a sport that was invented by an American professor called James Naismith. During the winter of 1891, students had no chance of getting outdoors to play sports. So he designed the game to allow boys to play indoors.

D: Go on, you know so much about it.

W: At first the game used two real baskets. So every time they shot the ball into baskets they had to get it out. That was a big problem, so they just got rid of the bottoms.

D: Interesting beginning, but how could that game prosper so well and sweep the whole world eventually?

W: For nearly half a century after the game was invented, it was ignored. Then in 1936, when the Olympic Games were held in Berlin, basketball became an international sport for the first time.

D: A long history. I wonder how those boys played the ball at first.

W: James Naismith made a few rules to regulate the game. At first each team had 10 players. Then the number got smaller and smaller, finally they settled on five.

D: Really good information, thanks a lot.

W: You are welcome.

丹尼：你知道篮球的历史吗？我需要写一些关于它的东西，这是我写作课的作业。

威利：据我所知，篮球作为一项运动，是美国一个叫做詹姆斯·奈史密斯的教授发明的。在1891年冬天来临的时候，学生没有机会做户外运动，所以他设计了这个游戏，好让男孩能在室内玩。

D：继续讲。你知道好多关于篮球的知识呀。

W：最初这个游戏用的是两个真正的篮筐，所以每次他们投中的时候都要把球取出来。这太麻烦了，所以他们才把篮筐的底部去掉了。

D：开始这段儿真有意思！那么这个游戏最终是怎样风靡整个世界的呢？

W：在这个游戏发明后的近半个世纪之中，它一直受冷落。1936年的柏林运动会上，篮球首次成为一项国际性的运动。

D：好长一段历史。我想知道男孩最开始是怎么玩球的？

W：詹姆斯·奈史密斯制定了一些规则来规范这个游戏。最初每队有10个队员，这个数字后来渐渐变少，最终成为5个。

D：不错的资料。真的太感谢了！

W：不客气。

**核心词汇记一记**

**Words Storm**

assignment [ə'sainmənt] *n.* 任务，作业

outdoors ['aut'dɔːz] *ad.* 在户外

indoors ['in'dɔːz] *ad.* 在室内

regulate ['regjuleit] *v.* 规范

**Phrases**

get rid of 去掉

# 38. American Football

## 美式足球

### 知识链接　拓展视野，掌握背景知识

美式足球（American Football）又称美式橄榄球，是橄榄球的一种衍生运动，也是美国最流行的竞赛运动之一。有时与加拿大足球并称为烤盘足球。由于球赛中往往会与对方球员有身体冲撞，因此球员需穿护具及头盔出赛。

### 难点点拨　知识难点看一看，情景实战热热身

1．in turn 轮流

Each team strikes in turn, meanwhile another defends.

每个队轮流进攻，同时另一支队防守。

2．fail to do sth. 做某事失败

If they try four times but still fail to achieve it, it will be their opponents' turn to move forward.

如果连续 4 次都失败的话，就轮到他们的对手进攻。

3．at will 随意，只要想就可以

They can use their hands and feet at will.

他们可以手脚并用。

4．hurl sth. at/towards sb. 向某人扔某物

You'll find your opponents hurl themselves madly towards you to pull you down.

你会发现你的对手们会疯狂地向你冲撞过来，想把你扑倒在地。

## 情景实战 跟着老外听一听，读一读，练一练

**会话 1**

Adam: Is football popular in your country?

Lucy: Yes. Guys like it. They love running with the ball as fast as possible and get a perfect touchdown.

A: What's a touchdown? I've never heard of that in football.

L: Football? You must mean soccer.

A: Yes. But football isn't soccer? Aren't they the same?

L: No. In America we call British football "soccer" because we play "gridiron" which is our own kind of football—the ball is oval shaped, you know?

A: Yes. I think I see what you mean. Sorry that I forgot this. Can you tell me something about American football?

L: Of course. There are 11 players in one team, just like soccer. Each team strikes in turn, meanwhile another defends. They have to move the ball forward by 10 yards at a time. If they try four times but still fail to achieve it, it will be their opponents' turn to move forward.

A: It seems complicated to me. I'm a bit confused.

L: They can use their hands and feet at will. Most often you can see a player running madly forward with the ball in his hand while his opponents are trying their best to tackle him.

A: So it's mainly a game to see who runs fast.

L: Not necessarily. One can pass the ball if he is intercepted by opponents. They can score by having a touchdown or a field goal.

亚当：足球在你们国家很流行吗？

露西：流行。男孩子们喜欢玩这个。他们喜欢带着球玩命地跑，直到得到一个完美的触地得分。

A：什么是触地得分？我从来没听说过足球里有这个规则。

L：football？你指的是"soccer"吧。

A：是的，但是 football 不是 soccer 吗？他们难道不一样吗？

L：不一样的，在美国我们称英式足球为"soccer"，因为我们玩橄榄球，那是我们的足球，球是椭圆形的，你知道吗？

A：知道。我想我知道你的意思了。不好意思我忘了这点了。你能告诉我一些关于美式足球的事情吗？

L：当然。一个队有 11 名队员，跟英式足球一样。每个队轮流进攻，同时另一支队防守。他们一次要把球带出 10 码远的距离，如果连续 4 次都失败的话，就轮到他们的对手进攻。

A：听起来有点复杂，我有点搞不清。

L：他们可以手脚并用。你经常会看到一个队员用一只手抱着球疯狂地向前冲，他的对手则竭尽全力地阻挠他。

A：所以这是一个看谁跑得快的游戏。

L：不全是。如果一个队员被对手们拦截，他可以把球传出去，他们可以通过触地或者射门来得分。

### 核心词汇记一记

**Words Storm**

touchdown ['tʌtʃdaun] *n.* 触地得分

yard [jaːd] *n.* 码（英制中丈量长度的单位，1 码 =3 英尺）

opponent [ə'pəunənt] *n.* 对手

tackle ['tækl] *v.* 阻挠，抢断

intercept [ˌintə'sept] *v.* 中途拦截

**Phrases**

American football 美式足球

at a time 一次

## 会话 2

Simon: Why do American boys like American football so much?

Richard: You see. If you can join a football team in a university, you'll be loved by many sexy girls, and get respected by your fellow students, because you must be tough, quick, brave, and smart to become a football player.

S: I see. That's the reason. If a boy can play the ball well he'll be loved.

R: Yes. But American football is a game in which you can get really hurt. You'll find your opponents hurl themselves madly towards you to pull you down. Therefore you need equipment to protect yourself.

S: Those players often wear helmets and pads. They very often get tackled to the ground or get hit.

R: Yes. So a player has to be strong enough to endure the pain. It's just like a war. Girls love warriors. That's the natural law of things.

S: Do you think I can play it?

R: Definitely not. You're so weak. You'll be easily knocked out of joint.

S: Don't be so sure. Maybe I can be a football star.

西　蒙：为什么美国男孩子那么喜欢美式橄榄球呢？

理查德：你看，如果你在大学加入足球队，就会有很多性感女孩喜欢你，而且你也会受到同学的尊敬，因为你必须要具备坚强、迅速、勇敢和聪明的品质才能成为一名足球运动员。

S：我明白了。这就是原因所在，如果一个男孩能玩足球，人人都爱他。

R：是的。但是美式足球运动可能会让你受很严重的伤。你会发现你的对手们会疯狂地向你冲撞过来，想把你扑倒在地。所以你需要一些保护自己的装备。

S：这些运动员经常戴着头盔，穿着各种护具。他们经常摔倒在地或者被撞到。

R：是的，所以一名橄榄球运动员必须要足够强壮，能忍受疼痛。这就像一场战争。女孩儿们喜欢勇士，这是自然法则。

S：你觉得我可以玩这个吗？

R：当然不成。你身体太虚弱了，很容易就会被撞脱臼。

S：你可别这么肯定，说不定我能成为一名橄榄球明星呢！

### 核心词汇记一记

**Words Storm**

| | | |
|---|---|---|
| university | [ju:ni'və:siti] | *n.* 大学 |
| equipment | [i'kwipmənt] | *n.* 装备 |
| helmet | ['helmit] | *n.* 头盔 |
| pad | [pæd] | *n.* 防护垫 |
| warrior | ['wɔ:riə] | *n.* 勇士 |

**Phrases**

natural law　自然法则

# 39. Poker

## 纸牌乐趣

### 知识链接 拓展视野，掌握背景知识

牌类游戏有很多种，而且大多数都可以开发人的智力，使人受益。这是牌类游戏不同于一般娱乐性游戏的最显著的特点。有些牌类游戏如桥牌等非常难玩，需要学很久才能掌握玩牌的技术，是一种非常有趣的游戏。但是人们却赋予了牌类游戏一种不那么高尚的使命——赌博。一旦跟这两个字眼联系在一起，打牌就成了一种闲杂人等才做的事情，他们有钱有闲，或者有闲没钱，害得牌类游戏背上了赌博的骂名。

### 难点点拨 知识难点看一看，情景实战热热身

1．correspond to 对应

Different cards correspond to different numbers.

不同的牌对应不同的号码。

2．be addicted to 迷恋，沉迷

Linda's husband is addicted to cards.

琳达的丈夫迷恋打牌。

4．day and night 整日，没日没夜地

He plays cards with his friends day and night.

他没日没夜地和朋友们打牌。

5．plunge sth. into... 把某物投入某地方

They plunge a lot of money into it.

他们投了很多钱进去。

## 情景实战 跟着老外听一听，读一读，练一练

**会话 1**

Nick: Tom, I've got a pack of cards here. Would you like to play poker with us?

Tom: But I know nothing about cards. Can you teach me a little first?

N: OK. There are four suits—diamonds, hearts, spades, and clubs.

T: I got it.

N: You need to shuffle your cards before you play, watch this.

T: Oh! You are an expert shuffler. You must have practiced a lot.

N: Yes, for sure! Then different cards correspond to different numbers. And you also get "Ace", "Jack", "Queen", and "King". Finally you see two "Jokers".

T: Can we tell which card it is from its back?

N: No! You can't see anything from the opposite side and you need to be careful not to let others see what cards you have during the play.

T: I see. I'll keep that in mind.

N: A large-number card can beat a small-number card. Powerful cards are called trumps. So you need to think carefully before using them.

尼克：汤姆，我这儿有一副牌。你想跟我们一起玩吗？

汤姆：但是我对打牌一窍不通呀。你能先教教我吗？

N：好的。一副牌总共有 4 种花色，方片、红桃、黑桃还有梅花。

T：知道了。

N：打牌前必须先洗一下牌，像这样。

T：你真是个洗牌专家。你一定练了很久吧！

N：肯定是呀。不同的牌对应不同的号码，我们还有 A、J、Q 和 K 这 4 种牌。最后你还能看到两张王牌。

T：我们能从牌的后面判断是哪张牌吗？

N：不能。从反面你是看不到任何东西的。而且你在打牌的时候要多加小心，防止别人偷看你的牌。

T：我明白了，我会记住的。

N：大牌可以打小牌，最大的牌叫王牌，在出之前一定要考虑好。

### 核心词汇记一记

**Words Storm**

diamond ['daiəmənd] *n.* 方片
spade [speid] *n.* 黑桃
club [klʌb] *n.* 梅花
shuffle ['ʃʌfl] *n.* 洗牌
trump [trʌmp] *n.* 王牌

**Phrases**

play poker 打牌
correspond to 对应

**会话 2**

Alex: Linda's husband is addicted to cards. He plays cards with his friends day and night.

Bill: Why? Is that so interesting a game?

A: Not really, the truth is—they gamble a lot. They plunge a lot of money into it.

B: So the game becomes exciting.

A: Yes. Every round becomes a game of life and death. They are so excited that if anyone tried to interrupt their playing they would become wildly agitated and hurl insults.

B: No. There must be someone who stops them.

A: In fact, they lose quite a lot of money. Sometimes Linda's husband brings no money home—all his salary is wasted in the game.

B: That's terrible, so what about Linda? She must feel heart-broken.

A: You are right. She cries all day, and begs her husband to stop gambling. But he doesn't listen.

B: The poor woman. It would be unfortunate to marry a man like that.

A: Playing cards is good, but never try to win money through it.

亚历克斯：琳达的丈夫迷恋打牌。他没日没夜地和朋友打牌。

比尔：为什么？这个游戏就那么有趣吗？

A：不是。事实是他们总是赌博。他们投了很多钱进去。

B：所以游戏就变得激动人心了。

A：是的。每一局都变成了生与死的游戏对决。他们打牌时情绪高涨，如果有人试图打断他们，他们就会变得歇斯底里并且出言不逊。

B：不，一定有人可以制止他们。

A：事实上，他们在这上面花了不少钱。有时琳达的丈夫回家时一点钱都没有，因为他的工资都被挥霍在打牌上了。

B：太可怕了。那琳达呢，她是不是觉得心都碎了？

A：是呀，她整天以泪洗面，求她丈夫不要赌博，但是他不听。

B：可怜的女人。嫁给那样一个男人太不幸了。

A：玩牌没什么不好，但是永远都别想靠打牌来赢钱。

### 核心词汇记一记

**Words Storm**

| | |
|---|---|
| gamble | ['gæmbl] *v.* 赌博 |
| plunge | [plʌndʒ] *v.* 投入 |
| interrupt | [ˌintə'rʌpt] *v.* 打断 |
| hurl | [hə:l] *v.* 扔，抛 |
| insult | ['insʌlt] *n.* 侮辱 |
| salary | ['sæləri] *n.* 工资 |

**Phrases**

heart-broken 心碎的

# 40. Chess

## 棋类游戏

### 知识链接 拓展视野，掌握背景知识

*棋盘游戏，又名板图游戏或图版游戏、纸上游戏，是桌上游戏的一类，指将图文符号画在硬板上作为纪录工具的游戏。棋类游戏有很多种，包括五子棋、连珠棋、中国象棋、国际象棋、围棋、跳棋、连珠棋、军旗等等。下棋可以锻炼思维，增强空间想象能力，提高智商，是人类智慧的伟大结晶。*

### 难点点拨 知识难点看一看，情景实战热热身

1．do the checkmate（棋）将死

Theoretically, there is no “least important role”, because even a pawn can get promoted and do the checkmate.

理论上是没有最不重要的角色的，因为即使是一个卒都能得到提升，并且可以将死国王。

2．fall into an enemy ambush 落入敌人埋伏

You must be very careful not to fall into an enemy ambush.

你必须十分小心以免落入敌人的埋伏。

3．while 表示“同时”

The most important thing is to kill the enemy king while protecting your own.

（下国际象棋）最重要的是在保护自己国王的基础上杀死敌人的国王。

4．lose one’s temper 发脾气

Some people are so serious that they lose their temper when they lose a game.

有些人太认真了，以至于输一盘棋，他们就大发雷霆。

## 情景实战 跟着老外听一听，读一读，练一练

**会话 1**

James: I like playing chess. It enhances my intelligence and cultivates my flexibility.

Sara: Chess? I don't know how to play it yet. Can you tell me the rules?

J: Of course. You see, here we get a chessboard. Then we place chessmen on it. Each side has eight pawns.

S: Pawns? Are they the least important roles in the game?

J: Theoretically, there is no "least important role", because even a pawn can get promoted and do the checkmate. You must be very careful not to fall into an enemy ambush.

S: It sounds hard. But I think I can handle it. You know, I'm good at mathematics.

J: Then there are a king, a queen, two bishops, two knights and two rooks.

S: What's the difference?

J: The king can move horizontally, vertically, and diagonally. But every time it can move only one square at a time. The most important thing is to kill the enemy king while protecting your own.

S: It's just like a war, isn't it? A fierce battle.

J: Yes. You must be clever. The queen maybe the most powerful piece because it can go as far as you want, vertically, horizontally, and diagonally.

詹姆斯：我喜欢下国际象棋。它能增加我的智慧，培养我的灵活性。

萨拉：国际象棋？我还不知道怎么玩呢！你能告诉我一些规则吗？

J：当然。你看，这是棋盘，我们把棋子摆上去。每一边都有8个卒。

S：卒？他们是这个游戏中最不重要的角色吗？

J：理论上是没有最不重要的角色的，因为即使是一个卒都能得到提升，并且可以将死国王。你必须十分小心以免落入敌人的埋伏。

S：听起来很难呀，但我觉得我可以玩。你知道的，我数学还不错。

J：然后还有一个国王，一个王后，两个象，两个马和两个车。

S：有什么不同吗？

J：国王可以走水平线，垂直线还有对角线，但是他一次只能移动一格。（下国际象棋）最重要的是在保护自己国王的基础上杀死敌人的国王。

S：就像一场战争一样，是吧？一场激烈的战斗。

J：是的，你很聪明。王后可能是这个游戏里最强大的角色了，因为她可以随心所欲地想走多远就走多远，无论是在垂直线，水平线还是对角线上。

### 核心词汇记一记

**Words Storm**

| | |
|---|---|
| pawn | [pɔːn] *n.* （国际象棋的）卒 |
| ambush | [ˈæmbuʃ] *n.* 埋伏 |
| bishop | [ˈbiʃəp] *n.* 主教，相（或象） |
| knight | [nait] *n.* 骑士 |
| rook | [ruk] *n.* （国际象棋的）车 |
| horizontally | [ˌhɔriˈzɔntli] *ad.* 水平地 |
| vertically | [ˈvəːtikəli] *ad.* 垂直地 |
| diagonally | [daiˈægənəli] *ad.* 对角线地 |

**Phrases**

play chess 下国际象棋

**会话 2**

Jack: Shall we have a game of chess?

Angela: I'm a beginner. I know only basic moves. You can beat me easily. Anyway, let's have a go at it.

J: Do you think playing chess is good?

A: Of course. It makes you work your intellect.

J: Yes, playing it over time will develop your abilities, it will do you good.

A: But some people are so serious that they lose their temper when they lose a game. I have an uncle who is mad keen on chess. He has good tactics, but still no one has the guts to challenge him because he can easily get mad.

J: That's too bad. A Game is a game. The most important thing is not to win, but to participate in good spirits.

A: Yes. Look at me. I'm a big loser in chess, but I keep trying to win. Sometimes I find myself being quite foolish, because I play so poorly.

J: You have to learn from your defeats, so that you can avoid making the same mistake next time.

A: I wonder how one can predict the moves of his enemy. I cannot do that and I often fall into traps.

J: Keep alert. You need to concentrate your mind.

杰克: 我们来下一盘国际象棋吧?

安吉拉: 我是个菜鸟，只知道基本的一些步骤。你很容易就可以打败我。不管了，我们来一局吧。

J: 你觉得下国际象棋好吗?

A: 当然好了，它能让人变聪明。

J: 是呀，长期下棋对你很有好处，使你越来越聪明。

A: 但是有些人太认真了，以至于输一盘棋，他们就大发雷霆。我有个叔叔是个疯狂的国际象棋爱好者，他的战术非常棒，但是很少有人有勇气向他挑战，因为他太容易抓狂了。

J: 这太不好了。游戏就是游戏嘛！最重要的不是赢而是快乐地参与。

A: 对，看看我，我可是个下国际象棋的大输家，但我一直都在努力让自己能赢一局。有时我觉得自己很滑稽，因为我棋艺太差了。

J: 你要从失败中学习，以使你下次避免犯同样的错误。

A: 我很纳闷的是，你要怎么预测对手的动机呢？我就做不到，所以我经常掉到对手的陷阱里。

J: 保持警觉，你需要集中自己的精力。

**核心词汇记一记**

**Words Storm**

temper ['tempə] *n.* 脾气

tactics ['tæktiks] *n.* 战略，战术

gut [gʌt] *n.* 勇气

participate [pɑː'tisipeit] *v.* 参与

**Phrases**

concentrate one's mind 集中精力

# 41. Electronic Games

# 电子游戏

## 知识链接 拓展视野，掌握背景知识

当今电子游戏发展迅速，有力地推动了计算机软硬件的发展。越来越多的人也开始把游戏当作他们的生活乐趣，用游戏排解生活的压力和痛苦。当然，大批缺乏自制力的青少年也沉迷于游戏中，造成了不良影响。但是我们应当正视游戏，它作为一种大众文化的产物，比电影更进一步，给人类带来了新的思维模式和艺术形式。许多学者用文化研究的方式来研究游戏的内涵外延，于是一门新的学科“游戏学”诞生了。

## 难点点拨 知识难点看一看，情景实战热热身

1．independent/integrated video card 独立 / 集成显卡

In the “minimum requirements” it says the computer should have an independent video card.

在“最低配置要求”这里说，必须得有一块独立显卡才行。

2．be confused 对某事感到迷茫，不解

Now computer games are developing so fast that I'm more and more confused.

现在电脑游戏发展太迅速，我越来越不懂了。

3．subject 学科，等于 discipline

Ludology is a new academic subject about computer games.

游戏学是关于电脑游戏的一门新的学科。

4．aim at 注重

Some scholars aim at cultural studies, and focus on the political and social connotations of the game.

有些学者着力把重点放在文化研究上，集中研究游戏的政治性和社会性。

## 情景实战 跟着老外听一听，读一读，练一练

**会话 1**

Arron: I cannot play this game on this computer—it's so slow and out of date.

Bill: You see, in the "minimum requirements" it says the computer should have an independent video card, but yours is an integrated one.

A: That's really a pity. *Medal of Honor* is a game which I love so much. Several years ago I went through all Mods of it. Now a new version comes out—*Medal of Honor: Airborne*, but my computer just can't handle it!

B: Don't worry. You can try other games.

A: How much do you know about games?

B: I have played games for decades. When I was young I played FC games—*Super Mario Bros*, *Tetris*... Then PC's became cheap enough for me to afford, so I brought one. At first I played *Command & Conquer* and *Starcraft*, then three-dimension began to prosper, *Counter-Strike*, and *Medal of Honor* became my favorite. At that time my computer had only a 128 Megabyte memory and a Pentium 3 CPU.

A: Great, you're so familiar with games.

B: But now computer games are developing so fast that I'm growing more and more confused.

艾伦：我没法用这台电脑玩这个游戏——这电脑太慢了，太落后了。

比尔：你瞧，在"最低配置要求"这里说，必须得有一块独立显卡才行，你的是集成的。

A: 真是可惜。《荣誉勋章》我非常喜欢。几年前我就玩过关了。现在新版本出来了——《荣誉勋章：空降奇兵》，可是我的电脑玩不了！

B: 别着急，你可以玩其他游戏。

A: 你对游戏了解多少？

B: 我玩了好几年了。我小的时候玩红白机游戏——《超级玛丽》、《俄罗斯方块》……之后电脑变得便宜的时候我就买了台电脑。刚开始我玩《命令与征服》和《星际争霸》。后来3D特效技术发展了，《CS》和《荣誉勋章》就成了我的最爱。在那个时候我的电脑只配有128兆内存和奔腾3处理器。

A: 很好，你对游戏很熟悉。

B: 可是现在电脑游戏发展太迅速，我越来越不懂了。

### 核心词汇记一记

**Words Storm**

| | | |
|---|---|---|
| integrate | ['intigreit] *v.* | 集成 |
| version | [ˌvəːʃən] *n.* | 版本 |
| prosper | [ˌprɔspə] *v.* | 兴起 |

**Phrases**

| | |
|---|---|
| out of date | 过时 |
| minimum requirements | 最低要求 |

**会话 2**

Andy: Have you heard of ludology?

Barry: No. What's that?

A: It's a new academic subject about computer games and their effect on people.

B: I don't think computer games are worth studying.

A: Why? Now we study films, dramas, music, paintings... Why can't we have a serious study of games? Games have now become a very important social phenomenon, and billions of people play computer games around the world.

B: So what do they study exactly?

A: For example, the aesthetic aspects such as visual effects and music used in the game. Some scholars aim at cultural studies and focus on the political and social connotations of the game. For example, they try to dig out the political and ecological implications in *S.T.A.L.K.E.R.: Shadow of Chernobyl*, a game about nuclear pollution.

B: I see. So it's a good subject. Computer games have long been regarded as just an entertainment, but ludology tries to challenge this public view.

A: Yes, a game is more than just an entertainment. Some early philosophers have already studied games and proposed different reasoning. For example, Schiller thought the game was the liberation of man from the yoke of his life. Herbert Spencer once said, "Games are the outpouring of excessive energy." Freud declared that "Games are an outlet for repressed desires."

安迪：你听说过游戏学吗？

巴利：没有，那是什么？

A：它是研究电脑游戏和游戏对大众影响的一门新的学科。

B：我不觉得电脑游戏值得研究。

A：为什么？我们现在研究电影、戏剧、音乐、绘画……为什么不能严肃地研究游戏呢？游戏现在变成了非常重要的社会现象，几十亿人都在玩电脑游戏。

B：那他们具体研究什么？

A：比如，美学方面，他们研究视觉特效和音乐。有些学者着力把重点放在文化研究上，集中研究游戏的政治性和社会性。比如，他们力图挖掘《潜行者：切尔诺贝利的阴影》这款游戏的政治和生态学寓意，这款游戏是关于核污染的。

B：我明白了。这学科很不错。电脑游戏长期以来只被看作是娱乐，游戏学是对这种大众观念的挑战。

A：是的。游戏不仅仅是娱乐。以前一些哲学家早就研究过游戏，还提出过不同的看法。比如，席勒认为“游戏是人从生活枷锁中的解放”。赫伯特·斯宾塞说“游戏是多余能量的发泄”。弗洛伊德称“游戏是受压抑的欲望的出口”。

**核心词汇记一记**

**Words Storm**

| | | |
|---|---|---|
| ludology | ['luːdəulədʒi] *n.* | 游戏学 |
| implication | [impli'keiʃən] *n.* | 寓意 |
| yoke | [jəuk] *n.* | 枷锁 |
| outpour | [aut'pɔː] *v.* | 发泄 |
| repress | [ri'pres] *v.* | 压抑 |

**Phrases**

| | |
|---|---|
| nuclear pollution | 核污染 |
| more than | 不只是 |

# 42. Singing and Dancing

## 载歌载舞

### 知识链接 拓展视野，掌握背景知识

*歌舞是人类表达自我情绪的一种很好的艺术形式。据艺术史学家的考证，人类最早产生的艺术就是舞蹈。在远古人类尚未产生语言以前，人们就用动作、姿态的表情来传达各种信息和进行情感、思想的交流。以后由各种声音发展成为语言和音调以后，才相继产生了诗歌和音乐。现代社会，人类已经将舞蹈和音乐完美地结合在了一起，形成了一种臻于完美的艺术表达形式。*

### 难点点拨 知识难点看一看，情景实战热热身

1. sing karaoke K 歌

   Yesterday I went singing karaoke with a bunch of friends.

   昨天我跟一帮朋友去 K 歌了。

2. be good at doing 擅长做某事

   I found myself not good at singing high notes.

   我发现自己不太擅长唱高音。

3. out of tune 走调，不协调

   I sing out of tune.

   我唱歌跑调。

## 情景实战 跟着老外听一听，读一读，练一练

**会话 1**

Edgar: Yesterday I went singing karaoke with a bunch of friends. I found myself not good at singing high notes. I don't know why. I tried hard only to get my throat sore.

Alisa: You have to get properly trained to do that. Straining your voice will hurt your vocal cord.

E: Why? Some people can sing hard songs with ease. I think it's a matter of natural endowments.

A: It's unquestionable that everyone's voice is unique. But if one can master the breathing and voicing techniques, he can sing beautifully.

E: I find a pattern like this. Every morning my larynx gets really shabby and I cannot sing at all, but when time goes on and afternoon comes, I become able to sing in some high pitch.

A: Er... It's a natural thing. Before, many people think it right to practice singing in the morning, but the best time to do that is in the afternoon.

E: Any other advices?

A: You have to choose suitable songs for your voice. If you cannot sing too high, you can try to be an excellent baritone.

E: The problem is—sometimes I sing out of tune.

埃德加：昨天我跟一帮朋友去 K 歌了。我发现自己不太擅长唱高音。我不知道为什么。我很用力但却搞得喉咙痛。

艾丽莎：你要经过适当的训练才能唱高音的。扯着嗓子唱会破坏你的声带。

E：为什么呢？一些人轻轻松松就可以唱很难的歌。我觉得这是个天赋问题。

A：毫无疑问每个人的声音都是独一无二的，但是一个人如果学会了控制呼气和发声技巧，那么他就能唱得很好听。

E：我发现这样一个现象，每天早上起来我的喉咙很糟糕，我根本没法唱歌，但是再过一段时间，到下午的时候，我就能唱一些高音了。

A：哦，这是很自然的。以前，很多人认为应该上午练声才对，但是其实最佳时间是在下午。

E：还有其他建议吗？

A：你要根据自己的声音选择合适的歌曲。如果你不能唱得太高，就试着做一个优秀的男中音吧。

E：问题是，有时我会唱跑调。

### 核心词汇记一记

**Words Storm**

| | |
|---|---|
| endowment | [in'daumənt] *n.* 天赋 |
| unquestionable | [ˌʌn'kwestʃənəbl] *a.* 毫无疑问的 |
| larynx | ['læriŋks] *n.* 喉 |
| shabby | ['ʃæbi] *a.* 低劣的，不好的 |
| suitable | ['sjuːtəbl] *a.* 合适的 |
| baritone | ['bæritəun] *n.* 男中音 |

**Phrases**

| | |
|---|---|
| a bunch of | 一群 |
| high notes | 高音 |
| vocal cord | 声带 |

**会话 2**

Colin: May I have a dance with you?

Rita: You must be kidding me. This is not a ball at all. Besides, I cannot dance.

C: You cannot dance? It's a pity. I think you need to learn.

R: Learn what? I want to know the origin of dance. Maybe it's related to music?

C: Maybe. Some anthropologists declare that dance is the earliest art form of human beings. When our ancestors heard some music, they began moving their bodies with the beat. There comes the dance. They may also imitate the act of hunting. Dance is a game rather than a performance.

R: Yes. Even now we dance to please ourselves more than spectators.

C: There are many kinds—ballet, waltz, cha-cha, Latin, samba... Now we have a new style, street dance.

R: So what's the most important thing for me if I want to learn dancing?

C: A strong sense of rhythm. You have to dance with the beat of music.

R: I'm good at music. I was the lead singer of a band when at university.

C: That's good. You can make it.

科林：我可以请你跳支舞吗？

瑞塔：你一定在开玩笑。这根本就不是个舞会。还有，我不会跳舞。

C：你不会跳舞？真可惜。我觉得你需要学一下。

R：学什么？我想知道舞蹈的由来。是不是和音乐有关呀？

C：可能吧。有些人类学家认为舞蹈是人类最早的艺术形式。当我们的祖先听到一些音乐时，他们就会有节奏地摆动身体。由此舞蹈就诞生了。舞蹈还可能是模仿了打猎的动作。舞蹈是一种游戏，而不是一种表演。

R：是的，甚至到现在我们跳舞也更多地是为了娱乐自己而不是观众。

C：舞蹈分很多种——芭蕾、华尔兹、恰恰、拉丁舞、桑巴等等。现在我们还有一种新形式的舞蹈叫街舞。

R：那么如果我想学舞蹈的话，最重要的是什么？

C：强烈的节奏感。你要能够随着音乐的节拍跳舞。

R：我对音乐很在行。在大学的时候，我还曾经是乐队的主唱呢！

C：很好，你可以学好舞蹈的。

### 核心词汇记一记

#### Words Storm

| | | |
|---|---|---|
| origin | ['ɔridʒin] | *n.* 起源，由来 |
| ancestor | ['ænsestə] | *n.* 祖先 |
| imitate | ['imiteit] | *v.* 模仿 |
| spectator | [spek'teitə] | *n.* 观众 |
| ballet | ['bælei] | *n.* 芭蕾 |
| waltz | [wɔ:lts] | *n.* 华尔兹 |
| samba | ['sæmbə] | *n.* 桑巴 |
| rhythm | ['riðəm] | *n.* 节奏 |

#### Phrases

| | |
|---|---|
| street dance | 街舞 |
| lead singer | 主唱 |

# 43. Kung Fu

## 中国功夫

### 知识链接 拓展视野，掌握背景知识

*中国武术如同浩瀚大海，深不可测，门派拳种，枝繁叶茂，竭尽毕生精力能得其九牛之一毛，已属不易。中国功夫也称中国武术，是以技击为主要内容，以套路和搏斗为运动形式，注重内外兼修的中国传统体育项目，是中国人民长期积累起来的一项宝贵文化遗产。作为古老东方文化的标志之一，武术已经作为一个文化符号被引入好莱坞电影，并且进入西方人的文化视线。一批以中国武术为题材的电影或动画片在好莱坞成为票房赚钞机，叫好又叫座，如《卧虎藏龙》、《花木兰》、《功夫熊猫》等。*

### 难点点拨 知识难点看一看，情景实战热热身

1. make efforts to do 努力做某事

   It seems easy, but you have to make great efforts to practice.

   看起来挺简单的，但是要学好你可得多加努力练习。

2. reach out one's arm(s) 伸出手臂

   Reach out your arms like tree limbs, naturally and softly.

   让你的手臂像树枝一样伸展开来，自然点，轻柔些。

3. martial arts 武术

   I love all kinds of martial arts.

   我喜欢各种武术。

4. cultivate 修养，修炼

   Not only to improve your body, but also to cultivate your mind and personality.

   不只要让身体变得强壮，还要修炼头脑和性格。

## 情景实战 跟着老外听一听，读一读，练一练

**会话 1**

Johnny: Hey! I'm just practicing Tai Chi. Would you like to join me?

Tom: I know nothing about it. Is it difficult?

J: It seems easy, but you have to make great efforts to practice. You just follow me like this.

T: OK. Don't laugh at me. I may look funny.

J: Bend your knees slightly and reach out your arms like tree limbs, naturally and softly. Try to keep your body erect. Move slowly, then be sure to keep your balance and don't let your body shake.

T: I cannot control my body well. My thighs become sore and painful.

J: Keep holding your gesture for a while. It helps develop your strength and flexibility. Raise your leg and let it stay in the air for seconds.

T: I feel my legs getting stiff. I cannot do this any longer.

J: Be patient! Tai Chi is also called "shadow boxing". It asks you to act like water—to be flexible, but also strong. In real combat a Tai Chi master borrows the strength of his enemy and uses this energy to fight back. The harder you try to beat him, the harder you will get hit. He controls you!

T: Unbelievable!

约翰尼：嗨！我正在练太极呢，你想一起练吗？

汤姆：我一点都不懂呀。难吗？

J：看起来挺简单的，但是要学好你可得多加努力练习。你就跟着我来练吧，就像这样。

T：好的。你可别笑话我呀。我看起来可能很好笑。

J：轻轻地弯下你的膝盖，让你的手臂像树枝一样伸展开来，自然点，轻柔些。身体要保持直立，慢慢转动。然后还要保持平衡，不要让身体抖动。

T：我还不能很好地控制自己的身体。我的大腿现在又酸又疼。

J：保持那个姿势一段时间。这样会增强气力和灵活性。抬起腿来，让它在半空中停几秒钟。

T：我觉得我的腿僵掉了，我坚持不住了。

J：要耐心一点。太极在英语里又叫"影子拳"，它要求你表现得像水一样，刚柔相济。在真正的战场上，太极高手会借助敌人的力量反打回去。你越是想伤害他，你自己挨的拳头就越重。高手始终控制着你。

T：太神奇了，简直太不可思议了！

### 核心词汇记一记

**Words Storm**

erect [i'rekt] *v.* 直立的
thigh [θai] *n.* 大腿
flexibility [fleksi'biliti] *n.* 灵活性

**Phrases**

Tai Chi 太极拳
laugh at 嘲笑
keep balance 保持平衡
in combat 在战场上

## 会话 2

Mark: Do you like Chinese martial arts?

Jim: I love all kinds of martial arts—Karate, Judo, Taekwondo and Chinese Kung Fu. I want to develop superhuman power by practicing martial arts. With this I will fear nobody!

M: Yes. Kung Fu strengthens you, making you more skillful in combat, but its main purpose doesn't lie here.

J: What?

M: Kung Fu is to help you keep fit and defend yourself, not to give you the strength to bully others.

J: But it is a human desire to show your strength and let others fear you, isn't it?

M: No. Kung Fu calms you down. Through moving and fighting, you will learn peace and the best way to overcome others is not by conflict, but by wit. Kung Fu helps you think philosophically and understand the world better. To be superior, it is not enough for you to have only strength. But more importantly you need wisdom as well as a sense of justice and responsibility.

J: Not only to improve your body, but also to cultivate your mind and personality…

M: You are right!

马克：你喜欢中国武术吗？

吉姆：我喜欢各种武术，包括空手道、柔道、跆拳道，还有中国功夫。我想通过练习武术得到一种超人的力量，那我就不用怕任何人了。

M：是的，功夫能够增强你的力量，使你在战场上更加有技巧。但是它的主要目的却不在于此。

J：那是什么呢？

M：功夫是为了让你强身健体和自卫，而不是给你力量去欺负别人。

J：但是展示自己的力量让他人感到害怕是人的一种天性，不是吗？

M：不是的。功夫会让人平静下来。通过打斗，你会学到和平的意义。征服他人最好的方法不是通过战争，而是通过智慧。功夫会让你学会哲学性思考，更好地理解这个世界。要变得强大起来，光拥有力量是不够的，更重要的是智慧、正义感和责任感。

J：所以不只要让身体变得强壮，还要修炼头脑和性格。

M：这就对了！

### 核心词汇记一记

**Words Storm**

| | | |
|---|---|---|
| karate | [kə'rɑːti] | *n.* 空手道 |
| judo | ['dʒuːdəu] | *n.* 柔道 |
| taekwondo | [ˌtaiˌkwɔn'dəu] | *n.* 跆拳道 |
| bully | ['buli] | *v.* 威吓 |
| philosophically | [ˌfilə'sɔfikli] | *ad.* 哲学上 |

**Phrases**

| | |
|---|---|
| keep fit | 保持健康 |
| as well as | 也，又，以及，同……一样 |

# 44. Olympics

## 奥运赛场

### 知识链接　拓展视野，掌握背景知识

奥林匹克运动会是国际奥林匹克委员会主办的包含多种体育运动项目的国际性运动会，每4年举行一次。奥林匹克运动会最早起源于古希腊，因举办地在奥林匹亚而得名。19世纪末由法国的顾拜旦男爵创立了真正意义上的现代奥林匹克运动会。从1896年开始奥林匹克运动会每4年就举办一次（曾在两次世界大战中中断过3次），会期不超过16天。由于1924年开始设立了冬季奥林匹克运动会，因此奥林匹克运动会习惯上又称为“夏季奥林匹克运动会”。奥林匹克运动会现在已经成为了和平与友谊的象征。

### 难点点拨　知识难点看一看，情景实战热热身

1．the quintessence of ……的本质，精华

The quintessence of Chinese culture was well shown.

中国文化的精髓得到了很好的展示。

2．I never thought... 我从未想到……

I never thought they would have such an innovative design.

我从来没想到他们能想出如此有创意的设计。

3．main dish 主菜

The main dish is the games rather than the opening ceremony.

最主要的是比赛而不是开幕式。

4．be forbidden to do 被禁止做某事

At that time, women were forbidden even to watch the game.

在那个时候，女性甚至被禁止观看比赛。

## 情景实战 跟着老外听一听，读一读，练一练

**会话 1**

Rick: Last year we held Olympic Games in Beijing. How do you like them?

Amy: Superb! The opening ceremony was a real fantastic thing.

R: Did you watch it in the Bird's Nest or on TV?

A: I got a ticket from a friend, so I had the chance to watch the ceremony in the Bird's Nest. You can never imagine the flamboyance of those fireworks and the dazzling beauty of the performances. The quintessence of Chinese culture was well shown.

R: I was not as lucky as you. I could only sit before the television. The ignition ceremony was the most breath-taking. I never thought they would have such an innovative design.

A: But the main dish is the games rather than the ceremony. I was surprised to see how fast those runners can be. They dashed like lightening.

R: I love to see Ping Pong best. It's our national sport, and we have absolute predominance in this game.

A: You won a lot of gold medals. China has become a giant in sports.

R: We have made a great effort to get stronger and broken a lot of records.

A: I admire those athletes who win honor for their nations.

里克：去年北京举行了奥运会，你喜欢吗？

艾美：非常壮观！开幕式真是不错！

R：你是在鸟巢里看的还是电视上看的？

A：我从朋友那儿弄了张票，所以有机会在鸟巢里看开幕式。你永远无法想象那些焰火有多华丽，表演有多美丽耀眼！中国文化的精髓得到了很好的展示。

R：我没你那么幸运，我只能坐在电视机前看。点燃仪式是最激动人心的一刻。我从来没想到他们能想出如此有创意的设计。

A：最主要的是比赛而不是开幕式。令我感到惊奇的是这些运动员怎么跑得那么快。他们像闪电一样冲了出去。

R：我最爱看乒乓球了。这是中国的国家运动，在这项运动中中国占绝对优势。

A：你们赢了很多金牌。中国现在已经成为体育大国了。

R：我们付出了很多努力来让自己变得强大。我们打破了很多项记录。

A：我佩服那些为祖国赢得荣誉的运动员。

### 核心词汇记一记

**Words Storm**

flamboyance [flæm'bɔiəns] *n.* 华丽
firework ['faiəwəːk] *n.* 焰火
dazzling ['dæzliŋ] *a.* 头晕目眩的
quintessence [kwin'tesns] *n.* 精华
innovative ['inəveitiv] *a.* 创新的
predominance [pri'dɔminəns] *n.* 优势

**Phrases**

Olympic Games 运动会
opening ceremony 开幕式
Bird's Nest 鸟巢

**会话 2**

Bryan: What's the motto of the Olympic Games?

Grant: "Swifter, higher, stronger". Athletes strive hard to challenge themselves, and all the while, sportsmanship is highly valued.

B: When was the first Olympics held?

G: Thousands of years ago in ancient Greece, people held a match to decide who the strongest man on earth was, but at that time, women were forbidden to even watch the games. Then in 1896 the first modern Olympics were held in Athens.

B: What's the significance of the Olympics in your opinion?

G: The spirit to challenge and make a breakthrough. Human beings may be weak compared with nature, but we have the wisdom and courage to get better and better. Friendship is the eternal objective. Sportsmen are supposed to be graceful and affectionate toward each other. They have to respect their opponents.

B: But I think it's more of a competition about the countries' overall strength. Only a country with a well-developed economy can afford to train its athletes well and besides, different races have their own physical advantages—the yellow race is excellent in flexibility; the white, strength; the black, speed and endurance.

布莱恩：奥运会的口号是什么？

格兰特：“更快，更高，更强”。运动员们努力奋斗去挑战自己。同时，运动精神也是极为可贵的。

B：第一届奥运会是什么时候举行的？

G：在几千年前的古希腊，人们举行了一次比赛，来看看谁是世界上最强壮的人。但是在那个时候，女性甚至被禁止观看比赛。1896 年第一届现代奥运会在雅典举办。

B：你认为奥运会的意义是什么？

G：挑战和突破的精神。同大自然相比，人类可能是弱势的，但是我们有智慧和勇气不断完善自我。然后，友谊是永恒的主题，体育人应当优雅并且彼此关爱，要尊重他们的对手。

B：但是我觉得这更像是一个关于国家整体实力的竞赛。只有经济发达的国家才有资金来训练运动员。除此之外，不同的种族，他们自身的身体优势也不一样——黄种人在灵活性上比较有优势，白种人有力量，而黑种人则有速度和耐力。

**核心词汇记一记**

**Words Storm**

| | |
|---|---|
| sportsmanship | ['spɔːtsmənʃip] *n.* 运动精神 |
| forbid | [fə'bid] *v.* 禁止 |
| significance | [sig'nifikəns] *n.* 意义 |
| wisdom | ['wizdəm] *n.* 智慧 |
| graceful | ['greisful] *a.* 优雅的 |
| overall | ['əuvərɔːl] *a.* 全面的 |
| endurance | [in'djuərəns] *n.* 耐力 |

**Phrases**

make a breakthrough 突破

# Life as Art 生活即艺术

# 45. Red Letter Days

## 中外假日

**知识链接** 拓展视野，掌握背景知识

各民族和地区都有自己的节日。一些节日源于传统习俗，如中国的春节、中秋节、清明节、重阳节等。有的节日源于宗教，比如西方的圣诞节。有的节日源于对某人或某件事件的纪念，比如中国的端午节、国庆节、青年节等等。另有为国际组织提倡的运动而指定的日子，如劳动节、妇女节、母亲节。随着时间推移，节日的内涵和庆祝方式也在发生着变化。

**难点点拨** 知识难点看一看，情景实战热热身

1. stay up 熬夜，不睡

   On New Year's Eve, many people stay up the whole night.

   在除夕夜，很多人都通宵不睡。

2. in the hope of doing 希望以此达成某种心愿

   We also paste "Spring Festival Couplets" on gates in the hope of bringing good luck to the family.

   我们还在门上贴春联，希望可以带给家里好运气。

3. kowtow to sb. 给某人磕头

   Children will kowtow to their paternal grandparents.

   孩子们会向他们的爷爷奶奶磕头。

4. make resolution 下决心

   We make New Year's resolution for New Year's Day.

   我们在新年表新年决心。

5. make a commitment to sb. 对某人承诺

   It's a kind of commitment we make to ourselves.

   这是我们对自己的承诺。

## 情景实战 跟着老外听一听，读一读，练一练

**会话 1**

Ben: The National Day of China will come, and there will be a mass parade at Tian'anmen Square.

Donald: Gorgeous. What's the most important day in China?

B: Spring Festival, of course. On that day, everyone eats dumplings and sets off firecrackers to celebrate the New Year of the Lunar Calendar. Before that, on New Year's Eve, many people stay up the whole night. We also paste "Spring Festival Couplets" on gates in the hope of bringing good luck to the family.

D: Firecrackers… I like to hear all kinds of explosions…Bang!

B: On that day we are all dressed up in new clothes, and go visiting friends and relatives all around the town to give them New Year greetings.

D: Will you go and worship your ancestors on that day?

B: Children will kowtow to their paternal grandparents. There will also be a table set with pork, fish, and tofu, as the tributes for ancestors.

D: Wonderful! Are these activities nationwide on this day?

B: No. But on the eve of Spring Festival, there is a program on CCTV, called "New Year's Gala", and many famous actors and singers get on the stage to show for us. It is rather a nationwide activity, because every family will stay together to watch this show.

本: 中国的国庆日就要到了，天安门广场将会有一场声势浩大的阅兵。

唐纳德: 太棒了，在中国最重要的日子是什么？

B: 当然是春节了。那天每个人都会吃饺子放炮仗，以此来庆祝农历新年的到来。在那之前，在除夕夜，很多人都通宵不睡，我们还在门上贴春联，希望可以带给家里好运气。

D: 炮仗啊，我喜欢听各种各样爆炸的声音，嘣嘣！

B: 而且那天我们都会穿新衣服，去访亲串友，带给他们新年的祝福。

D: 那你们那天会去祭祖吗？

B: 孩子们会向他们的爷爷奶奶磕头。而且每家都会有张摆着猪肉、鱼，还有豆腐的桌子，这些是给祖宗的供品。

D: 不错啊。那天你们有什么全国性的活动吗？

B: 没有。但是在除夕夜中国中央电视台有一档节目，叫“春节联欢晚会”。很多著名的演员和歌手都会登台表演。这真的是一个全国性的活动，因为家家户户老老小小都会凑在一起观看这场晚会。

### 核心词汇记一记

**Words Storm**

firecracker ['faiəkrækə] *n.* 鞭炮，爆竹

explosion [ik'spləuʒən] *n.* 爆炸

worship ['wəːʃip] *v.* 敬神，拜神

tribute ['tribjuːt] *n.* 贡品

**Phrases**

mass parade 阅兵

dressed up 打扮，穿上盛装

**会话 2**

Shawn: What holidays do you have?

Phred: Quite a lot in America—New Year's Day, Valentine's Day, Easter, Independence Day, Thanksgiving, Halloween, Christmas...

S: What will you do on these days?

P: We make New Year's resolutions for New Year's Day. It's a kind of commitment we make to ourselves, for example, to lose weight, to find a new job, or a new girlfriend.

S: Valentine's Day is a day for lovers, I know that one.

P: Yes, a day for romance. We send chocolates, cards, and flowers to our lovers to show how much we love them. Then Easter comes, it is believed that Jesus's Resurrection was on that day.

S: I know that, we have Easter eggs!

P: The Independence Day then comes on the Fourth of July. It is the National Day of our country, because it was on the Fourth of July of 1776 that we American people became independent. We made *The Declaration of Independence* and liberated ourselves from the rule of the British government.

S: Thanksgiving is particularly American, isn't it?

P: Yes. The Indians helped the early settlers a lot, so we thank those kind-hearted Indians. Then we have Halloween, the day for ghosts. On that day we make the Jack-o'-lantern out of a pumpkin.

S: Christmas is the birthday of Jesus. Now we Chinese also celebrate this festival.

肖恩：你们都有什么假期？

弗莱德：美国有很多节日，包括新年、情人节、复活节、独立日、感恩节、万圣节、圣诞节等等。

S：这些节日里你都会干什么呢？

P：我们在新年表新年决心，这是我们对自己的承诺，比如减肥啊、找工作啊，或者是找女朋友等等。

S：情人节是情人们的节日，这个我知道。

P：是的，浪漫的日子，我们把巧克力，贺卡还有鲜花送给我们的爱人，来表示有多爱对方。然后就是复活节，大家相信耶稣复活就是在那天。

S：我知道那个，我们有复活节彩蛋。

P：独立日是每年的 7 月 4 日。这是美国的国庆日，因为 1776 年 7 月 4 日我们美国人民独立了。我们发表了《独立宣言》，把自己从英国政府的统治下解放了出来。

S：感恩节是美国独有的节日，是吗？

P：是的。印第安人为早期的定居者们提供了很多帮助。所以我们感谢那些好心的印第安人。然后我们还有万圣节，也就是鬼节。那天我们都用南瓜做南瓜灯。

S：圣诞节是耶稣的诞生日。现在我们中国人也庆祝这个节日呢。

### 核心词汇记一记

**Words Storm**

| | |
|---|---|
| Easter | ['iːstə] *n.* 复活节 |
| Thanksgiving | ['θæŋksˌgiviŋ] *n.* 感恩节 |
| Halloween | [ˌhæləu'iːn] *n.* 万圣节 |
| resolution | [ˌrezə'luːʃən] *n.* 决心 |
| commitment | [kə'mitmənt] *n.* 承诺 |
| pumpkin | ['pʌmpkin] *n.* 南瓜 |

**Phrases**

| | |
|---|---|
| Valentine's Day | 情人节 |
| lose weight | 减肥 |

# 46. Are You Punctual

## 时间观念

### 知识链接 拓展视野，掌握背景知识

*现代社会竞争日益激烈，人们的时间观念也越来越强。大部分经济发达的国家和地区的人对时间有着很强的观念，如日本人、美国人等。曾有专家进行统计，一个人看着手表的次数越多，那么他很有可能在以后相同条件下比其他的人更有发展的潜力。而一些经济较为落后的地区，比如一些非洲的土著部落，对于时间则没有什么概念。*

### 难点点拨 知识难点看一看，情景实战热热身

1．on time 准时

I come right on time.

我来的时间刚刚好。

2．heavy rain/fog/snow 大雨、雾、雪

It says due to the heavy fog, the flight will be postponed.

上面说由于大雾天气，航班会延迟。

3．the lack of 缺乏某物

I guess it runs slow due to the lack of electric power.

我猜它走得慢是因为电池快没电了。

4．come and go 来去匆匆，一闪即逝

Good chances come and go.

好机会总是来去匆匆。

## 情景实战 跟着老外听一听，读一读，练一练

**会话 1**

Nicole: Tom, you are late again!

Tom: What time is it? It's just seven thirty. I am right on time.

N: But we've been waiting for you for ten minutes. Please come earlier next time. By the way, does your watch keep good time?

T: No. I'm really sorry. That clock there says seven forty already. My watch is a bit slow.

N: We must hurry. The plane takes off at eight o'clock. We've got twenty minutes left, we have to run.

T: I thought I arrived on time. Sorry for making you wait.

N: Don't worry. Look at that board. It says due to the heavy fog, the flight will be postponed. I think we have enough time now. Relax.

T: Goodness. That's bad for other passengers, but good for us. Now I'll examine my watch. I guess it runs slow due to the lack of electric power. I should change the battery.

N: Why not get rid of your quartz watch and get a mechanical one? You just have to wind it to keep it running.

尼科尔：汤姆，你又迟到了！

汤 姆：这才几点呀？刚刚 7:30 而已，我来的时间正好呀。

N：但是我们大家已经等了你 10 分钟了。下次记得早点来。顺便问一下，你的表准吗？

T：真抱歉，不太准。我看到那儿的钟显示已经 7:40 了，我的表慢了些。

N：我们必须要抓紧了，飞机 8 点整就要起飞。还剩 20 分钟，我们得跑步前进了。

T：我还以为我来的正好呢，实在抱歉让你们等我。

N：没关系。看看那个公告牌，上面说由于大雾天气，航班会延迟。所以我们现在有足够的时间了，不要着急。

T：天哪，这对其他乘客来说简直糟透了，但是对我们来说却是个好消息。现在我得看看我的手表到底怎么了。我猜它走得慢是因为电池快没电了，我想我换换电池就好。

N：为什么不直接把你的石英表换成机械表呢？这样你只需要动手上弦它就可以继续转了。

### 核心词汇记一记

**Words Storm**

| | | |
|---|---|---|
| board | [bɔːd] *n.* | 公告牌 |
| fog | [fɔg] *n.* | 雾 |
| flight | [flait] *n.* | 航班 |
| postpone | [pəust'pəun] *v.* | 推迟 |
| quartz | [kwɔːts] *n.* | 石英表 |

**Phrases**

| | |
|---|---|
| keep good time | 走得准 |
| take off | 起飞 |

### 会话 2

Mike: Are people quite punctual in your country?

Kathy: Yes. In China, we value punctuality. Those who are always late will be disliked and considered undependable.

M: So if we agree that we should meet at seven o'clock, we should come at sixty fifty-five?

K: Yes. But we usually come earlier, say, six forty-five. Sometimes we come even much earlier, say, six fifteen.

M: But in America things are different, especially when you are going to visit someone. It is unwise for you to come too early because when you arrive they may be still making preparations for your coming. Nevertheless, you have to be punctual.

K: You know, in some countries people never think about punctuality. They just have no conception of time. When you agree that you'll meet at seven, he might well come at half past seven.

M: Terrible. In the modern world, the competition becomes keener. It demands that we should be punctual. Good opportunities come and go, if we don't pay attention to time, we'll easily miss them.

迈克：你们国家的人很守时吗？

凯西：是的。中国人很看重一个人是否守时。那些总迟到的人不太讨人喜欢，而且被认为是些靠不住的人。

M：那么如果我们约好要 7 点见面，我们是不是应该在 6:55 就到呢？

K：是呀。但是通常我们会到的更早一些，比如说 6:45 到。某些时候我们甚至要提前很多，可能 6:15 就要到。

M：但是在美国却不是这样的，尤其是当你要去拜访一个人的时候。提前很早到别人家里是不明智的，因为这时候他们可能还在为你的到来而做各种准备。但是，你还是得守时。

K：你知道吗，一些国家的人非常没有守时观念。他们脑子里对时间完全没概念。你跟他约定 7 点见面，他可能 7:30 才到。

M：太糟糕了！现代社会的竞争越来越激烈了，这要求我们必须要守时。好机会总是来去匆匆，如果我们没有时间观念，我们就抓不住机遇。

#### 核心词汇记一记

**Words Storm**

| | |
|---|---|
| punctual | ['pʌŋktjuəl] *a.* 守时的 |
| dislike | [dis'laik] *v.* 讨厌 |
| undependable | [ʌndi'pendəbl] *a.* 靠不住的 |
| nevertheless | [nevəðə'les] *ad.* 然而 |
| conception | [kɔn'sepʃən] *n.* 概念 |

**Phrases**

| | |
|---|---|
| make preparations for | 为……做准备 |
| pay attention to | 注意 |

# 47. Job and Income

## 职业和收入

### 知识链接 拓展视野，掌握背景知识

职业在一定时期包含了社会地位的成分。《敬业与乐业》中梁启超提出一些有关职业的东西。敬业的意思是“凡做一件事，便忠于一件事，将全副精力集中到这事上头，一点不旁骛，便是敬。”乐业的意思是“人生能从自己职业中领略出趣味，生活才有价值。”

### 难点点拨 知识难点看一看，情景实战热热身

1．graduate school 研究生院
Should I just step into society and find a job, or go to graduate school?
我应该踏入社会找一份工作呢，还是读研呢？

2．entrance exam 入学考试
If you want to get a master's degree you need to pass the entrance exam first, and that is hard for you.
如果你想获得硕士学位，需要先通过入学考试，那对你来说很难。

3．try one's luck 碰运气
Then if they call me for an interview, I'll go to try my luck.
如果他们让我去面试，我就去碰碰运气。

4．big money 大钱，厚利
I want to establish a small business myself, so that I can be my own boss, and make the big money.
我想自己创建个小公司，那样我就可以做自己的老板，赚大钱了。

5．go bankrupt 破产
Now competition in the market is so hot that many small companies go bankrupt.
现在市场竞争这么激烈，好多小公司都破产了。

## 情景实战 跟着老外听一听，读一读，练一练

### 会话 1

Celia: What should I do? I feel so confused. Should I just step into society and find a job, or go to graduate school?

James: I think you should find a job. If you want to get a master's degree you need to pass the entrance exam first, and that will be hard for you. To be honest, you are not a good scholar.

C: But my roommates are all getting prepared for it.

J: Don't mind others. Just consider yourself. You can be a good whitecollar office lady, because you talk well and you can really put things in order.

C: I am afraid that I may not get promoted and get a good salary in the future.

J: Don't worry, you get along well with your friends and you were also the president of the Student Union. You could be a good leader in the future. I have no doubt of that.

C: I have to send my resume to those companies I spoke to you about, and then if they call me for an interview, I'll go and try my luck.

J: Landing a well-paid job is what job seekers dream about, but you have to make a good CV that is well prepared and professional. Try to present what qualifications and honors you've achieved during the past four years and put them in your CV.

C: I'll think it over. After all, it's a big choice in my life.

J: Good luck.

西莉亚：我应该做什么呢？我觉得好困惑，我应该踏入社会找一份工作呢，还是读研呢？

詹姆斯：我觉得你应该去找一份工作。如果你想获得硕士学位，需要先通过入学考试，那对你来说很难。坦白说，你不适合做研究。

C：但是我的舍友都在准备这个呀！

J：不要管其他人怎么做，做你自己就好。你可以成为一位不错的女白领，因为你很会说话，而且可以把东西整理得井井有条。

C：我害怕不能升职，拿不到高薪。

J：别担心，你总是能跟你的朋友们相处融洽，你还是学生会主席，将来一定是个好的领导者。我一点都不怀疑。

C：我得把简历发给以前跟你说过的那些公司。如果他们让我去面试，我就去碰碰运气。

J：找到一份薪水不错的工作是所有找工作的人梦寐以求的事。但是首先你得制作一份精美的简历。找找你在过去的 4 年里挣得的荣誉和证书，填到你的简历上。

C：我会考虑一下的。不管怎样，这是我人生的一次重大选择。

J：祝你好运。

#### 核心词汇记一记

**Words Storm**

| | | |
|---|---|---|
| confused | [kən'fjuːzd] *a.* 困惑的 | |
| resume | [ri'zjuːm] *n.* 简历 | |
| interview | ['intəvjuː] *n.* 面试 | |

**Phrases**

| | |
|---|---|
| to be honest | 坦白说 |
| white collar | 白领 |
| in order | 整齐 |
| Student Union | 学生会 |

**会话 2**

George: Your friends are all devoted job-seekers. Why don't you move?

Sherry: I want to establish a small business myself, so that I can be my own boss, and make the big money.

G: Are you mad? Now competition in the market is so hot that many small companies go bankrupt. Are you sure that you can win? What will you do if your business fails and your money is all wasted?

S: I know it's a high-risk task, but I'll consult some real clever people to figure out every step we should take. I'll open up a store selling electronic gadgets, I have always been mad keen on laptops, mobile phones and such in the past four years and I know the exact situation about these commodities and the market. I think this will give me an advantage.

G: I am still apprehensive about your chances of success. Why do you have to start your own business?

S: It's boring to work for others, to make them wealthy. I want freedom. I may be occupied all day, but I want to decide my own life, and to fill it with challenges. Life to me is a gamble!

乔治：你的朋友都在全力以赴找工作，为什么你还不行动呢？

雪莉：我想自己创建一个小公司，那样我就可以做自己的老板，赚大钱了。

G：你疯了？现在市场竞争这么激烈，好多小公司都破产了。你确定可以搞下去吗？如果你的生意失败了，钱都打水漂了，你怎么办？

S：我知道这是个高风险的事情，但是我会请教一些行业内专业人士来指导，我要开一家经营电子产品的商店。在过去的 4 年里我一直都狂热爱好笔记本电脑和手机之类的东西，而且我知道目前有关这些产品和市场的准确行情。我觉得这是我的一个优势。

G：我还是担心你可能失败。为什么你非要开个自己的公司呢？

S：我觉得为别人工作赚钱很无聊。我想要自由。我可能每天都没空，但是我应该决定我自己的生活，让生活充满挑战。生活对于我就像是一场赌博。

### 核心词汇记一记

**Words Storm**

| | | |
|---|---|---|
| devote | [di'vəut] | v. 投入 |
| bankrupt | ['bæŋkrʌpt] | n. 破产 |
| gadget | ['gædʒit] | n. 小器具，小配件 |
| laptop | ['læptɔp] | n. 笔记本电脑 |
| commodity | [kə'mɔditi] | n. 商品 |
| gambling | ['gæmbliŋ] | n. 赌博 |

**Phrases**

figure out　算出，看出

# 48. Hobbies

## 兴趣爱好

### 知识链接 拓展视野，掌握背景知识

兴趣爱好是最好的老师。它可以让你的生活变得丰富而充实，也可以让你在与朋友交往时分享自己的快乐幸福。对于一个家庭主妇来说，如果她没有兴趣爱好，那么她的全部生活就是围着老公孩子团团转，稍有变故，就会引起歇斯底里的情绪。所以，培养一项兴趣爱好不仅有利于打发闲暇时光，更有利于身心健康。

### 难点点拨 知识难点看一看，情景实战热热身

1. like doing 喜爱做某事（作为爱好）
   I like collecting stamps.
   我喜欢集邮。
2. spend time on sth. 在某事上花费时间
   I spend a lot of time on stamp collection.
   我在集邮上花了很多时间。
3. make friends (with sb.)（与某人）交朋友
   I've made a lot of friends in this way.
   通过这种方式我交了很多朋友。
4. various kinds of 多种多样的
   I grow various kinds of beautiful flowers, sometimes trees, and cultivate them.
   我种植各种各样美丽的花卉或者树木，培育它们（长大）。
5. fall in love with 与……共坠爱河
   I thought you would drop this hobby soon when you said you fell in love with carpentry.
   你跟我说你爱上木工活的时候，我还以为你只是 3 分钟热度呢。

## 情景实战 跟着老外听一听，读一读，练一练

**会话 1**

Emma: Come gardening with me, John.

John: No, I'm re-examining my stamps. I like collecting stamps.

E: Why, to earn money or to show off?

J: For my amusement, it's just a hobby. Don't you think stamps are beautiful? I spend a lot of time on stamp collecting and I have a circle of friends who also love doing it. Sometimes we have parties together, to swap or sell our stamps. I've made a lot of friends in this way.

E: I cannot understand where the fun can be in it. For me, gardening is everything! I grow various kinds of beautiful flowers, sometimes trees, and I cultivate them and watch them grow. I often spend a whole weekend doing this. It really pleases me.

J: By the way, I'm also a radio buff. I like building radios with my own hands.

E: Oh. Can you show me some of your radios? I'm interested and I think everyone needs at least one hobby. Then we can get together to share our hobbies—you give me a radio, and I give you a bunch of flowers, or whatever.

J: Great. I need the flowers, because tomorrow is my girlfriend's birthday. But she hates radios.

爱玛：跟我一起去搞园艺，约翰。

约翰：不行，我在查看我的邮票呢，我喜欢集邮。

E：为什么呢？为了挣钱还是炫耀？

J：为了娱乐，只是个人爱好而已。难道你不觉得邮票是种很美的东西吗？我在集邮上花了很多时间，而且我有一群热爱集邮的朋友。有时候我们会搞一个派对来交换我们收集的邮票。我通过这种方式交了很多朋友呢。

E：我不能理解这有什么好玩的。对我来说，搞园艺才是我的一切。我种植各种各样美丽的花卉或者树木，培育它们长大。我经常会花一整个周末来搞园艺，因为这使我觉得心情舒畅。

J：顺便提一下，我还是个业余的无线电爱好者，我喜欢亲手来制作无线电设备。

E：你能给我展示一下你做的收音机吗？我挺感兴趣的。每个人至少需要有一个爱好，这样我们在一起才能分享我们的快乐——你给我台收音机，我给你一束花，诸如此类。

J：太棒了，我正需要花呢，明天是我女朋友的生日，但是她讨厌收音机。

### 核心词汇记一记

**Words Storm**

| | | |
|---|---|---|
| gardening | ['gɑːdniŋ] | *n.* 园艺 |
| hobby | ['hɔbi] | *n.* 爱好 |
| swap | [swɔp] | *v.* 交流，交换 |
| buff | [bʌf] | *n.* 爱好者，迷 |
| bunch | [bʌntʃ] | *n.* 束，捆 |

**Phrases**

collect stamps 集邮

**会话 2**

Jenny: You are doing this again. Saw, nail, hammer, plane…

Chuck: I like carpentry. I like things made of wood and doing this makes me happy.

J: Yes, a hobby can really make your life enjoyable. I thought you would drop this hobby soon when you said you fell in love with carpentry. I really didn't think the romance would last, guess I was wrong.

C: I changed my hobby frequently before because I never really felt happy about those things. I loved cooking for a while, but I found it too hard. I collected stamps too, but I found that too boring. I never thought I would discover a hobby as appealing as carpentry.

J: Maybe you can make something for me. I need a small stool.

C: No problem, tomorrow you'll have a nice new stool, just you wait!

J: I'll give you a painting in exchange. You know I've been learning to paint for years. I guarantee it won't disappoint you.

C: Great! Just the other day I was thinking about buying one to decorate my new room.

J: Hobbies can always give us so much pleasure—and sometimes save us money.

珍妮：你又在鼓捣这些了，锯、钉子、锤子、刨子……

查克：我喜欢木工活，就是喜欢用木头制作的东西，搞这些东西让我觉得很开心。

J：是呀，爱好会让你的生活更加有意思。你跟我说你爱上木工活的时候，我还以为你只是 3 分钟热度呢。我真没想到你这么执着，看来我错了。

C：以前我经常改变爱好是因为我不能从中获得乐趣。我有段时间喜欢上了烹饪，但是后来我发现它太难了。我也曾喜欢集邮，但是又觉得集邮太无聊了。我从来没有想过我会这么喜欢干手工活。

J：也许你可以为我做些小玩意儿。我需要一个小板凳。

C：没问题。你就等着吧，明天你就会拿到一个崭新漂亮的小板凳。

J：那么我就给你一幅油画作为回报。你也知道，我已经学了好多年油画了，所以一定不会让你失望的。

C：太棒了！我本来还想买一幅挂在家里作装饰用呢。

J：爱好总是能带给我们许多欢乐，有时还能给我们省点钱呢！

**核心词汇记一记**

**Words Storm**

saw [sɔː] *n.* 电锯
nail [neil] *n.* 钉子
hammer ['hæmə] *n.* 锤子
carpentry ['kɑːpəntri] *n.* 木工活
stool [stuːl] *n.* 板凳

**Phrases**

no problem 没问题

# 49. Cute Pet

## 可爱宠物

**知识链接** 拓展视野，掌握背景知识

*宠物是指人们不是为了经济目的，而是为了精神目的而豢养的动植物。以前的宠物一般是哺乳纲或鸟纲的动物，因为这些动物大脑比较发达，容易和人交流。实际生活中的宠物包括鱼纲、爬行纲、两栖纲甚至昆虫，一般都是体型比较小的动物。而现在宠物已经不再是动物的专利，植物也可以作为宠物，因为很多人喜欢安静，动物的声音有时相对嘈杂，且会有不清洁的排泄物，因此导致了植物宠物的产生。*

**难点点拨** 知识难点看一看，情景实战热热身

1．I never thought you did... 我没想到你……

   I never thought you had a cat!

   没想到你居然有只猫！

2．somewhat 有点，后跟形容词或副词

   Cat is somewhat like a girl, beautiful, quiet, lovely, and small.

   猫有点像女孩子，美丽、安静、可爱，而且一副小鸟依人的样子。

3．be affectionate to 很喜爱某人

   The cat is very affectionate to me.

   这猫很喜欢我。

## 情景实战 跟着老外听一听，读一读，练一练

**会话 1**

Jack: Hey! I never thought you had a cat!

David: You see. I don't have a girlfriend. So I got a cat as my friend.

J: Ha-ha. A cat is somewhat like a girl, beautiful, quiet, lovely, and small.

D: She is quite naughty. Every night she jumps on my bed and wants me to cuddle her.

J: So cute. What's her name?

D: Emily.

J: Emily? Isn't that the name of your ex-girlfriend?

D: Yes... I miss her a lot. So I named the cat Emily.

J: I'm sorry. But at least the cat won't betray you.

D: Yes, she's very affectionate to me. She likes being caressed. Usually a cat is supposed to be haughty and cool, but Emily is so kind to me.

J: Does she like fish?

D: I often give her fish burgers.

J: That reminds me the other Emily who loves fish burgers too.

D: Don't mention that again, please.

杰克：嘿！没想到你居然有只猫！

大卫：你看，我没有女朋友，所以就养了只猫当朋友。

J：哈哈，猫有点像女孩子，美丽、安静、可爱，而且一副小鸟依人的样子。

D：她很淘气的。每天晚上都会跳到我床上，想让我搂着睡。

J：太可爱了。她叫什么名字？

D：艾米丽。

J：艾米丽？这不是你前女友的名字吗？

D：嗯，我很想她。所以就管这只猫叫艾米丽。

J：不好意思。但至少猫是不会背叛你的。

D：是的，她很喜欢我。她喜欢被我抚摸。通常来说猫是冷傲的，但是艾米丽对我很好。

J：她喜欢吃鱼吗？

D：我经常喂她鱼肉汉堡。

J：这让我想到了另一个爱吃鱼肉汉堡的艾米丽。

D：请别再提了。

### 核心词汇记一记

**Words Storm**

somewhat ['sʌmhwɔt] *ad.* 稍微，有点

naughty ['nɔti] *a.* 淘气的

cuddle ['kʌdl] *v.* 拥抱，搂着

affectionate [ə'fekʃənət] *a.* 充满深情的

caress [kə'res] *v.* 爱抚

haughty ['hɔːti] *a.* 傲慢的

**Phrases**

be supposed to 认为……

## 会话 2

Paul: Honey. Here is Mike. Do you like it?

Kate: What? You bring a dog into our house! It will mess up everything and shit everywhere. Don't let it enter the house! I've just swept the floor.

P: But honey, don't you think it's cute? It can give you a sense of security. Burglars will not dare to enter our house from now on.

K: No! It looks horrible. Look at its teeth! It's bearing its teeth to me!

P: Easy. Easy, honey. It has noble blood—its father has won the championship of a worldwide dog show.

K: So are you sure it is tame? It won't bite me? It won't bark at us?

P: Yes, I'm sure. It will be a nice boy. This afternoon I'll take it out for a walk, and play frisbee with it. It'll love the game.

K: You have to feed it with meat, don't you?

P: Yes. We can also buy some dog food from the supermarket.

K: It will cost a lot of money.

P: Never mind. I'll work harder and earn more money. It will bring pleasure to our lives.

保罗：亲爱的，这是迈克，你喜欢它吗？

凯特：什么？你居然带着一只狗进了我的房子！它会把一切都弄乱的，还会随处大小便。不要让它进屋！我刚擦过地。

P：但是亲爱的，你不觉得它很可爱吗？它能给你安全感。从此以后盗贼就不敢再闯进家门了。

K：不行！它看上去很恐怖。看看这牙齿，它正向我龇牙呢！

P：放轻松点，亲爱的。它是有贵族血统的，它父亲赢得了世界狗展锦标赛的冠军呢。

K：那你确定它很温驯吗？它不会咬我？不会朝我们叫？

P：是的，我确定。它是只乖乖狗。今天下午我会带它出去遛遛，跟它玩玩飞盘。它会爱上这个游戏的。

K：你得喂给它肉吃，是吗？

P：是的，我们也可以从超市买点狗粮喂它。

K：这很费钱的。

P：没关系，我会努力工作赚更多钱的。它会给我们的生活增添很多乐趣的。

### 核心词汇记一记

#### Words Storm

security [si'kjuriti] *n.* 安全

burglar ['bəːglə] *n.* 夜贼

championship ['tʃæmpiənʃip] *n.* 锦标赛

bark [bɑːk] *v.* 吠

frisbee ['frizbiː] *n.* 飞盘

#### Phrases

mess up 弄乱

sweep the floor 扫地

noble blood 贵族血统

# 50. Keeping Fit

# 养生保健

## 知识链接 拓展视野，掌握背景知识

养生保健是一种综合的维持健康的行为，养生和保健的侧重点不同，却殊途同归。养生保健追求的不仅仅是长寿，更重要的是生活质量的提高，使人活得更健康、更快乐。中国传统医学认为养生保健指保养、调养、颐养生命，即以调阴阳、和气血、保精神为原则，运用调神、导引吐纳、四时调摄、食养、药养、节欲、辟谷等多种方法，以期达到健康、长寿的目的。

## 难点点拨 知识难点看一看，情景实战热热身

1. He is a big drinker.

   他可是个大酒鬼。

2. have something to do with 与……有关

   The doctor said this has something to do with his illness.

   医生说这些都跟他的病有关。

3. a pack of cigarettes 一包烟

   I smoke one pack everyday, sometimes two packs.

   我每天抽一包，有时两包。

4. nothing but 除了……不会……

   Smoking gives you nothing but an early death.

   抽烟除了让你过早死亡外不会带给你任何好处。

## 情景实战 跟着老外听一听，读一读，练一练

**会话 1**

Neil: It's so terrible. My boss has cancer of the stomach. A week ago he got a simple stomachache and didn't know why, so he went to the hospital for a checkup and got a surprisingly bad result.

Clive: Does he drink a lot?

N: Yes, he is a big drinker and he loves barbecue and pickles as well. The doctor said this has something to do with his illness.

C: Excessive alcohol harms your stomach very badly and things roasted and pickled may cause cancer if you eat them often and to excess.

N: My boss just cannot live without all this. He very often got drunk and vomited in front of us. What a shame.

C: We should be very careful not to lead such a lifestyle. Do you drink?

N: A little, I'm the kind of person who can easily get the Asian flush. I can never drink more than two bottles of beer in a row.

C: That's a good thing. You know, in some countries, drinking is a social activity. If someone makes a toast to you, you simply cannot refuse—any kind of refusal to a toast will be regarded as impolite. It's hard to stop drinking.

尼尔: 太可怕了，我的老板得了胃癌。一周以前他肚子痛但不知道为什么，所以就去医院检查了一下，结果竟然这么严重。

克莱夫: 他喝酒喝得很多吗？

N: 是呀，他可是个大酒鬼。此外，他还喜欢吃烤肉和腌制品。医生说这些都跟他的病有关。

C: 过量的酒精会严重伤胃，如果一个人经常吃很多烧烤和腌制品，很容易致癌。

N: 但是我的老板没有这些不能活。他经常喝醉，当着我们的面就呕吐。真是丢脸。

C: 我们可要注意，不要过这样的生活。你喝酒吗？

N: 喝一点。我是那种喝一点酒就上脸的人。我喝啤酒从来都不超过两瓶。

C: 那样挺好的。你知道吗，在一些国家，喝酒是一项社交活动。如果别人敬你酒，你根本无法拒绝——任何形式的拒酒都被看做是不礼貌的。这样就很难戒酒了。

### 核心词汇记一记

**Words Storm**

barbecue ['bɑːbikjuː] *n.* 烤肉
pickle ['pikl] *n.* 腌制品
vomit ['vɔmit] *v.* 呕吐

**Phrases**

Asian flush （饮酒）脸红
make a toast 敬酒

**会话 2**

Matt: Hey. Do you smoke?

Miller: No thanks! You are a big smoker, aren't you?

Matt: I am a chain-smoker. I smoke one pack everyday, sometimes two packs.

Miller: I think you should try to give it up. It's harmful to your health.

Matt: I know, but it seems hard to stop now. If I don't have a cigarette, I feel terrible and weak. I think I'm addicted to nicotine.

Miller: Nicotine is only one of the many elements in cigarettes that can hurt you, you have to stop. Every cigarette can shorten your life expectancy by eleven minutes, which means, if you smoke twenty a day, you'll waste nearly four hours of your lifetime.

Matt: It is terrible. I know smokers are far more prone to get cancer of the lungs, but as you know I'm a writer and I need to get inspired. Smoking gives me inspiration!

Miller: That's totally non-sense. Smoking gives you nothing but an early death. Think about it. One day you'll be lying on your death bed in agony waiting for your miserable end. Stop it now my friend!

Matt: How should I stop? I need some help.

Miller: Go to see a doctor, try to smoke less and less each day and finally you'll quit smoking.

马特：嘿，你抽烟吗？

米勒：不，谢谢。你抽烟很厉害，是吧？

M: 我可是个大烟鬼。每天抽一包，有时两包。

M: 我觉得你应该试着戒掉。抽烟有害健康。

M: 我知道，但是现在很难戒了。如果不抽，我就觉得难受和虚弱。我觉得我已经吸食尼古丁成瘾了。

M: 尼古丁只是香烟里众多危害你身体的因素之一。你必须停止抽烟。每根烟都会让你的寿命缩短 11 分钟，这意味着如果你抽 20 根烟，你将会消耗将近 4 个小时的生命。

M: 太恐怖了。我知道吸烟者很容易得肺癌，但是你知道我是个作家，我必须获取灵感，抽烟使我产生灵感。

M: 这简直是胡闹。抽烟除了让你过早死亡外不会带给你任何好处。好好考虑一下吧。你会痛苦地躺在床上等待你的生命悲哀地终结。赶紧戒烟吧。

M: 我怎么戒？我需要一些帮助。

M: 去看医生。试着慢慢减少抽烟，最后你会发现你已经戒掉了。

**核心词汇记一记**

**Words Storm**

| | | |
|---|---|---|
| harmful | ['hɑːmful] | *a.* 有害的 |
| nicotine | ['nikətiːn] | *n.* 尼古丁 |
| cancer | ['kænsə] | *n.* 癌症 |
| inspiration | [ˌinspə'reiʃən] | *n.* 灵感 |

**Phrases**

| | |
|---|---|
| be addicted to | 上瘾 |
| life expectancy | 寿命 |
| quit smoking | 戒烟 |

# 51. Give up Your Seat

## 让座的艺术

### 知识链接 拓展视野，掌握背景知识

让座看起来是件小事儿，其实里面学问大着呢，小到道德问题，大到可以反映出一个社会的文化传统和思维模式。在中国，让座给老弱病残者是一种社会公德，如果不这么做就会遭到周围人的道德谴责。而在美国，很多老年人都有一颗年轻不服老的心，他们不愿意被当做特殊人群对待，你如果直接让座给他或她可能会引起不愉快，必须要确认他们是否想接受你的帮助才能让座。

### 难点点拨 知识难点看一看，情景实战热热身

1. respect for sb. 对某人的尊重
   The respect for the old is always a virtue to be praised.
   尊重老年人一直都是一种被提倡的美德。
2. more and more 越来越多
   More and more of them become affectionate to the aged.
   越来越多的人开始关爱老人了。
3. grey-haired 白发的，不说“white”
   Some people, though they are grey-haired, don't like to be regarded as old.
   有些人尽管头发已经白了，但他们却不愿意被当成老人。
4. joke about 调侃
   Some people will feel embarrassed, and they will joke about their age.
   有些人会觉得尴尬，他们会拿自己的年龄调侃一下。
5. an act of 某种行为
   I think it's an act of selfishness.
   我觉得这是一种自私的行为。

## 情景实战 跟着老外听一听，读一读，练一练

**会话 1**

Lily: Do we need to give up our seats when there are old people on the bus?

Wang Yan: In China, to give up your seat for an old man is a virtue. There are seats reserved for the old, the weak, sick, the disabled and pregnant women, but very often these seats have been occupied. So when you see some old man getting on the bus, you'd better voluntarily offer your seat to him, to show your love and respect for our seniors. In Chinese culture the respect for the old is always a virtue to be praised.

L: Will those senior citizens feel shy and refuse the offerings?

W: They usually accept the seats willingly. Some of them will praise the seat-givers by word. Now if an old man stands near you and you don't offer your seat to him, other people will dislike you and offer their seats.

L: So in China the old are respected and loved. They have their privileges.

W: People are being educated this way as part of our culture. More and more of them are becoming affectionate toward the aged.

莉莉：公车上有老人的时候我们需要让座吗？

王岩：在中国，给老人让座是一种美德。公车上设有专门为老、弱、病、残、孕准备的座位，但是这些座却经常被占。所以你看到一位老人上车的时候，最好主动让座给他，来表示你对老人的关爱和尊重。在中国文化里，尊重老年人一直都是被提倡的美德。

L：那这些老市民会不会觉得不好意思，然后拒绝我的好意呢？

W：他们通常会很愿意接受你的让座。有些还会口头表扬让座的人。如果一个老人站在你身边而你却不让座，其他人就会厌恶你，并且主动让座。

L：原来中国的老人是受尊敬和关爱的，他们拥有自己的特权。

W：作为我们中国文化的一部分，人人都会受到这样的教育。越来越多的人开始关爱老人了。

### 核心词汇记一记

**Words Storm**

| | |
|---|---|
| virtue | ['vəːtjuː] *n.* 美德 |
| reserve | [ri'zəːv] *v.* 保留 |
| disabled | [dis'eibld] *a.* 残疾的 |
| pregnant | ['pregnənt] *a.* 怀孕的 |
| occupy | ['ɔkjupai] *v.* 占据 |
| voluntarily | ['vɔləntərili] *ad.* 自愿地，主动地 |
| privilege | ['privilidʒ] *n.* 特权 |

**Phrases**

| | |
|---|---|
| give up | 放弃 |
| offer one's seat | 让座 |

## 会话 2

Zhang Yun: In America, do we need to give up our seats to the old people on the bus?

Tony: It depends. Some people, though they are grey-haired, don't like to be regarded as "old". Being old means being weak, and they don't like to be looked down upon as such.

Z: So if we offer our own seats to them, they will be angry?

T: Some people will feel embarrassed, and they will joke about their age. Some may feel displeased.

Z: But if we meet someone who is really old, what should we do?

T: Go ahead and inquire quite politely whether he needs a seat. If he gives an affirmative answer, just show him your own seat.

Z: Anyway, we should show care for the aged, this is a universal ethos.

T: In some nations and in modern times the young never give their seats to the old. I think it's an act of selfishness. To love the old is always a virtue, wherever you go.

张云：在美国，乘公交的时候我们需要给老人让座吗？

托尼：看情况吧。有些人尽管头发已经白了，但他们却不愿意被当成老人。变老意味着变得虚弱，而他们却不想被看不起。

Z：那么是说如果我们把座位让给他们，他们会生气？

T：有些人会觉得尴尬，他们会拿自己的年龄调侃一下，还有些人可能会觉得不开心。

Z：但是当我们真的遇到一位老人的时候，该怎么办呢？

T：那就上前去非常礼貌地询问一下他是否需要一个座位。如果他同意了，那就把座让给他。

Z：不管怎么说，我们都需要关心老人。这是基本的道德素质。

T：在一些国家，现代的年轻人从来不会把座让给老人。我认为这是一种自私的行为。无论你身处何方，关爱老人总是一种美德。

### 核心词汇记一记

**Words Storm**

inquire [in'kwaiə] *v.* 询问
affirmative [ə'fə:mətiv] *a.* 确定的
selfishness ['selfiʃnis] *n.* 自私

**Phrases**

look down upon 轻视

# 52. The English National Sport: Queuing

## 英国人的排队

### 知识链接 拓展视野，掌握背景知识

人类社会中，一般认为排队是文明的表现。在不同的社会中，有一定的文化差异。排队是有限资源的分配方法之一，排队是“先到先得”，以消除“价高者得”或者“亲疏有别”、“私相授受”等的不公平行为。排队可以体现一定的公平性。

### 难点点拨 知识难点看一看，情景实战热热身

1．on average 平均来说

On average, in his life, a British man spends six months queuing.

一个英国人的一生中平均要有6个月的时间花在排队上。

2．do the queuing 排队

We do a lot of queuing.

我们经常排队。

3．get bored 无聊

Don’t you get bored when you stand there doing nothing?

当你站在那儿无事可做的时候，你不觉得无聊吗?

4．be aware of 意识到，考虑到

They are often poorly educated, and they are not aware of the importance of order.

他们通常受教育程度不高，没有意识到秩序的重要性。

5．at work 起作用

It’s the dark side of human nature at work.

这是人性的阴暗面在作祟。

## 情景实战 跟着老外听一听，读一读，练一练

**会话 1**

Holly: On average, in his life, a British man spends six months queuing for something. Do you believe it?

Amanda: For sure, if you go there you'll see everybody queuing. We wait in a queue in the supermarket to pay. We stand in a queue to buy liqueur in a bar, the same for drawing money from an ATM. This also can take a long time. We do a lot of queuing.

H: Don't you get bored when you stand there doing nothing?

A: It's our tradition. We have to do this because we need order, and if we don't follow the order we'll fall into chaos.

H: Yes. I think that's right. We need order. We have to do things one at a time.

A: Very often, if I need to wait, I will take a newspaper or a book to kill time. Now boys take their PSPs and play games while queuing.

H: Good idea. That will turn boredom into pleasure.

A: I don't think queuing is particularly a human activity. For example, wild geese fly in a V formation, and penguins, buffalos, goats all follow each other one by one. They understand they have to keep things in the right order. This is just like our queuing.

霍利：一个英国人的一生中平均要有 6 个月的时间花在排队上。你相信吗？

阿曼达：相信。如果你来我们国家，你会发现每个人都在排队。我们在超市里排长队来结账，我们在酒吧里排队买酒，我们从自动取款机里取款也要花很长时间。我们经常排队。

H：站在那儿无事可做的时候你不觉得无聊吗？

A：这是我们的传统。我们不得不这么做，因为我们需要秩序。如果不遵守秩序我们就会陷入混乱。

H：是，我觉得很对。我们需要秩序。我们做事应当井井有条。

A：通常如果我要排队的话，就会拿一份报纸或者一本书来消磨时间。现在的男孩子都带着 PSP，排队的时候就玩游戏。

H：好主意。那会化无聊为快乐的。

A：我想排队不是人类特有的活动。比如，大雁排成 V 字形在天上飞，企鹅、水牛还有山羊都一个接一个地排队。它们知道必须要保持正确的顺序。这跟我们的排队是一样的。

### 核心词汇记一记

**Words Storm**

| | | |
|---|---|---|
| queue | [kjuː] | *v.* 排队 |
| formation | [fɔːˈmeiʃən] | *n.* 编队 |
| penguin | [ˈpeŋgwin] | *n.* 企鹅 |
| buffalo | [ˈbʌfələu] | *n.* 水牛 |
| goat | [gəut] | *n.* 山羊 |

**Phrases**

| | |
|---|---|
| follow the order | 遵守秩序 |
| kill time | 消磨时间 |

**会话 2**

Rudy: Do you Chinese people often wait in a queue?

Nelson: Years ago we didn't queue well. Now we queue a lot. Nevertheless, there are always people who want to jump the queue. They are often poorly educated, and they are not aware of the importance of order.

R: I would disagree. I tend to think that's a problem of personality and morality rather than education. If you have the consideration of others' interests, you will surely not violate them. The problem for those who jump the queue is that they are selfish and impatient and they never care about anything but themselves.

N: Maybe it's the dark side of human nature at work. We need to continue educating our people, to let them pay more attention to others than to themselves. Now we still don't queue on many occasions, especially when we are waiting for a bus.

R: It might be a tradition, or a cultural thing that cannot be changed easily.

N: Another problem is that we don't have enough resources for everyone. If we don't rush and scramble for a good seat on the bus, there will be no place for us to sit. Therefore we have to develop our industry to meet the needs of all people.

鲁迪：你们中国人经常排队等候吗？

尼尔森：很多年前我们不怎么排队，但现在经常排队。但是总是有些人想要插队。他们通常受教育程度不高，没有意识到秩序的重要性。

R：我觉得不是这样。这不是教育问题，而是人格和道德品质的问题。如果你关心他人的利益，当然你就不会冒犯他们。那些插队者的问题是，他们很自私，除了自己，谁也不关心。

N：可能是人性的阴暗面在作祟。我们需要继续教育人民，让他们多加考虑别人而不是自己。现在我们在很多场合依然不排队，尤其是在等公交的时候。

R：这可能是一种传统或者是一种文化，不能轻易改变吧。

N：另外一个问题是我们没有足够的资源来提供给每一个人。如果我们不冲上车去抢位子，那我们就没地方坐了。所以我们必须发展我们的工业来满足全体人民的需求。

### 核心词汇记一记

#### Words Storm

| | | |
|---|---|---|
| nevertheless | [nevəðə'les] *ad.* | 然而，不过 |
| morality | [mə'ræliti] *n.* | 道德 |
| consideration | [kənsidə'reiʃən] *n.* | 考虑 |
| selfish | ['selfiʃ] *a.* | 自私的 |
| occasion | [ə'keiʒən] *n.* | 场合 |
| scramble | ['skræmbl] *v.* | 抢夺 |

#### Phrases

| | |
|---|---|
| jump the queue | 插队 |
| dark side | 阴暗面 |

# 53. Electronic Life

## 电子生活

### 知识链接　拓展视野，掌握背景知识

*人类现在已经生活在电子时代的地球村了。电子时代的到来给我们的生活提供了很多便利，但不可否认的是，它也带来了诸多隐性或显性的问题。人工智能就算再精密，也永远无法像人一样可以随机应变。甚至当人类过度依赖电子产品的时候，还可能异化为这些工具性物品的奴隶。*

### 难点点拨　知识难点看一看，情景实战热热身

1．think of doing 考虑做某事

I'm thinking of buying one for my car to report my position when I'm lost.

我正考虑给我的车也买一个（GPS 定位系统），在我迷失方向的时候，它就可以报告我的位置了。

2．be competent at doing sth. 有能力做

You seem to be very competent at playing with electronic gadgets.

看起来你好像对电子小玩意儿很有研究啊。

3．bargain with sb. 与人讨价还价

I know how to bargain with those salesmen.

我知道怎么和商家讨价还价。

## 情景实战 跟着老外听一听，读一读，练一练

**会话 1**

Abby: I don't know which way we should go now, there's a fork in the road up ahead, can you see?

Bill: Wait. I'll consult my mobile phone. It has a build-in GPS.

A: Great. I'm thinking of buying one for my car to report my position when I'm lost.

B: Turn left, please. With this, you won't make a mistake.

A: Good. You seem to be very competent at playing with electronic gadgets.

B: Yes, I have an arsenal of them. Every season I have a new mobile and every year I get a new laptop. I also have a UMPC, which is a little bit bigger in size than a phone but as useful as a computer.

A: You are so extravagant. That must be money-consuming.

B: I know. But I sell my old phones to get money for new ones. This is not about the money, but about the lifestyle. I always try my best to update my knowledge, to keep up with the development of technology, to enjoy the benefits of technological progress.

A: So next time I want to buy something, can I call on you for some advice?

B: Sure, leave it to me. I'm an expert!

艾比：不好意思，我不知道我们应该走哪条路了，在路尽头有个岔路口，看到了吗？

比尔：等一下。我用我的手机查一下，上面有内置的 GPS 定位系统。

A：太棒了。我正考虑给我的车也买一个 GPS 定位系统，迷路的时候它就可以报告我的位置了。

B：左拐吧。有了这个，你就不会走错了。

A：很好。看起来你好像对电子小玩意儿很有研究啊。

B：是的，我有好多电子产品呢。每个季节我都会换一个新手机，每年换一台新笔记本。我还有个超便携式电脑，这玩意儿比手机大一些，但是在用途方面却跟电脑一样。

A：你好奢侈呀，那些东西一定很费钱。

B：我知道，但是我用卖旧手机的钱来买新的，这不是钱的问题，而是一种生活方式。我总是尽最大努力去更新我的知识，紧跟技术发展的潮流，并且享受科技进步的乐趣。

A：那我下次要是买什么类似的东西，你能给我些建议吗？

B：当然了，交给我好了，我可是个专家。

### 核心词汇记一记

**Words Storm**

fork [fɔːk] *n.* 岔路

arsenal [ˈɑːsnəl] *n.* 储藏，军火库

extravagant [ikˈstrævəgənt] *a.* 奢侈的，浪费的

**Phrases**

turn left 左拐

as useful as 像……一样有用

keep up with 与……并行

**会话 2**

Daci: Have you heard of netbook?

Cady: Yes. It's a small laptop. But I don't know much else about it.

D: It's small in size, thus being convenient to take. You can take it everywhere you want. Most netbooks are energy-saving, and can run a long time without external power.

C: Then what about its performance?

D: That's another question. Because it consumes less power, it cannot run as fast as an ordinary laptop. You can do your office jobs with it. But many games cannot run on it.

C: That's enough for me. I don't play games at all.

D: There are many choices. If you need one, maybe I can go shopping with you. I know how to bargain with those salesmen and check the thing to make sure there is no defect.

C: Thanks. I have some apprehension about being deceived by dishonest sales people. If you go along with me, I will feel far more confident.

D: Yes. You may rest assured, I will be sure you get a good deal.

达希：你听说过上网本吗？

凯迪：听说过。是一种小型笔记本电脑。但是其他的我就不知道了。

D：它体积小，因此便于携带。你可以带着它去任何你想去的地方。大部分上网本都是节能的，在没有电源的情况下能长时间运转。

C：它的性能如何？

D：这就是另外一回事了。因为它不是很耗电，所以运行起来不如普通的笔记本电脑快。你可以用它来工作，但却不能玩很多游戏。

C：这对我来说已经足够了。我根本就不玩游戏。

D：你可以有很多选择的。如果你需要的话，也许我可以陪你一起去买。我知道怎么和商家讨价还价，而且可以检查一下确保电脑没有瑕疵。

C：多谢了，我害怕被不讲诚信的卖家欺骗。如果你能陪我一起去，那我就安心了。

D：好了，你就放心吧，肯定能买个好的。

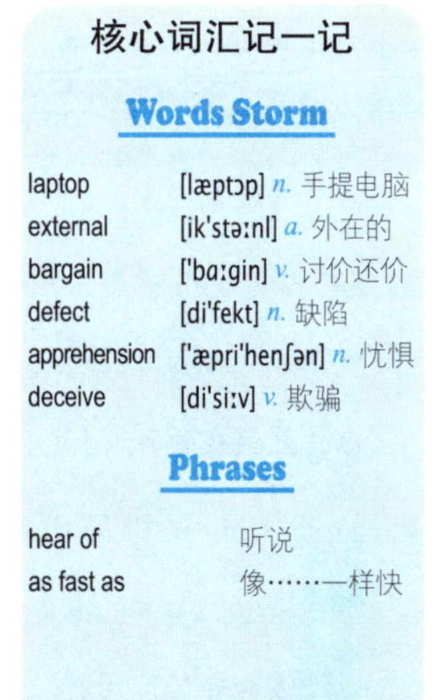

**核心词汇记一记**

**Words Storm**

laptop [læptɔp] *n.* 手提电脑
external [ik'stəːnl] *a.* 外在的
bargain ['bɑːgin] *v.* 讨价还价
defect [di'fekt] *n.* 缺陷
apprehension ['æpri'henʃən] *n.* 忧惧
deceive [di'siːv] *v.* 欺骗

**Phrases**

hear of 听说
as fast as 像……一样快

# Love and Family 爱情与家庭

## 54. Men and Women

## 男人和女人

**知识链接** 拓展视野，掌握背景知识

男人和女人之间亘古以来就弥漫着一场没有硝烟的战争，紧张而激烈。男人来自火星，女人来自金星，两种不同星球的生物走到一起时，情感关系就会面临诸多的问题。男人错误地期待女人按照他的方式进行思考和交流，做出他理想中的反应。女人错误地期待男人按照她的方式加以感受和沟通，展示她愿望中的姿态。他们忘记了"你是你，我是我"的道理。其实，最有效的解决方式也是最简单的解决方式，即沟通。

**难点点拨** 知识难点看一看，情景实战热热身

1．kiss sb. on her lips 吻某人的嘴唇

I saw you kissing a girl on the lips this afternoon.

我今天下午看到你在吻一个女孩。

2．jump to conclusions 轻率地判断

You've jumped to conclusions.

你下结论太轻率了。

3．find fault with 挑刺，找毛病

You are always finding fault with me!

你总是找我的茬儿！

4．gossip with sb. 跟人闲聊

She always gossips with neighbors.

她经常和邻居们闲聊。

## 情景实战 跟着老外听一听，读一读，练一练

**会话 1**

Carrie: Tell me the truth. Are you cheating on me?

Steve: No! Why do you ask me this?

C: I saw you kissing a girl on the lips this afternoon.

S: Impossible, you must be kidding!

C: No. I'm serious. She was tall and beautiful, wearing a pink skirt. You were at the post office.

S: Ah! I see. You have jumped to conclusions. That's my sister, Kate. We were sending air mail to our uncle.

C: You're making my blood boil! You're lying! Don't think I am stupid! I saw you caressing her affectionately!

S: Yes. We usually do this, it's a family tradition.

C: I'm about to explode! You will never tell the truth!

S: What's wrong with you? You are always finding fault with me!

C: The day before yesterday, a girl called you "baby" on the phone, and I heard it. A week ago you just couldn't keep your eyes off a hot girl on the street. A month ago you said you loved next door's little girl.

S: She is just ten years old! I beg you, calm down!

C: Ten years old? Perhaps you think of her as a good nymph, like Lolita.

凯 利：跟我说实话，你是不是背叛了我？

斯蒂夫：没有！你为什么要这样问？

C: 我今天下午看到你在吻一个女孩。

S: 不可能，你在开玩笑吧！

C: 没有，我是认真的。她高挑漂亮，穿着粉色衬衫。你们当时正在邮局。

S: 哦，我知道了，你下结论太轻率了。那是我妹妹。她叫凯特，我们那时正在给我们的叔叔发航空邮件呢。

C: 你简直要把我气疯了，你在撒谎！不要以为我傻，我看到你含情脉脉地抚摸她了！

S: 是啊，我们经常这样啊，这是家族传统。

C: 我简直忍无可忍了！你根本就不打算说实话。

S: 你究竟怎么了？总是找我的茬儿！

C: 前天我听到一个女孩在电话里叫你"宝贝"。一星期前你在大街上目不转睛地盯着一个美女看。一个月前你还说你喜欢住在隔壁的小女生。

S: 她只有 10 岁啊！我求你了，平静一下好吗？

C: 10 岁？你以为她是美少女洛丽塔呢吧！

### 核心词汇记一记

**Words Storm**

lip [lip] *n.* 嘴唇

impossible [im'pɔsəbl] *a.* 不可能的

nymph [nimf] *n.* 美丽的少女

**Phrases**

cheat on 背叛

family tradition 家庭传统

calm down 平静一下

**会话 2**

Samantha: I'm reading a book. It proclaims that man comes from Mars and woman from Venus. They are two totally different species.

Miranda: Man is supposed to be tough, serious, rational, and calm, while the woman is supposed to be soft, light-hearted, emotional, and sometimes hysterical.

S: I think it's true because I can see it in my family. My father speaks far less than my mother, but when he speaks, he always talks about serious things such as politics and history. He is especially interested in international relations and warfare.

M: And your mother?

S: She is an ordinary woman. She loves soap operas, cosmetics. She always gossips with neighbors. Sometimes she cries and shouts like mad—my father will never do that.

M: Do they quarrel?

S: No, not very often, but if they are unhappy they will keep silent for a while.

M: You know, in my family my parents often fight. My mother scratches my father, kicks him, but he never fights back. He just runs away.

S: A good man will never beat his wife. I think what your father does is the right thing to do.

萨曼莎：我正在读一本书，书上说男人来自火星，女人来自金星。他们完全是两种不同的物种。

米兰达：是的，男人应该是坚强、严肃、理性和沉着的。而女人则应该是柔弱、无忧无虑、感性的，有时是歇斯底里的。

S：嗯，从我的家庭中就能看出来。我爸爸说话就比我妈妈少，但是每次只要他一开口，谈论的就是像政治、历史那样的严肃话题。他尤其对国际关系和战争感兴趣。

M：那你妈妈呢？

S：她就是一个普通女人。她爱看肥皂剧，喜欢化妆品之类的东西。她经常和邻居们闲聊，有时她还会像疯了一样哭喊，可是我爸爸就从来不这样。

M：那他们吵架吗？

S：不经常吵。但是如果他们闹矛盾的话，他们就会冷战一段时间。

M：你知道吗，在我家，父母经常吵架。我妈妈会厮打我爸爸，还踢他。但我爸爸从来都不还手，他只是躲开我妈妈。

S：好男人是不会打妻子的。我觉得你爸爸做得很对。

### 核心词汇记一记

**Words Storm**

| | | |
|---|---|---|
| Mars | [mɑːs] *n.* | 火星 |
| Venus | ['viːnəs] *n.* | 金星 |
| rational | ['ræʃənl] *a.* | 理性的 |
| neighbor | ['neibə] *n.* | 邻居 |
| scratch | [skrætʃ] *v.* | 抓，挠 |

**Phrases**

| | |
|---|---|
| international relations | 国际关系 |
| fight back | 还手 |

# 55. Love Is Like a Soap Opera

## 爱如肥皂剧

### 知识链接 拓展视野，掌握背景知识

*现代爱情越来越戏剧化了。传统上，我们讲求男耕女织，相夫教子的家庭美德。而现在，越来越多的人开始追求一种戏剧性的爱情，把电影、电视上看到的情节照搬到现实中来。尤其在西方，女权与男权的斗争使得婚恋越来越像是演戏或者战争，而传统上的幸福感却在一点点地丧失。*

### 难点点拨 知识难点看一看，情景实战热热身

1．first love 初恋

She was his first love.

她是他的初恋。

2．new love 新欢

cheat on 背叛，欺骗

His girlfriend found a new love, and cheated on him.

他的女朋友找到了新欢，背叛了他。

3．have a crush on sb. 喜欢某人

I have had a secret crush on you for long.

我已经暗恋你很久了。

4．在重复句式中某些词可省略，如：

Your eyes are brighter than stars; your lips fresher than roses; your voice sweeter than honey.

你的眼睛比星光还明亮，你的嘴唇比玫瑰还鲜红，你的声音比蜜还甜美。

## 情景实战 跟着老外听一听，读一读，练一练

**会话 1**

Larry: John is constantly changing his girlfriends. What's wrong with him?

Terry: I think he sleeps with them, and then dumps them one by one.

L: He was not a playboy before, but he was once deeply hurt by a girlfriend. She was his first love.

T: So he has a tragic love story?

L: I believe so. He did everything for her. He led a miserable life to save money and then buy his girl a present, but he was happy because he was in love.

T: What happened then?

L: His girlfriend found a new love, and cheated on him. He eventually discovered her deceit and it tore him apart.

T: Maybe this is the reason why he plays with girls now. Perhaps he secretly harbors intense hatred for girls and wants to take revenge.

L: He was really angry when he found what his girl had done to him. He swore then he would get all girls to share his hell.

T: We should see if we can help. I'll try to have a talk to him about all this.

拉里：约翰正在频繁更换女朋友，他到底怎么了？

特里：我觉得他只是跟她们上床，然后就一个一个把她们都甩了。

L：他以前不是个花花公子呀。但是他曾经被一个女友深深伤害过。她是他的初恋。

T：所以他有个悲情故事咯？

L：应该是吧。他为她做任何事情。攒钱给那个女孩买礼物，自己却过着惨淡的生活。但是那时他很开心因为他还沉浸在恋爱中。

T：然后发生了什么？

L：他的女朋友找到了新欢，背叛了他。他最终发现了这件事，心都碎了，伤得很深。

T：也许这就是他现在玩弄女孩的原因了吧。他可能对女孩心存怨恨，想要报复她们。

L：当他发现他女朋友对他所作的事情后，几近疯狂。然后他发誓他要让所有的女孩子都跟他一起下地狱。

T：我们应该考虑帮他一把。我想试着跟他谈一谈。

### 核心词汇记一记

**Words Storm**

playboy ['pleibɔi] *n.* 花花公子
miserable ['mizərəbl] *a.* 悲惨的
eventually [i'ventʃuəli] *ad.* 最终
harbor ['hɑːbə] *v.* 怀有

**Phrases**

tear apart 撕碎
take revenge 复仇

**会话 2**

Tom: Jane, listen to me, you can slap me, kick me, punch me, shout at me... Whatever you want me to be! I'll become like a tame dog if that's what you want. I have had a secret crush on you for long. Will you be my girlfriend?

Jane: You are kidding me!

T: I beg you! I implore you. Jane, I love you with all my heart and soul. Your eyes are brighter than stars; your lips fresher than roses; your voice sweeter than honey. I ache for you in the lonely nights. I feel lost when I cannot see you. I'm incurably in love with you...

J: Don't say these sweet nothings to me. I know you are a good boy, but we are too different—I'm full of passion all day, but you are always unhappy and upset, besides, we have nothing in common.

T: Don't you love Shakespeare? Don't you love writing and reciting? We are the same.

J: No. I don't love these things any longer, we are just good friends and that's all.

T: Oh! My heart breaks!

J: Why do you perform so. You have no problems at all.

汤姆：听着，简，你可以扇我耳光、踢我、打我、吼我，你想怎么对我都行。要是你愿意，我将变成一只温顺的小狗。我已经暗恋你很久了，你能做我女朋友吗？

简：你开玩笑呢吧！

T：我请求你，我乞求你，我哀求你。简，我是全心全意地爱着你的。你的眼睛比星光还明亮，你的嘴唇比玫瑰还鲜红，你的声音比蜜还甜美。我在孤独的夜里想你想到心痛，当我看不到你的时候就会觉得失落。我无可救药地爱上了你。

J：别跟我说这些没用的甜言蜜语了。我知道你是个好男孩，但是我们差异太大了。我整天充满了热情，而你总是闷闷不乐感到烦闷，而且我们没有任何共同点。

T：难道你不爱莎士比亚吗？难道你不爱写作和朗诵吗？我们是一样的。

J：不，我已经不再热衷于这些东西了。我们只能做好朋友，就这样吧。

T：噢，我的心都碎了！

J：你装什么呀？你一点问题都没有！

**核心词汇记一记**

**Words Storm**

| | | |
|---|---|---|
| punch | [pʌntʃ] *v.* | 打 |
| tame | [teim] *a.* | 驯服的 |
| implore | [im'plɔː] *v.* | 哀求 |
| incurably | [in'kjuərəbli] *ad.* | 不可救药地 |

**Phrases**

| | |
|---|---|
| shout at | 吼叫 |
| heart and soul | 全身心地 |

# 56. Marriage and Family

## 婚姻与家庭

### 知识链接 拓展视野，掌握背景知识

一位社会学博士在做毕业论文时产生了疑惑，因为他在归纳两份相同性质的材料时发现结论相互矛盾。一份是杂志社提供的4800份抽样调查报告，问的是“什么在维护婚姻中起着决定作用？”90%的答案是“爱情”。可是从法院民事法庭提供的资料看，根本不是那么回事。在4800宗协议离婚案中，真正因感情彻底破裂而离婚的占不到10%，看来真正维持婚姻的并不是爱情。经过仔细地调查和研究，他得出的结论是：无论从哪个角度来看，婚姻仅仅拥有爱情那是远远不够的。一段美满的婚姻，它不仅需要爱情来滋润，更需要彼此的尊重理解、忍让与信任，而更重要的是责任。

### 难点点拨 知识难点看一看，情景实战热热身

1．put aside 放一边

Will you just put aside your newspaper and tell me something interesting?

你能不能把报纸先放一边，跟我讲点有趣的事情？

2．a line of 一套

She told me I would look pretty if I tried a new line of cosmetics.

她说如果我能尝试一下新的化妆品，就会看起来更漂亮。

3．preside over 主持

The priest presided over the wedding.

牧师主持了婚礼。

4．at the point 在某时某刻

At the point when we made our vows, John placed the wedding ring on my left ring finger.

我们宣誓的时候，约翰给我的左手无名指戴上了结婚戒指。

## 情景实战 跟着老外听一听，读一读，练一练

### 会话 1

Laura: What's wrong with you, honey? You haven't spoken a word the whole day.

Nathan: Er... Nothing to say.

L: Why don't you put aside your newspaper, talk to me, and tell me something interesting! A housewife gets bored, stuck at home all day.

N: In a minute Honey, let me finish this paper first.

L: Will you at least just look at me, and tell me something about your business? You got promoted, huh? How do you like your new position?

N: Good.

L: Good... Yesterday I went shopping with Mrs. Green, and she told me I would look pretty if I tried a new line of cosmetics.

N: Buy it then.

L: This morning, Mike told me he has a new girlfriend now. Tomorrow afternoon he will bring her home. Maybe I should get prepared for it.

N: Yes, you should.

L: Listen, Nathan! I cannot stand it any longer, throw the paper away, stand up, look at me and talk to me!

N: Let me finish this paper first.

劳拉：你怎么了，亲爱的？你一整天都没说话了。

内森：哦，没什么要说的。

L：你能不能把报纸先放一边，跟我讲点有趣的事情？一个家庭主妇整天待在家里挺无聊的。

N：亲爱的，等一会儿，让我先把这张报纸看完。

L：你能不能看着我，告诉我一些你生意上的事情呢？你升职了吧？喜欢你的新职位吗？

N：挺好的。

L：那就好。昨天我和格林太太去逛街，她说如果我能尝试一下新的化妆品，就会看起来更漂亮。

N：那就买了吧。

L：今天早上，迈克跟我说他现在又有新女朋友了，明天下午会把她带回家。也许我应该准备一下了。

N：是应该准备一下。

L：听着，内森！我再也受不了了，你赶紧把这报纸给我扔一边去，起立，看着我，跟我说话！

N：你让我先看完这一页。

#### 核心词汇记一记

**Words Storm**

tongue [tʌŋ] *n.* 舌头
housewife ['hauswaif] *n.* 家庭主妇
position [pə'ziʃən] *n.* 职位
cosmetics [kɔz'metik] *n.* 化妆品

**Phrases**

get prepared for 为……做准备
throw away 丢掉

**会话 2**

Chris: I can never forget the day when I got married.

Benny: You are married? I never knew you were married!

C: Yes, I've been married for two years. John proposed and I accepted. Then we set a date and went to the church.

B: You were wearing a gorgeous wedding gown?

C: Yes, I got the nicest one that I could find, and then we went to the church. We were accompanied by the maid of honor and the best man. The priest presided over the wedding service. Then at the point when we made our vows, John placed the wedding ring on my left ring finger, and I became his wife.

B: You must have been very excited and happy on that day.

C: It was the happiest day of my life. We had a wonderful reception and a big wedding cake. John was so handsome as a groom.

B: Did you video your wedding?

C: Of course, it's right here in my computer. If you'd like to have a look at it I can show you.

B: Great! I would love to share the happiness. Perhaps in a few years I will get married also. I need to know something about a wedding.

克蕾斯：我永远都忘不了我结婚的那天。

本尼：你结婚了？我从来都不知道你居然结婚了！

C：是的，我已经结婚两年了。约翰向我求婚，我就答应了。然后我们就选订了婚期去了教堂。

B：你穿着华丽的结婚礼服吧？

C：是的，我找到了我所能找到的最好的礼服。然后我们就在伴郎和伴娘的陪伴下，步入了婚姻的殿堂。牧师主持了婚礼，我们宣誓的时候，约翰给我的左手无名指戴上了结婚戒指，我成了约翰的妻子。

B：你那天一定很激动、很开心吧。

C：那是我生命中最幸福的一天。我们举行了盛大的结婚典礼，婚礼上订了一个大号的结婚蛋糕。约翰是那么帅。

B：你有关于你们婚礼的视频资料吗？

C：当然有了，就在我电脑里。如果你想看，我可以放给你看。

B：太棒了！我想要分享你的幸福。也许过几年我也要结婚了。我需要知道一些关于婚礼的事情。

### 核心词汇记一记

**Words Storm**

| | | |
|---|---|---|
| propose | [prə'pəuz] | *v.* 求婚 |
| church | [tʃə:tʃ] | *n.* 教堂 |
| gorgeous | ['gɔ:dʒəs] | *a.* 华丽的 |
| accompany | [ə'kʌmpəni] | *v.* 陪伴 |
| priest | [pri:st] | *n.* 牧师 |
| groom | [gru:m] | *n.* 新郎 |

**Phrases**

| | |
|---|---|
| maid of honor | 女傧相 |
| best man | 男傧相 |

# 57. After the Honeymoon

## 蜜月之后

### 知识链接 拓展视野，掌握背景知识

*爱情需要保鲜，可是这往往说起来容易做起来难。新婚夫妇怀着激情度蜜月，可是谁又知道以后的爱情会不会逐渐退却呢？蜜月容易，婚后的平淡生活却往往困难。我们先来看看标准的"激情退却"的故事吧，西方如此，东方也是如此。*

### 难点点拨 知识难点看一看，情景实战热热身

1．spend the honeymoon 度蜜月

He's spending the honeymoon with Kate.

他正在和凯特度蜜月呢。

2．know about 了解，认清

As they know more about each other, their weak points are exposed.

随着他们对彼此了解的增多，他们的弱点也就暴露了。

3．only to do 却只是……

We pursue our happiness, only to find sadness.

我们追求幸福，结果却发现是悲剧一场。

4．at the first sight 第一眼

Four years ago I fell in love with him at the first sight.

4 年前我对他一见钟情。

5．He was all I wanted.

他简直就是我想要的那个人。

## 情景实战 跟着老外听一听，读一读，练一练

**会话 1**

John: I have not been able to find Tom recently. Where is he?

Peter: He's spending his honeymoon with Kate. They are now in Europe, didn't you know this?

J: We Chinese people never enjoy a honeymoon. What's a honeymoon all about?

P: It is a western custom that after marriage, the happy couple often spends a month somewhere far from home. They can enjoy their time there, just the two of them.

J: But after that month?

P: After that, they will return to daily life. Their passion gradually fades away.

J: This is so very true. When a boy meets a girl for the first time, he feels excited and full of fiery passion. He thinks he is in love and he woos her, sends her bunches of roses and presents, just to win her heart. After that they stay together. Then they know more about each other, and their weak points are exposed. They begin to hate each other, and quarrel a lot.

P: This is a pattern. Few couples can avoid it. Maybe they are tired of each other.

J: It's a pity that human life is full of misery and disappointment. We pursue our happiness, only to find sadness. It's our lot to be sure!

P: Don't say that! At least Tom and Kate are getting along well with each other.

约翰: 我最近联系不上汤姆，他在哪儿呢?

彼得: 他正在和凯特度蜜月呢。他们现在在欧洲，难道你不知道吗?

J: 我们中国人从来不度蜜月的。蜜月是什么?

P: 结婚以后，夫妇俩人就会到远离家乡的某个地方待 1 个月，他们可以在那里单独享受欢乐时光。

J: 那个月之后呢?

P: 之后他们就回到日常生活了，然后激情就逐渐退却了。

J: 这倒是真的。当一个男孩第一次遇到女孩的时候，他觉得很兴奋，并且满腔充满如火的热情。他觉得自己爱上她了。他追求她，大把大把地送她玫瑰和礼物，只是为了赢取她的芳心。然后他们就在一起了。随着他们对彼此了解的增多，他们的弱点也就暴露了。他们就开始讨厌对方，并且经常吵架了。

P: 这是一个模式。很少有人可以避免。也许他们会对彼此感到厌倦。

J: 多可惜呀！人类的生活充满悲剧。我们追求幸福，结果却发现是悲剧一场。这真是我们的宿命！

P: 不要这样说！至少汤姆和凯特现在相处得很好。

### 核心词汇记一记

**Words Storm**

| | | |
|---|---|---|
| honeymoon | ['hʌnimuːn] *n.* | 蜜月 |
| marriage | ['mæridʒ] *n.* | 婚姻 |
| couple | ['kʌpl] *n.* | 夫妇 |
| passion | ['pæʃən] *n.* | 热情 |
| woo | [wuː] *v.* | 追求 |
| disappointment | [ˌdɪsə'pɔɪntmənt] *n.* | 失望 |

**Phrases**

| | |
|---|---|
| daily life | 日常生活 |
| weak point | 弱点 |
| be tired of | 厌倦 |

## 会话 2

Kaelin: My boyfriend dumped me a week ago…

Serena: That's terrible. Weren't you good to him? Did you often quarrel? Perhaps he found a new lover?

K: Four years ago I fell in love with him at first sight. I thought he was my prince charming—handsome, tough, and humorous—he was all I wanted. I expressed my love to him, we became lovers soon after. But after three months' happiness, we began to quarrel a lot. We just didn't seem to get along well and I took every word of him as the absolute order that I should follow, but this didn't delight him at all. He became more and more demanding and peevish, and I came to the end of my rope. We fought, then he slapped me and I cried. Instead of comforting me he left for a bar to drink with another girl. My heart was broken.

S: It's really a pity. You were too good to him. I think this is where the problem lies—and he didn't appreciate you. Don't worry, a good boy will come soon and you'll be glad that you have left him.

K: If I could find another boy, I will never make this mistake again. By the way, you are really my true friend. I feel much better now.

凯林：我男朋友一周前把我甩了。

塞丽娜：太糟糕了。你不是对他很好吗？你们经常吵架吗？还是他找到新欢了？

K：4年前我对他一见钟情，我以为他就是我的白马王子，他帅气、坚强，又不失幽默，简直就是我想要的那个人。我向他表白后，我们就成了情侣。但是3个月的甜蜜过后，我们就开始频繁吵架。我们就是相处不来。我把他说的每句话都当做命令来执行，但是即使这样都不能让他开心。他的要求越来越多，并且脾气暴躁。我的忍耐也到了极点。我们打起来了，他扇了我耳光，我哭了，他不但不安慰我，反而去酒吧和另一个女孩喝酒去了，我的心都碎了。

S：太遗憾了。你一开始对他太好了。我想这就是问题所在——你对他太好了，但是他并不领情。不要担心，很快你就会遇到好男孩的，你会发现离开你前男友是个明智的选择。

K：如果我能找到另外一个男孩，我再也不会这么错下去了。不管怎样，我想说的是，你真是我的贴心朋友，我现在感觉好多了。

### 核心词汇记一记

**Words Storm**

dump [dʌmp] *v.* 抛弃
quarrel ['kwɔrəl] *v.* 吵架
peevish ['pi:viʃ] *a.* 暴躁的
slap [slæp] *v.* 掴耳光
comfort ['kʌmfət] *v.* 安慰

**Phrases**

fall in love with 爱上，迷恋

# 58. Baby Shower

## 宝贝来了

### 知识链接 拓展视野，掌握背景知识

西方人有各种各样的派对，什么生日派对、商业派对、舞会、宴会、新年派对、单身派对、庆功宴，甚至还有迎婴聚会。为了迎接宝宝出生，大家给未来的妈妈送各种宝宝将来用得着的礼物，并且聚在一起聊关于宝宝的各种话题。下面就让我们来看一下迎婴聚会究竟是什么吧。

### 难点点拨 知识难点看一看，情景实战热热身

1．expect a baby/be expectant 怀孕

Bella has been expectant for several months.

贝拉已经怀孕好几个月了。

2．move sb. to tears 感动得落泪

When I was pregnant you arranged party for me, which moved me to tears.

我怀孕那会儿，你为我安排了一次这样的聚会，我都感动得落泪了呢。

3．dress sb. up 打扮

She once told me if it was a girl she would buy beautiful clothes for her to dress her up like a princess.

她曾经告诉我，如果她有个小女孩，一定会给她买很多漂亮衣服，把她打扮得像小公主一样。

4．shower sth. on sb./ shower sb. with sth. 送（很多）礼物

We showered her with a lot of gifts, from diapers to toys.

我们给了她很多礼物，从尿布到玩具应有尽有。

## 情景实战 跟着老外听一听，读一读，练一练

### 会话 1

Julie: Bella has been expectant for several months. I think we should do something for her.

Rachel: Let's plan a baby shower then. When I was pregnant you arranged one for me, which moved me to tears.

J: OK. So we'll do that again maybe it will move Bella to tears as well. I'll call her to make sure she wants one, and then gather together a large group of friends to have the party.

R: So we have to get prepared. What gift do you want to send her?

J: Some little quilts for the baby will do.

R: I can get some little clothes for the baby. I think Bella will be satisfied.

J: Good. Then we'll talk about how to take care of the baby. You have a lot of experience about this. You've got three children.

R: Yes, I'll give some advice. I'm a veteran.

J: I think Bella will give birth within this season, so we have to be quick.

R: Do you know if it's a girl or a boy?

J: No idea. I am guessing it's a girl.

R: Me too. She loves little girls so much. She once told me if it was a girl she would buy beautiful clothes for her to dress her up like a princess.

茱莉：贝拉已经怀孕好几个月了。我觉得我们应该为她做点什么。

瑞秋：那我们就为她办一个迎婴送礼会吧。我怀孕那会儿，你为我安排了一次这样的聚会，我都感动得落泪了呢。

J：好呀，那么我们就办一次，让贝拉也落泪。我会打电话给她，确认一下她的想法，然后再召集一大批朋友来参加这个聚会。

R：所以我们要着手准备了。你想送她什么礼物？

J：送给她的宝宝一些小被褥什么的就行。

R：我可以给她的宝宝准备些小衣服。我觉得贝拉一定会满意的。

J：不错。然后我们可以谈谈怎样照顾婴儿。你一定很有经验，因为你已经有 3 个孩子了。

R：是的，我会给她一些建议。我可是个老手了。

J：我觉得贝拉应该会在这段时间生下宝宝。所以我们得快点了。

R：你知道是男孩还是女孩吗？

J：一点都不清楚，我猜是个女孩。

R：我猜也是。她特别喜欢小女孩。她曾经告诉我，如果她有个小女孩，一定会给她买很多漂亮衣服，把她打扮得像小公主一样。

#### 核心词汇记一记

**Words Storm**

expectant [iks'pektənt] *a.* 期盼的，怀孕的

arrange [ə'reindʒ] *v.* 安排

satisfied ['sætisˌfaid] *a.* 满意的

experience [iks'piəriəns] *n.* 经验

princess ['prinsis] *n.* 公主

**Phrases**

be moved to tears 被感动落泪

take care of 照顾

**会话 2**

Jane: You know what? Yesterday I went to a baby shower and shared the experience of taking care of the baby.

Henry: For whom?

J: For Mary Walker. She is expecting a baby. Don't you know that?

H: I don't know Mary. Anyway, you had a good time there.

J: We showered her with many gifts, from diapers to toys. She said she never expected so many presents. I gave her a set of baby tableware. Then we chatted happily and talked about how to raise a child. I told many stories about little Jack to amuse them. Some ladies also told their own stories—their babies sounded so cute.

H: I've never been to a baby shower. What a pity, it sounds like such a special event.

J: Hey. You're a guy!

H: I don't think a guy cannot be invited to a baby shower nowadays.

J: We play a lot of games at the party. For example, we eat some baby food and guess what it is.

H: I envy you mothers, you have such a great time!

简：你知道吗？昨天我去了一个迎婴送礼会，分享了一些育婴经验。

亨利：为谁举办的？

J：为玛丽·沃克举办的。她快要生宝宝了，你不知道吗？

H：我甚至都不认识那个玛丽。不管怎样，看来你在那儿玩得很开心。

J：我们给了她很多礼物，从尿布到玩具应有尽有。她说她从来没想到会有这么多礼物。我给了她一套儿童餐具，然后我们聊得很愉快，并且探讨了关于如何养育孩子的问题。我讲了很多关于小杰克的故事，逗得大家很开心。还有些女士也讲了她们自己的一些故事，她们的宝宝真地好可爱呀。

H：我还从来没有去过迎婴送礼会呢。真可惜，应该非常有趣吧。

J：嘿，你可是个大男人啊！

H：可我不认为现在的男人就不能被邀请参加迎婴送礼会呀！

J：我们在聚会上会玩很多游戏。比如，我们可能吃一些婴儿食品，然后猜猜是什么。

H：我好羡慕你们这些做母亲的，你们肯定玩得特别开心。

**核心词汇记一记**

**Words Storm**

anyway ['eniwei] *ad.* 无论如何
diaper ['daiəpə] *n.* 尿布
tableware ['teiblwɛə] *n.* 餐具
amuse [ə'mju:z] *v.* 使开心

**Phrases**

raise a child 养育孩子
at the party 在聚会上

# 59. Are You a Family Man

## 居家好男人

### 知识链接 拓展视野，掌握背景知识

时下的“新男性”被定位为“在社会重大转型时期被寄予重大社会期望的角色”，这类新男性与传统的“不食人间烟火”的英雄人物迥然有别的是，他们“上得厅堂，下得厨房”。“尊重和体谅女性”、“脾气好”、“对太太忠心”、“家务好手”等被男人和女人推为理想男性的标准。这也许与西方的骑士精神、绅士风度和女权的兴起都有紧密联系。

### 难点点拨 知识难点看一看，情景实战热热身

1．be tied up = be occupied 忙碌，没时间

He's tied up all day long.

他一天到晚都在忙。

Mike is really occupied with so many things in business.

迈克真的是在忙生意上的事情（公务缠身）。

2．hang out with 与……混在一起

Jonny always hangs out with his friends.

乔尼总是和他的朋友们混在一起。

3．count on = depend on 指望，依靠

We women shouldn't count on men too much.

我们女人是不该太依赖男人的。

4．wear lipstick 涂口红

a teddy bear who wears lipstick and has long hair

一只涂着口红留着长头发的泰迪熊

## 情景实战 跟着老外听一听，读一读，练一练

**会话 1**

Jane: My husband is so busy. He's tied up all day long.

Liz: I have the same problem. Johnny never comes back home before ten o'clock in the evening. I begin to sense something untoward.

J: Mike is really occupied with so many things in business. That's what I know. He works overtime and exhausts himself pitifully. He told me he wanted to get promoted quickly and become a manager in his department. That's his dream.

L: Johnny always hangs out with his friends. They drink a lot, and play cards. He seems already tired of me. I don't know how to please him.

J: Sometimes I think myself deplorable. When I was young and beautiful, he was very concerned about me. But now I am not sure anymore!

L: I'm afraid to say we are totally ignored. We women shouldn't count on men too much.

J: But Cathy's husband is so caring. He does the cooking everyday for his beloved wife, and even writes love letters to her. Besides, he is a good father. He buys everything for his daughter, trying his best to please her.

L: I envy her.

简：我丈夫太忙了，一天到晚都在忙。

丽兹：我也有同样的问题。乔尼晚上 10 点前从没回过家。我开始觉得有点不正常了。

J：据我所知，迈克真的是在忙生意上的事情。他总是加班加点，把自己弄得筋疲力尽，让人心疼。他跟我说想快点得到提升，成为他们部门的经理，这是他的梦想。

L：乔尼总是和他的朋友们混在一起。他们既喝酒又玩牌。他好像厌倦我了。我不知道怎样才能取悦他。

J：有时候我觉得自己很可悲。在我年轻美丽的时候，他很关心我，但是现在不这样了！

L：恐怕我们已经被彻底遗忘了。我们女人是不该太依赖男人的。

J：但是凯西的丈夫就很体贴。他每天都为他心爱的妻子煮饭，甚至给她写情书。此外，他还是个好爸爸。他肯为女儿买任何东西，竭尽全力地让她开心。

L：我真羡慕她。

### 核心词汇记一记

**Words Storm**

overtime ['əuvətaim] *ad.* 超时
exhaust [ig'zɔːst] *v.* 耗尽
pitifully ['pitifulli] *ad.* 无情地
deplorable [di'plɔːrəbl] *a.* 可悲的
beloved [bi'lʌvd] *a.* 深爱的

**Phrases**

love letter 情书

## 会话 2

Daisy: Daddy, look! It's my new drawing.

Shawn: Hey. Dear. You have drawn a picture! Let me have a look. Is this a little piggy? It's so cute isn't it?

D: No. It's not a piggy, daddy. It's you. Look, you are playing with me. We're dancing.

S: Er…Yes, I see. Who's that girl? Let me guess. She must be your mum. I can see her big smile.

D: You are wrong again, daddy. It's a teddy bear.

S: A teddy bear who wears lipstick and has long hair? Look, it even has breasts…

D: It's Mr. Teddy's muscles. It is a handsome and strong bear. Other girl bears love it.

S: Do you love it then?

D: No. It is a dandy. It plays with girl bears but never marries them.

S: So cute. You are so cute a girl. How do you know all this?

D: Yesterday it and its girlfriend, a girl bear, came to visit me. I found it had changed its girlfriend. He will never get married.

S: You can write all this in your diary. You should keep a diary.

D: But I cannot write yet. Daddy, can you help me?

S: Yes. I can teach you how to write.

D: Thank you. As a reward, I'll marry you.

黛西：爸爸，看，这是我新画的。

肖恩：呵，亲爱的，你画了一幅画呀！让我来瞧一瞧，这是一只小猪吗？太可爱了，是不是呀？

D: 不，不是小猪，爸爸，那是你。看，你在跟我玩呢，我们在跳舞！

S: 呃，是的，我知道了。那个女孩是谁呢？让我猜猜，她一定是你妈妈，我看到她灿烂的笑容了。

D: 你又错了爸爸。那是泰迪熊。

S: 一只涂着口红留着长头发的泰迪熊？看，它甚至还有胸呢！

D: 那是泰迪先生的胸肌。它是一只又帅又强壮的熊，其他的小熊姑娘都爱它。

S: 你也爱它吗？

D: 不，它是个花花公子。它和那些小熊姑娘只是玩玩的，不会跟它们结婚。

S: 真可爱，你真是个可爱的小姑娘。你怎么知道这些的？

D: 昨天它和它的小熊女朋友来拜访我了，我发现它换女朋友了，它永远都不会结婚的。

S: 你可以把这些都写在你的日记里，你应该记日记的。

D: 但是我现在还不会写呢，爸爸，你能帮我吗？

S: 可以啊，我来教你怎么写。

D: 太感谢了，作为回报，我要嫁给你。

### 核心词汇记一记

**Words Storm**

| | | |
|---|---|---|
| piggy | ['pigi] *n.* | 小猪崽 |
| lipstick | ['lipstik] *n.* | 口红 |
| breast | [brest] *n.* | 胸 |
| muscle | ['mʌsl] *n.* | 肌肉 |
| dandy | ['dændi] *n.* | 花花公子 |
| diary | ['daiəri] *n.* | 日记 |

**Phrases**

| | |
|---|---|
| teddy bear | 泰迪熊 |
| keep a diary | 记日记 |

# 60. The Life of a Housewife

# 主妇生活

## 知识链接 拓展视野，掌握背景知识

*现代的家庭主妇要负责的事情非常繁重，她们需要是好妈妈、好妻子，还要是好厨师和清洁员，她们要保障全家人的健康。表面上没有工作的家庭主妇其实比一般的女性更忙一些，她们的大部分时间都是在家里度过，没有与社会沟通，因此很容易产生抑郁等状况，情况严重者甚至可能走上自杀之路。美剧《绝望主妇》就讲述了四个绝望主妇的故事。*

## 难点点拨 知识难点看一看，情景实战热热身

1．whatever 什么都行

I just eat whatever I can find as a humble lunch.

我只是随便吃点东西。

2．nothing but 只有

Then nothing but soap opera can comfort my lonely heart.

然后就只有肥皂剧能安抚我寂寞的心了。

3．leisure time 闲暇时光

You can see how those Chinese housewives spend their leisure time.

你可以看看那些中国的家庭主妇们是如何度过闲暇时光的。

4．take care of 照顾

I have to take care of the whole family.

我要照顾好整个家庭。

5．no wonder 怪不得

No wonder many westerners now love oriental girls.

怪不得现在很多西方人都爱东方女孩呢。

## 情景实战 跟着老外听一听，读一读，练一练

**会话 1**

Donna: I feel bored everyday.

Sara: Have you seen the TV series *Desperate Housewives*?

D: Yes, I am becoming desperate now. Every morning I wake I know it will be a boring day. I prepare breakfast for John and Tom, and send Tom to the kindergarten. After that I have nothing to do till noon.

S: John comes back at noon?

D: No, of course not. He dines at a cafeteria near his company. I just eat whatever I can find as a humble lunch. In the daytime I do the laundry and sweep the floor. Then nothing but soap operas can comfort my lonely heart.

S: That's too bad. You should join some club. Cathy and I now go to a reading group every afternoon. We read and gossip, and feel quite satisfied. Will you join us?

D: Cathy! I think I must join you. I love her—she is so beautiful. I want to learn how she does the facial skin care.

S: Ha-ha, she uses a special cream. Tomorrow we'll read a novel *The Joy Luck Club*. You can read it and see how those Chinese housewives spend their leisure time.

D: OK. See you tomorrow!

多娜：我每天都觉得很无聊。

萨拉：你看过电视连续剧《绝望主妇》吗？

D：看过。我现在变得绝望了。每天早上醒来我都意识到这会是无聊的一天。我为约翰和汤姆准备早餐，送汤姆去幼儿园，然后直到中午我都没事可做。

S：约翰中午回来吗？

D：不，当然不了。他在公司附近的一家自助餐厅吃饭。我只是随便吃点东西。白天我就洗衣服擦地板，然后就只有肥皂剧能安抚我寂寞的心了。

S：那太糟了。你应该参加一些俱乐部。我和凯西现在每天下午都去一个阅读小组。我们一起读书，一起聊天，感觉特别满足。你要不要加入我们？

D：凯西！我觉得我必须要加入！我太喜欢她了——她很漂亮的。我想知道她是怎么做脸部皮肤护理的。

S：哈哈，她用的是一种特殊面霜。明天我们要读一本叫做《喜福会》的小说。你可以读一下，看看那些中国的家庭主妇是如何度过闲暇时光的。

D：好的，明天见！

### 核心词汇记一记

**Words Storm**

| | | |
|---|---|---|
| desperate | ['despərət] | *a.* 绝望的 |
| kindergarten | ['kində,gɑːtn] | *n.* 幼儿园 |
| cafeteria | [,kæfi'tiəriə] | *n.* 自助餐厅 |
| humble | ['hʌmbl] | *a.* 粗陋的 |
| daytime | ['deitaim] | *n.* 白天 |
| cream | [kriːm] | *n.* 面霜 |

**Phrases**

| | |
|---|---|
| do the laundry | 洗衣服 |
| sweep the floor | 擦地板 |
| facial skin care | 脸部皮肤护理 |

## 会话 2

Alisa: Are you working at the moment?

Emily: No. I'm a housewife. I have to take care of the whole family. It's a big deal.

A: So your husband is the only breadwinner?

E: Yes. My child and I depend on him. Are you working?

A: Of course. Most Chinese women don't stay at home. Even the married ladies have to work hard.

E: Why?

A: Maybe it's because the salary of the husband alone cannot well support the whole family. So we Chinese women have to shoulder some responsibility.

E: But you have to take care of your children and the house. Do you have enough time to accomplish all this?

A: We are under heavy pressure then, but we are tough. We can handle it.

E: No wonder many westerners now love oriental girls. You are really terrific! We should learn from you.

A: We live in different cultures, and the economic situations of our nations differ. That can explain all this. Maybe in a few years I'll become a housewife too, if my husband can earn more money.

爱丽莎：你现在在工作吗？

艾米丽：没有，我是个家庭主妇。我要照顾好整个家庭。这可是个大事。

A：这么说只有你老公一个人养家糊口？

E：是呀，我和孩子都指望他呢。你工作吗？

A：当然了。很多中国女人都不待在家里。即使那些结婚的女人也要努力工作。

E：为什么呢？

A：可能是因为老公一个人的薪水不能负担整个家庭的花销吧。所以我们中国女人要负起一些责任。

E：但是你还需要照顾孩子和收拾房子呀。你有充足的时间来做这些事吗？

A：我们面临着沉重的压力，但是我们很坚强，能够处理两者间的关系。

E：怪不得现在很多西方人都喜欢东方女孩呢。你们真是太棒了！我们应该向你们学习。

A：我们生活的文化不一样，国家的经济情况也不一样。这才是我们不一样的原因。也许过几年我也会变成家庭主妇，如果我老公能赚更多的钱的话。

### 核心词汇记一记

#### Words Storm

breadwinner ['bredˌwinə] *n.* 养家糊口的人

accomplish [ə'kʌmpliʃ] *v.* 完成

handle [hændl] *v.* 处理

oriental [ˌɔːri'entl] *a.* 东方的

#### Phrases

depend on 依赖，指望

shoulder responsibility 负起责任

# 61. Divorce

## 离婚风潮

### 知识链接 拓展视野，掌握背景知识

*离婚制度是婚姻家庭制度的重要组成部分，它的发生、发展和演变受到社会物质生产关系的制约，并且受到政治、文化、道德、宗教等因素的深刻影响。在不同的社会和民族中，离婚的原因和难度也各不相同。在肯尼亚的古希人中，不育或阳萎是离婚的理由。而在一些印第安人中，比如雅甘人，如果人们认为丈夫残忍或者无法抚养家庭，那么离婚是被视为公正的。而现代社会中，人们对婚姻的态度越来越无所谓，闪婚闪离成为普遍的现象。*

### 难点点拨 知识难点看一看，情景实战热热身

1．used to do/be 以前，曾经（如何）

They used to be tightly attached to each other.

他们以前可是如胶似漆呀。

2．give sb. a good hiding 把某人打一顿

Next time I see him, I'll give him a good hiding. I promise.

下次我见到他的时候一定好好揍他一顿，我保证。

3．trickle down 流下，滚落

The moment she saw me, I noticed tears trickling down her cheeks.

她一见到我，眼泪就顺着脸颊流了下来。

4．be obliged to do 有义务做某事

I feel obliged to go and comfort her.

我觉得我们应该去安慰她。

5．short-lived 短暂的，短命的，不长久的

Ten years ago we never had such kind of short-lived marriage.

10 年前我们根本没有如此短命的婚姻。

## 情景实战 跟着老外听一听，读一读，练一练

**会话 1**

Steven: Have you heard Mary divorced her husband?

Mathew: For real? You must be kidding me. They used to be tightly attached to each other.

S: I met Mary yesterday. She was quite pale. She said Bob betrayed her, and he got a new lover.

M: Bob is a good guy, isn't he? Last year when they got married he told me he would never leave Mary and he was so sincere when he said it.

S: I hate him now. He is a total phony. He cheated on Mary, my best friend!

M: Next time I see him, I'll give him a good hiding. I promise.

S: But I think we should pay more attention to Mary, she is so down. The moment she saw me, I noticed tears trickling down her cheeks.

M: I feel obliged to go and comfort her. She needs friends now.

S: You said it. It's hard to recover from that pain. I still remember three years ago Mary called me excitedly and told me she found a good boyfriend. She vowed to stay with him forever. Such an innocent girl!

M: Hope she can find a good man in the future.

斯蒂芬: 你听说了吗？玛丽和她老公离婚了。

马 修: 真的？你在开玩笑吧。他们以前可是如胶似漆呀。

S: 我昨天遇到玛丽了。她很憔悴。她说鲍勃背叛了她，他有了新的爱人。

M: 鲍勃是个好男人，不是吗？去年他们结婚的时候，他告诉我说他永远都不会离开玛丽。他说的时候很真诚。

S: 我现在恨他了。他是个大骗子。他背叛了玛丽，我最好的朋友。

M: 下次我见到他的时候一定好好揍他一顿，我保证。

S: 但是我觉得我们应该多关心一下玛丽。她现在很绝望。她一见到我，眼泪就顺着脸颊流了下来。

M: 我觉得我们应该去安慰她，她现在很需要朋友在身边。

S: 你说得很对，从这种伤痛中恢复是很难的。我还记得 3 年前的那一幕，玛丽开心地打电话告诉我她找到了一个很好的男朋友，她说要永远和他在一起。多么纯真的一个女孩啊。

M: 希望她将来能够找到一个好男人。

### 核心词汇记一记

**Words Storm**

sincere [sin'siə] *a.* 真诚的

phony ['fəuni] *n.* 骗子

hiding ['haidiŋ] *n.* 痛打

trickle ['trikl] *v.* 滴，淌

innocent ['inəsənt] *a.* 天真的

**Phrases**

be attached to 依恋

cheat on 背叛

**会话 2**

Diana: Now more and more couples get divorced. I don't know why.

Marina: They marry too soon after getting to know each other. I have a friend who got married with a girl three weeks after their acquaintance, and then three weeks later their marriage broke up.

D: It's really depressing. Ten years ago we never had such short-lived marriages.

M: We call this marriage in haste "flash marriage"—it's just like a meteor or a lightening that sweeps across the sky and then disappears.

D: The young people now don't know the real significance of marriage. They are so childish to approach marriage as insignificant or unimportant.

M: Another phenomenon is the mixed marriage. A Chinese girl and a western man get married, but soon they may find they are so different that it's hard for them to move on. The cultural difference is a gap that they cannot stride over. So they divorce.

D: They are too impetuous. They should seriously think it over before making such a decision.

戴安娜: 现在有越来越多的夫妻开始离婚。我不知道为什么。

玛丽娜: 他们婚结得太快了，还没来得及好好了解对方。我有个朋友跟他女朋友认识不到 3 周就结婚了。3 周后他们的婚姻就破裂了。

D: 太可悲了。10 年前我们根本没有如此短命的婚姻。

M: 我们把这种草率的婚姻叫做“闪婚”，就像划过天际的流星或闪电，转瞬即逝。

D: 现在的年轻人不懂得婚姻的真谛。他们天真地以为婚姻是不重要的东西。

M: 另外一个现象是混合婚姻（异族通婚）。一个中国女孩和一个西方男人结婚了，但是很快他们可能会发现彼此之间的差异太多了，以致于很难再走下去。文化差异是他们无法逾越的鸿沟。所以他们会离婚。

D: 他们太冲动了。做决定之前应该认真思考一下的。

**核心词汇记一记**

**Words Storm**

| | | |
|---|---|---|
| meteor | ['miːtiə] | *n.* 流星 |
| lightening | ['laitniŋ] | *n.* 闪电 |
| disappear | [ˌdisə'piə] | *v.* 消失 |
| childish | ['tʃaildiʃ] | *a.* 孩子气的 |
| impetuous | [im'petjuəs] | *a.* 冲动的 |

**Phrases**

| | |
|---|---|
| break up | 破裂，分手 |
| in haste | 草率地 |
| flash marriage | 闪婚 |
| stride over | 跨过 |

# 62. Family Democracy

## 家庭民主

**知识链接** 拓展视野，掌握背景知识

家庭内部民主与否直接关系到家庭的健康和幸福。在一个民主的家庭里，爸爸不会天天只知道吃饭喝茶看报，妈妈不会天天被家务所累，孩子不会被无端呵斥，更不会出现父亲打骂妻子和孩子的情况。总之，家里每个人都互帮互助，遇到事情共同商量，民主解决。但是现代社会却催生出了越来越多的奇怪现象——单亲家庭、丁克家庭、同居、非婚生育。种种不安的社会现象造就出越来越多的家庭生活无能症患者。

**难点点拨** 知识难点看一看，情景实战热热身

1．order sb. to do sth. 命令某人干某事

He often orders me to do this and do that.

他经常命令我做这做那。

2．get rid of 摆脱

You are just trying to get rid of me.

你简直就是在想尽法子摆脱我。

3．Seat yourself down there.

你坐这儿。

4．be sorry for doing sth. 抱歉做了某事

I'm sorry for ignoring your feelings.

很抱歉忽略了你的感受。

## 情景实战 跟着老外听一听，读一读，练一练

**会话 1**

Lucy: My husband is an utter dictator. He often orders me to do this and do that and if I don't listen he just beats me angrily. Look at the bruise on my wrist. I cannot bear it any longer.

John: Oh, no. Mr. Anderson is always kind-hearted and mild to everybody. It's impossible for me to imagine him resorting to violence.

L: It is the truth. I tell you, the man behaves very differently when he is at home. He kicks me harshly and viciously, curses me with filth you can't imagine. He seems rather insane sometimes.

J: Your family is just like a country where a despotic king tortures and enslaves his subjects. Is Mr. Anderson also bad to little Mary?

L: No, he is good to her and tries his best to make her happy. It's so strange.

J: Mary is his dear daughter, but he should at least respect you and treat you with dignity. A good husband will never treat his beloved wife like that.

L: I don't know why he behaves so cruelly toward me, can you please help me. I guess he has a new lover, but I cannot verify it.

露 西：我的丈夫是个十足的独裁者。他经常命令我做这个做那个。如果我不听从他，他就会狠狠地打我。看我手腕上的瘀伤。我再也不能忍受了！

约翰：不可能吧。安德森先生总是又热心，对人家又和善的呀。很难想象他怎么可能那么暴力。

L：但我说的是真的。告诉你，一个男人在家里的表现跟在外面是完全不一样的。他在家里对我拳打脚踢，还用你想象不到的污秽语言咒骂我，有些时候他看起来简直就是个神经病。

J：你的家庭就像一个暴君统治的国家，他会折磨和奴役他的臣民。安德森先生对小玛丽也很不好吗？

L：不，他对她很好。他尽最大努力来让玛丽幸福。这太奇怪了。

J：玛丽是他亲爱的小女儿。但他对你也要有起码的尊重呀。一个好丈夫是绝对不会这样对待他心爱的妻子的。

L：我不知道为什么他那么粗暴地对我。你要帮帮我啊。我觉得他可能在外面有新欢了，但我无法证实这事。

### 核心词汇记一记

**Words Storm**

| | | |
|---|---|---|
| bruise | [bruːz] | *n.* 瘀伤 |
| wrist | [rist] | *n.* 手腕 |
| harshly | ['hɑːʃli] | *ad.* 严厉地 |
| viciously | ['viʃəsli] | *ad.* 敌意地 |
| insane | [in'sein] | *a.* 癫狂的 |
| despotic | [di'spɔtik] | *a.* 专制的 |
| torture | ['tɔːtʃə] | *v.* 折磨 |
| enslave | [in'sleiv] | *v.* 奴役 |

**Phrases**

resort to 诉诸

**会话 2**

Angela: Jason, I think we have to talk.

Jason: Talk about what? You know I'm busy. I have to write a lot of material for my work this morning. And then I'll see a customer this afternoon. After that, my secretary will…

A: Stop it! You are just trying to get rid of me, but I have to talk with you. We should negotiate. Seat yourself down there.

J: Negotiate what? I didn't know there is anything worth negotiating between us.

A: Listen. We have not been talking for a long time, ever since you got promoted and you became so busy. You think you do well by supporting the whole family, but a housewife is bored all day and she needs to be loved and cared for.

J: I'm sorry for ignoring your feelings…

A: Then when you make up your mind to do something you just go ahead without asking for my opinion. Last week you bought a new car, but I didn't even know about it until you drove it home.

J: I thought it would be a surprise.

A: But we have to save some money. I know you are better paid now, but that doesn't mean we can spend money like there is no tomorrow!

安吉拉: 詹森，我觉得我们需要谈一谈。

詹 森: 谈什么？你知道我很忙。我今天上午要写很多材料，然后我下午还要去见一个客户，然后我的秘书要……

A: 停！你这简直就是在想尽法子摆脱我！但是我必须要跟你谈一谈。我们要进行一次谈判。你赶紧给我坐下。

J: 谈什么呀？亲爱的，我不认为我们之间需要谈判什么。

A: 听着，我们已经很久没好好谈一谈了。你升职了，而且还变得很忙。你以为因为你供养着整个家庭就了不起了是吗？但是你的妻子待在家里天天很无聊，她需要你的爱和关心！

J: 对不起，我忽略了你的感受。

A: 而且，当你决定做一件事情的时候，你根本都没征求我的意见就去做了。上周你买了一辆新车，但是直到你开回家了我才知道这件事儿。

J: 我打算给你一个惊喜来着。

A: 可是我们必须省点钱出来。我知道你现在薪水涨了，可是我们也不能这么花钱，而不考虑以后的日子。

**核心词汇记一记**

**Words Storm**

negotiate [ni'gəuʃieit] *v.* 谈判
promote [prə'məut] *v.* 提升
housewife ['hauswaif] *n.* 家庭主妇
ignore [ig'nɔː] *v.* 忽略

**Phrases**

get promoted 得到升迁
make up one's mind 下定决心

# Culture and Society 文化与社会

# 63. Computer Culture

## 计算机文化

### 知识链接 拓展视野，掌握背景知识

*个人计算机简称 PC(Personal Computer)。现在越来越多的人在生活中离不开电脑，甚至到了早上醒来的第一件事就是开电脑的程度。电脑给人类带来了巨大便利，同时作为一种工具，也束缚了人的生活。但是我们无法忽略的是当今计算机的发展已经成了一种深刻的文化现象，并且计算机的发展也有悠久的历史。*

### 难点点拨 知识难点看一看，情景实战热热身

1. southeast to 方位词后跟 to，表示在某地的某个方向
   It's near Stanford University, southeast to San Francisco, famous for its computer technology.
   它靠近斯坦福大学，位于旧金山的东南部，以计算机技术而闻名天下。
2. by doing sth. 通过做某事（达到某种目的）
   Stanford University supports it by providing advanced technology and qualified technicians.
   斯坦福大学提供了先进的技术和资深科研人员。
3. purchase 采购
   The US government purchases many electronic gadgets and software for the construction of its military.
   美国政府从这里购买很多用于军事工程的电子配件和软件。
4. generally/honestly speaking 一般而言 / 说实话
   Generally speaking, all important IT firms are on the west coast of America.
   一般而言，所有重要的 IT 公司都集中在美国的西海岸。
5. only to 只是（表失望）
   We fight hard to design some good programs, only to find that they have already been pirated.
   我们辛辛苦苦才设计出一些好程序，结果却发现早已被盗版了。

## 情景实战 跟着老外听一听，读一读，练一练

**会话 1**

Brad: Have you heard of Silicon Valley?

Julie: Of course. It's near Stanford University, southeast of San Francisco, famous for its computer technology.

B: Are there many famous IT companies?

J: Yes. Intel and AMD are the world famous producers of CPU's and main boards. Actually they are the major competitors in this field. Apple is famous for iPod, iPhone, and laptop. Hewlett-Packard is one of the biggest computer producers.

B: Why can it be the center of IT industry?

J: Stanford University supports it by providing advanced technology and qualified technicians. The US government purchases many electronic gadgets and software for the construction of its military. Talented people immigrate from China and India, and settle down there to work for those high-tech companies.

B: Are the headquarters of Microsoft around there?

J: No. They are in Seattle. Generally speaking, all important IT firms are on the west coast of America.

B: In China, we also have a center for such kind of companies. It's located in the northwest part of Beijing, near Peking University and Tsinghua University. It's called Zhongguancun.

布拉德：你听说过硅谷吗？

茱莉 ：当然。它靠近斯坦福大学，位于旧金山的东南部，以计算机技术而闻名天下。

B：那里有很多著名的 IT 公司吗？

J：是的，因特尔和 AMD 都是世界著名的 CPU 和主板制造商，事实上他们是这个领域最主要的竞争者。苹果的 iPod, iPhone 和笔记本电脑比较出名。惠普是最大的电脑制造商之一。

B：为什么硅谷能成为 IT 产业的中心呢？

J：因为斯坦福大学提供了先进的技术和资深科研人员。美国政府从这里购买很多用于军事工程的电子配件和软件。来自中国和印度的人才定居在那里为高科技公司服务。

B：微软公司的总部是座落在那儿吗？

J：不是的，微软总部在西雅图。一般而言，所有重要的 IT 公司都集中在美国的西海岸。

B：在中国，我们也有这种地方。它坐落于北京的西北角，靠近北京大学和清华大学，叫做中关村。

### 核心词汇记一记

**Words Storm**

| | | |
|---|---|---|
| competitor | [kəm'petitə] | *n.* 竞争者 |
| qualified | ['kwɔlifaid] | *a.* 合格的，有限制的 |
| technician | [tek'niʃən] | *n.* 科技人员 |
| purchase | ['pəːtʃəs] | *v.* 购买 |
| immigrate | ['imigreit] | *n.* 移民 |
| headquarters | ['hed'kwɔːtəz] | *n.* 总部 |

**Phrases**

| | |
|---|---|
| main board | 主板 |
| electronic gadgets | 电子配件 |

**会话 2**

Susan: What's your opinion of Windows Vista?

Michael: I'm not so enthusiastic about it. It's such a capacity demanding operating system that I have had to get my computer hardware updated. I grant you that the interface is beautifully done. But we should put more emphasis on the performance rather than on the superficial things.

S: But I find it stable and user-friendly. It never collapses.

M: I don't think it is that much better than Windows XP though. You should really have a try of the Macintosh. That would have to be the best operating system that I've ever used.

S: Really? But I have to get an apple computer to run it. Now mine is a Dell. I still remember the good old days when we used DOS, and had a bunch of floppy disks. I loved those days.

M: So true, back then only IT elites knew how to use "basic" and operate a shell program, but now everyone can do it.

S: Now another problem is the act of piracy. Millions of disks are being copied, produced and sold illegally. The intellectual property rights of developers are being challenged.

M: Yes. It's a great threat to programmers. We fight hard to design some good programs, only to find that they have already been pirated. We lose money and feel discouraged.

S: It's a big problem.

苏 珊: 你喜欢 Windows Vista 系统吗?

迈克尔: 不怎么喜欢。它对硬件配置要求很高，我不得不升级电脑的硬件设备。我承认 Vista 的界面确实很漂亮，但是我们应该更加注重性能而不是一些表面性的东西。

S: 但是我觉得它很稳定而且易于使用，系统从来不瘫痪。

M: 但不如 Windows XP 好。你真的应该试试 Macintosh 操作系统，这是迄今为止我用过的最好的操作系统。

S: 真的吗? 但是我得买台苹果机才能用这个系统。我现在用的是戴尔。我还记得咱们使用 DOS 系统时的那些逝去的美好时光，那会儿我们有一堆的软盘，我喜欢那样的日子。

M: 是呀，以前只有 IT 精英才知道如何操作电脑系统，但是现在所有人都会玩了。

S: 现在另一个最大的问题是盗版行为。无数的光盘正在被复制、非法生产和售卖，知识产权正在受到严重的挑衅。

M: 是的，这对我们程序员来说是一个很大的威胁。我们辛辛苦苦才设计出一些好程序，结果却发现早已被盗版了。我们不仅损失了钱财，而且还觉得沮丧。

S: 这确实是个大问题。

### 核心词汇记一记

**Words Storm**

| | | |
|---|---|---|
| hardware | ['hɑːdwɛə] | *n.* 硬件 |
| interface | ['intə(ː)feis] | *n.* 界面 |
| superficial | [sjuːpə'fiʃəl] | *a.* 肤浅的 |
| collapse | [kə'læps] | *v.* 崩溃，坍塌 |
| piracy | [pairəsi] | *n.* 盗版 |
| illegally | [i'liːgəli] | *ad.* 非法地 |

**Phrases**

| | |
|---|---|
| operating system | 操作系统 |
| floppy disk | 软盘 |

# 64. About Cars

## 汽车文化

### 知识链接 拓展视野，掌握背景知识

汽车从发明到现在已有一百多年历史了。现在，西方各国都有自己的汽车工业，如美国福特、法国标志、德国大众等。美国是汽车工业大国，几乎家家户户都有汽车，而且许多家庭不止拥有一辆汽车。美国人从学生时代就有了自己的车，可以到处兜风，这是中国人暂时不能企及的。汽车数量的庞大催生了一些与汽车相关的文化，比如汽车的收藏、鉴赏、赛车等等。汽车象征着美国发达的工业和机械化的生活。

### 难点点拨 知识难点看一看，情景实战热热身

1. It's reported that... 据说，引导一个句子

   It's reported that Volvo is the safest car on earth.

   据说沃尔沃牌汽车是世界上最安全的车。

2. help sb. do sth. 帮助某人做某事

   Safety belts and airbags cannot really help you get out of danger.

   安全带和气囊不能真地保护你逃脱危险。

3. Pull over please.

   停一下车。

4. a sense of... 一种……感觉

   A car gives you a sense of security.

   车给人安全感。

5. unlike 不像（相反，可以用 like 表示“像”）

   Unlike you Chinese, we move around a lot.

   和你们中国人不一样，我们喜欢四处逛逛。

## 情景实战 跟着老外听一听，读一读，练一练

**会话 1**

Louis: Hey, I've got a new car, a Volvo. It's reported that "Volvo" is one of the safest cars on earth.

Carol: Safety belts and airbags cannot really help you get out of danger. What's most essential is that you drive carefully.

L: I'm a good driver. I was an excellent student in the driving school, and then I got my license very easily. I think I have a talent for driving.

C: This is a really nice car, beautiful and comfortable. Can you take me for a ride?

L: Hop in. It has a convertible top and an automatic transmission. We can drive cool and easy.

C: Good. Can you slow down a little? You drive too fast.

L: Don't you think it's cool?

C: Pull over please. I feel a bit sick.

L: If you like I can even drift it a little.

C: Please stop now. Driving like this you will kill us both.

L: Sorry, buddy. But don't you think it's a nice car?

C: The car's great, but I hope you don't go driving it like this, because you're scary!

路易斯：嘿，我买了辆新车，沃尔沃牌的。据说沃尔沃牌汽车是世界上最安全的车。

卡罗：安全带和气囊不能真地保护你逃脱危险。最重要的是你得小心开车。

L：我驾驶技术很好的。在驾校的时候我表现得很出色，很容易就拿到了驾照。我觉得我在开车这方面有天赋。

C：这真是辆好车，又漂亮又舒服。你能载我一程吗？

L：可以，上车吧。这车有活动顶篷，还有自动档。我们开起来既轻松又酷。

C：不错。你能开慢一点吗？你开得太快了。

L：你不觉得这样很酷么？

C：停一下吧。我有点晕车。

L：如果你喜欢，我甚至还能给你做点漂移动作。

C：停下吧。你都快成马路杀手了。

L：对不起，哥们儿。可是你不觉得这车很棒吗？

C：是很不错，可是我希望你以后别这么开了，太危险了。

### 核心词汇记一记

**Words Storm**

| | | |
|---|---|---|
| airbag | ['ɛəbæg] *n.* | 气囊 |
| essential | [i'senʃəl] *a.* | 本质的，基本的 |
| excellent | ['eksələnt] *a.* | 优秀的 |
| talent | ['tælənt] *n.* | 天赋 |
| comfortable | ['kʌmfətəbl] *a.* | 舒服的 |

**Phrases**

| | |
|---|---|
| safety belt | 安全带 |
| automatic transmission | 自动档 |

**会话 2**

Amanda: Do you have a car?

Brad: No. You see, I'm still a university student, and in China a student cannot afford a car.

A: You can do some part-time jobs and get some money.

B: I know what you mean. In China, labor is cheap. Maybe in your country working as a waiter in a restaurant means a good income, but in China this doesn't work. Besides, we have a large population. If everyone had a car, the roads would be crowded.

A: But without a car how can you get around?

B: I can take a bus or a train. It's easier for you to have a car in America, isn't it?

A: Yes. The car is an important symbol for modern Americans. Unlike you Chinese, who would rather stay than move, we move around a lot. We need cars.

B: So everyone has a car?

A: Almost, a car gives you a sense of security. You can jump in your car and feel you're safe and secure. It takes you anywhere you want.

B: Do you have a lot of car accidents?

A: We do have accidents. I believe you also have such a problem in China. Vehicles are a threat to human life. Drunk-driving is one of the major causes, of course.

阿曼达: 你有车吗?

布拉德: 没有。你看，我还在上大学，在中国，大学生是买不起车的。

A: 你可以做点兼职挣点钱啊。

B: 我知道你的意思。在中国劳动力很廉价。也许在你们国家在餐厅当服务员就可以赚不少钱，可是在中国这行不通。而且我们人口很多，如果每个人都有车，那公路就太拥堵了。

A: 可是没有车你怎么去旅行呢?

B: 我可以坐公共汽车或者火车。在美国很容易就拥有一辆车对吧?

A: 是的。汽车是现代美国的重要标志。你们中国人更安于故土，而我们喜欢四处逛逛。我们需要车。

B: 每个人都有车咯?

A: 几乎是。车给人安全感。你躲进车里，就会觉得你很安全。车能带你到处走动。

B: 可是你们也有很多车祸吧?

A: 是的。我想在中国你们也会碰到这个问题的。车祸严重威胁人类的生命。当然，酒后驾车是最主要的原因。

### 核心词汇记一记

#### Words Storm

afford [ə'fɔːd] *v.* 供应得起
income ['inkʌm] *n.* 工资
population [ˌpɔpju'leiʃən] *n.* 人口
symbol ['simbl] *n.* 标志
threat ['θret] *n.* 威胁

#### Phrases

part-time job 兼职
car accident 车祸
drunk-driving 酒后驾驶

# 65. Pollution and Environmental Protection

## 污染和环保

### 知识链接 拓展视野，掌握背景知识

人们一直以为地球上的水源、空气是无穷尽的，所以从不担心把千万吨废气送到天空去，又把数以亿吨计的垃圾倒进海洋。大家都认为世界这么大，这一点废物算什么。我们错了，其实地球虽大，但生物只能在海拔8千米到海底11千米的范围内生活，而占了95%的生物都只能生存在中间约3公里的范围内，人类却肆意地弄污这有限的生活环境。每一个环境污染的实例，可以说都是大自然对人类的一声警钟。为了保护生态环境，为了维护人类自身和子孙后代的健康，必须积极防治环境污染。如果不保护环境，人类将面临着灭亡。

### 难点点拨 知识难点看一看，情景实战热热身

1. ...to death ……致死

   Billions of people are frozen to death.

   几十亿人都被冻死了。

2. be conscious of 意识到，认识到

   People have already become conscious of the necessity of environmental protection.

   人们已经意识到了环境保护的必要性。

3. cut down 减少，减弱

   Cars are strictly limited to a certain number to cut down the gas consumption and the carbon dioxide emission.

   车辆被限制在一定数量之内以减少汽油的消耗和二氧化碳的排放。

4. used to do sth. 过去常常做某事

   We used to catch rabbits and grasshoppers in it. But now skyscrapers have occupied that place.

   我们过去常常在那里抓兔子和蚂蚱，但是现在那片地已经被摩天大楼占据了。

## 情景实战 跟着老外听一听，读一读，练一练

**会话 1**

Alice: Recently I saw a movie *The Day After Tomorrow*. It is a story about pollution, global warming, and the disastrous consequences. The earth, having reached a certain high temperature, suddenly becomes extremely cold, and billions of people are frozen to death.

Mike: I've seen the movie. It really horrified me, making me worry about global warming. If we don't stop emitting carbon dioxide into the atmosphere, soon the ice caps will melt, and the sea level will rise to devour many coastal cities. People living there will suffer a lot.

A: People have already become conscious of the necessity of environmental protection. In our country, cars are strictly limited to a certain number to cut down the gas consumption and the carbon dioxide emission. We encourage people to take buses and the metro instead of driving. Cycling is also a good way to reduce pollution.

M: Have you heard about the Kyoto Protocol? Many countries have signed it and promised that they will pay attention to global warming.

爱丽丝：最近我看了一部叫做《后天》的电影。它讲的是关于污染、全球变暖及其灾难性后果的故事。地球在达到了一定的高温后，突然间变得极其寒冷，几十亿人都被冻死了。

迈克：我看过这部电影。真的把我吓到了，我开始担心全球变暖的问题。如果我们还不停止向大气排放二氧化碳，很快冰盖就会融化，海平面就会上升，海水会吞噬沿海城市，那儿的居民也会跟着遭殃。

A：人们已经意识到了环境保护的必要性。在我们国家，车辆被限制在一定数量之内，以减少汽油的消耗和二氧化碳的排放。我们还鼓励人们乘坐公交和地铁出行来代替私家车。骑自行车也是减少污染的一个好方法。

M：你听说过《京都议定书》吗？很多国家都签署了，并且承诺他们会重视全球变暖问题。

### 核心词汇记一记

**Words Storm**

pollution [pə'lu:ʃən] *n.* 污染
disastrous [di'zɑ:strəs] *a.* 灾难性的
consequence ['kɔnsikwəns] *n.* 后果
temperature ['temprətʃə] *n.* 温度
consumption [kən'sʌmpʃən] *n.* 消费

**Phrases**

global warming 全球变暖
carbon dioxide 二氧化碳
ice cap 冰盖

**会话 2**

Jim: There are many forms of pollution—we burn fossil fuels to pollute the air; we run chemical factories to contaminate the rivers; we use fertilizers and pesticides in the fields to poison our own crops.

Kate: Yes, war can also make a great pollution to the battlefield. The American army is now using a kind of depleted uranium shell—it is made of radioactive waste, and is harmful to men living in the war zone.

J: Because of pollution, many species are gone forever. They can never be recreated. It's such a pity.

K: When I was young, there were many fish in the river around my town. The water was crystal clear and we used to catch big fish. But now the river has already dried up.

J: When I was young there was a large wheat field near my house. We used to catch rabbits and grasshoppers in it, but now skyscrapers have occupied that place. What we can see is only cement walls and asphalt roads.

吉姆：污染分很多种，我们燃烧化石燃料会污染空气，我们经营化工厂会污染河流，我们在地里用化肥农药会毒害自己的庄稼。

凯特：是的，战争也会对战场造成很大的污染。美军现在正在使用一种贫铀弹，这种炮弹是由核废料制成的，危害战区的居民。

J：由于污染，很多物种都灭绝了。它们永远都不可能再生，真是遗憾。

K：在我小的时候，我们镇上的河里还有很多鱼，水如同水晶般晶莹剔透，我们经常能抓到大鱼。但是现在河流已经干涸了。

J：我小时候，我家附近有一大片麦地，我们过去常常在那里抓兔子和蚂蚱，但是现在那片地已经被摩天大楼占据了，我们能看到的只有水泥墙和沥青路。

**核心词汇记一记**

**Words Storm**

| | | |
|---|---|---|
| contaminate | [kən'tæmineit] *n.* | 污染 |
| fertilizer | ['fəːtilaizə] *n.* | 肥料 |
| pesticide | ['pestisaid] *n.* | 杀虫剂 |
| crystal | ['kristl] *a.* | 水晶般的 |
| grasshopper | ['græshɔpə] *n.* | 蚂蚱 |
| cement | [si'ment] *a.* | 水泥的 |
| asphalt | ['æsfælt] *a.* | 沥青的 |

**Phrases**

| | |
|---|---|
| war zone | 战争区 |
| dry up | 干涸 |

# 66. Historical Relics

## 文物古迹

### 知识链接 拓展视野，掌握背景知识

世界各地都有一些文物古迹，时刻提醒我们文明的历史是多么悠远。人生在世不过百年，而这些文明古迹却以多种形式流传下来，象征着人类的延续和发展。追根溯源，我们在游览的时候，也要怀着敬畏之心，而不能随意破坏。

### 难点点拨 知识难点看一看，情景实战热热身

1．exhaust 使精疲力竭

In fact, the project beleaguered and exhausted many people.

事实上，这是个劳民伤财的工程。

2．royal 皇家的，高贵的

It was the royal palace, the home of emperors.

它是皇家宫殿，是皇帝的家。

3．birthplace 诞生地，发源地

It's the birthplace of European civilization, full of historical relics.

它是欧洲文明的发源地，有很多历史遗迹。

4．wear and tear 磨损

They suffer wear and tear, as well as human damage.

它们经历了时间的磨损和人为的破坏。

5．appeal for 呼吁

Scholars and scientists should stand out and appeal for the preservation of our heritage, culture, architectural, history or whatever.

一些学者和科学家应当站出来呼吁社会保护我们的历史文化遗产和古建筑。

## 情景实战 跟着老外听一听，读一读，练一练

**会话 1**

Albert: You should really go to Beijing for a visit. I'll show you around.

Scott: I don't know what fun there is. Tell me something about the city.

A: Beijing enjoys a long history. There are many scenic spots and historical relics.

S: You mean the Great Wall?

A: It's one of the greatest things in China, thousands of miles long. On the outskirts of Beijing you can see a part of it snaking through the mountains. It was built to defend against the Mongols and protect the whole nation.

S: It was so huge a project that many workers toiled on it for a long time.

A: That's true. In fact the project beleaguered and exhausted many people. It also wasted lots of money.

S: But now it's a symbol of your nation?

A: Yes. In Beijing you can also see some other great buildings, such as the Forbidden City, right in the center of Beijing. It was the royal palace, the home of emperors.

S: So is it quite big?

A: Yes. There are more than eight thousand rooms in it—a city within the city.

艾伯特：你真的应该去北京转转，我会带你去游览的。

斯科特：我不知道那儿有什么好玩的。你可以跟我说说。

A：北京历史悠久，那里有很多优美的景点和历史遗迹。

S：你是指长城？

A：这只是中国伟大的景观之一，绵延万里。在京郊你可以看到它的一部分在山间蜿蜒盘旋。它是用来抵御蒙古人的进攻和保护整个国家的。

S：它是个非常巨大的工程，是很多工人花了很多心血建造的。

A：是啊。可事实上，这是个劳民伤财的工程。

S：但现在它是你们国家的象征对吗？

A：是的。在北京你还可以看到其他雄伟的建筑，如位于北京正中央的紫禁城，它是皇家宫殿，是皇帝的家。

S：所以它很大是吗？

A：是的。那里有 8000 多个房间，是一个城中城。

### 核心词汇记一记

**Words Storm**

| | | |
|---|---|---|
| outskirt | ['autskə:t] *n.* | 郊区 |
| royal | ['rɔiəl] *a.* | 皇家的 |
| palace | ['pælis] *n.* | 宫殿 |
| emperor | ['empərə] *n.* | 皇帝 |

**Phrases**

| | |
|---|---|
| show around | 带领（某人）四处转转 |
| a symbol of | ……的标志 |

**会话 2**

Shannon: I dream of going to Athens. It's the birthplace of European civilization, full of historical relics.

Tim: Athens? It's a city full of mythological tales.

S: The Parthenon is one of its greatest places. It's the microcosm of the Greek history, architecture, and philosophy. You can see the accuracy of its design and construction.

T: I prefer Rome to Athens. It is the capital city of the Roman Empire.

S: Are there any historical relics in Rome?

T: So many. The Pantheon, for example.

S: But there is a common problem for all these relics. They suffer wear and tear, as well as human damage. For example, in China, many old buildings are being torn down because the government wants to clear the field for new buildings, especially for sky-scrapers.

T: Many people don't possess the awareness for protecting old things. We should raise their awareness. Once older treasures are gone, they never come back.

S: Some scholars and scientists should stand out and appeal for the preservation of our heritage, culture, architectural history or whatever. Government should take action and make rules to stop people from doing careless things with our heritage.

香农：我做梦都想去雅典。它是欧洲文明的发源地，有很多历史遗迹。

蒂姆：雅典？那是一个充满神话故事的城市。

S：帕台农神庙是其最伟大的地方之一。它是希腊历史、建筑和哲学的缩影。从中你可以看到它的设计和建筑的精巧。

T：比起雅典，我更喜欢罗马。它是罗马帝国的首都城市。

S：罗马有什么历史遗迹吗？

T：很多，比如万神殿。

S：但是所有这些遗迹都面临着一个共同的问题，它们都经历了时间的磨损和人为的破坏。比如在中国，很多古建筑都被拆除了，因为政府想要为新建筑尤其是摩天大楼腾出土地。

T：很多人没有保护古建筑的意识。我们应当提高他们的意识。一旦我们失去了这些古建筑，那可是无法挽回的。

S：一些学者和科学家应当站出来呼吁社会各界保护我们的历史文化遗产和古建筑。政府应当采取行动并制定法规来阻止人们破坏文化遗产。

### 核心词汇记一记

**Words Storm**

| | | |
|---|---|---|
| civilization | [siˌvilaiˈzeiʃən] | *n.* 文明 |
| microcosm | [ˈmaikrəukɔzəm] | *n.* 微观世界 |
| architecture | [ˈɑːkitektʃə] | *n.* 建筑 |
| awareness | [əˈwεənis] | *n.* 意识 |
| preservation | [ˌprezəˈveiʃən] | *n.* 保留 |
| heritage | [ˈheritidʒ] | *n.* 遗产 |

**Phrases**

| | |
|---|---|
| historical relics | 历史遗迹 |
| wear and tear | 磨损 |

# 67. Landmarks

## 地标建筑

### 知识链接 拓展视野，掌握背景知识

政府热衷的是政治地标、新城地标、商业地标、产业地标，这是摩登天空；百姓钟情的是怀旧地标、美食地标、约会地标、精神地标，这是充满记忆的大地。随着作为城市名片的建筑越来越多，人们对新地标的喜悦、惊讶、不适或陌生感使得城市地标成为人们茶余饭后的交谈话题。

### 难点点拨 知识难点看一看，情景实战热热身

1. symbol 象征，符号
   Big Ben is a symbol of the Great Britain and especially London
   大本钟是大英帝国尤其是伦敦的象征。
2. make a decision 做决定
   Members of the Parliament come here to make important decisions for the nation.
   国会议员都到这里来决定国家大事。
3. a bird's view of 鸟瞰
   You can get a bird's view of the whole city from it.
   从这里你可以鸟瞰到整个城市的风光。
4. (be) located in 坐落在
   It's a Gothic cathedral, located in the centre of Paris.
   这是一座哥特式大教堂，位于巴黎中心区。
5. work of art 艺术品
   It now serves as a museum, within which many great works of art are being shown.
   它现在是一个博物馆，收藏着很多伟大的艺术品。

## 情景实战 跟着老外听一听，读一读，练一练

**会话 1**

Rob: What can I see if I go to London?

Jim: Great buildings! Big Ben is the world famous bell and clock tower, a symbol of Great Britain and especially London. It celebrated its 150th anniversary in May 2009.

R: Does the bell ring sonorously?

J: Yes. Every fifteen minutes the bell rings. Its deep sound overwhelms everyone.

R: Is the tower attached to a larger building?

J: Yes, it's attached to Westminster Palace. Members of the Parliament come here to make important decisions for the nation.

R: Great! Any other landmarks?

J: Have you heard of the London Eye?

R: Yes, it's a great wheel.

J: It's the world's largest, near the Thames River. You can get a bird's view of the whole city from it.

R: I'll try it if possible.

J: The Tower Bridge is also a great symbol of London. It spans the River Thames, and joins the two bands into one whole. From the bridge you can see the warship "Belfast", a veteran of the Second World War.

R: Thank you for telling me so much.

罗伯：如果我去伦敦的话会看到什么？

吉姆：一些很伟大的建筑。大本钟是世界著名的钟楼，是大英帝国尤其是伦敦的象征。它在 2009 年 5 月份度过了第 150 个周年纪念日。

R：钟声响亮吗？

J：响亮呀，每 15 分钟响一次。它低沉的声音震撼了每个人的心。

R：这个塔是附属于一个更大一些的建筑吗？

J：是的，它附属于威斯敏斯特宫，国会议员都到这里来决定国家大事。

R：不错。还有别的地标建筑吗？

J：你听说过伦敦眼吗？

R：听说过，它是个很大的摩天轮。

J：是全世界最大的一个，位于泰晤士河边，连接两岸。从这里你可以鸟瞰到整个城市的风光。

R：如果可以我一定要去试试。

J：伦敦塔桥也是伦敦的伟大标志。它横跨泰晤士河，把两岸连结了起来。从桥上你可以看到“贝尔法斯特”战舰，这可是二战遗留下来的老战舰。

R：感谢你告诉我这么多东西。

### 核心词汇记一记

**Words Storm**

anniversary [æni'vəːsəri] *n.* 周年纪念日

sonorous [sə'nɔːrəs] *a.* 响亮的

overwhelm [ˌəuvə'hwelm] *v.* 压倒

parliament ['pɑːləmənt] *n.* 国会

**Phrases**

be attached to 附属于

Thames River 泰晤士河

**会话 2**

Reid: Paris has a lot of famous structures, hasn't it?

Samuel: Yes, for sure. If you live in Paris, you'll be lucky enough to see many great landmarks.

R: Can you tell me about them?

S: Shall we begin with Notre Dame de Paris? It's a Gothic cathedral, located in the centre of Paris. Have you read Victor Hugo's *Notre-Dame de Paris*?

R: Yes. It's a tragic love story, isn't it?

S: Le Louvre is an old palace, first built in the beginning of the thirteenth century. It now serves as a museum, within which many great works of art are being shown.

R: I know there is a glass pyramid in front of it now.

S: That's correct and it was a Chinese architect Ieoh Ming Pei who designed it. At the beginning many French people protested this design, thinking it ugly and weird, but now they accept it as an important landmark. Then we have Arc de Triomphe—the Arch of Triumph.

R: What significance does it have?

S: It was built to celebrate the victory of the French army in the war against Russia. Oh. I just forgot the most important landmark—Le Tour Eiffel, it used to be the tallest building on earth. When Mr. Eiffel proposed his design of it, many people protested, asserting that the tower would be as ugly as a monster. But now they are proud of it.

瑞 德：巴黎有很多著名的建筑，是吗？

塞缪尔：是的。如果你住在巴黎，你就有幸看到很多伟大的地标建筑。

R：你能告诉我吗？

S：我们从巴黎圣母院开始好吗？这是一座哥特式大教堂，位于巴黎中心区。你读过维克多·雨果的《巴黎圣母院》吗？

R：读过这是个爱情悲剧，是吗？

S：卢浮宫是一个旧宫殿，始建于 13 世纪初，现在是一个博物馆，收藏着很多伟大的艺术品。

R：我知道它前面有一个玻璃金字塔。

S：是的。是一个中国建筑师贝聿铭设计的。一开始的时候法国人民都反对这个设计，觉得又丑又奇怪，但是现在他们已经接受它并将其作为一个重要的建筑地标了。接下来我们说说凯旋门。

R：它有什么意义吗？

S：它的建立是为了庆祝法国在对俄战争中的胜利。哦，我刚才忘记了介绍一个重要的地标——埃菲尔铁塔。它是地球上最高的建筑。当埃菲尔先生提出设计方案的时候，很多法国人都反对，认为这个塔将会像怪物一样丑陋，但是现在他们非常引以为豪。

**核心词汇记一记**

**Words Storm**

landmark ['lændmaːk] *n.* 地标建筑

pyramid ['pirəmid] *n.* 金字塔

architect ['aːkitekt] *n.* 建筑师

**Phrases**

be proud of 以……而骄傲

# 68. City and Countryside

## 城市与乡村

### 知识链接 拓展视野，掌握背景知识

城市是繁华的代名词，高楼林立，时尚典雅，深夜的灯光依然璀璨。站在摩天大楼的顶层，城市人用高傲和自信俯视大地。乡村是淳朴的代名词，白墙黑瓦，小桥流水，清新的空气和满目的苍绿。站在静谧空旷的田野，乡村人用淳厚和坦诚仰望星空。一直以来，城市与乡村站在天平的两端，权衡各自的份量。城市为乡村的落后叹息，乡村为城市的世俗摇头。城市嘲讽着乡村的土气，乡村感慨着城市的傲慢。

### 难点点拨 知识难点看一看，情景实战热热身

1．in the city/in the suburbs 在城市 / 郊区

I live in the suburbs.

我住在郊区。

2．spend time doing 花时间做某事

Every morning I spend one and a half hours commuting.

每天早上我光花在公交车上的时间就有 1 个半小时。

3．a large population 众多的人口

The population is so large and the land is limited for cultivation.

人口太多了，而可耕种的土地太有限了。

4．means 意味着

As a result, being a farmer means to toil and moil a lot.

所以，当一个农民就意味着艰苦的劳作。

## 情景实战 跟着老外听一听，读一读，练一练

**会话 1**

Robert: Where do you live?

Monica: I live in the suburbs.

R: So you can enjoy the fresh air. It's good for you.

M: No. It's a problem. It's very difficult for you to buy an apartment in downtown Beijing, because it is usually quite expensive. Many people, including whitecollar workers, cannot afford an apartment there. This is why I'm now living in the suburbs.

R: But in my country, it is the rich who live in the suburbs. The environment is better. We have our houses and gardens there, and live a peaceful and sweet life.

M: But the traffic jams must be quite horrible. Every morning I spend one and a half hours commuting.

R: Terrible indeed.

M: I'm now thinking about buying a car, but the price of gas is so high, and driving is a bit hazardous. In rush hour I may also get caught in traffic.

R: I don't mind waiting so much. I really appreciate those skyscrapers downtown.

罗伯特：你住哪儿？

莫妮卡：我住在郊区。

R：你能呼吸到郊区的新鲜空气，这对你非常有好处。

M：不是这样的，实际上问题是，北京市区的房了实在是太贵了，根本买不起。包括白领在内的很多人都买不起市区的房子。这才是我住在郊区的真正原因。

R：但是在我们国家，住在郊区的是那些有钱人。郊区的环境比市区更好些，在那儿我们有房子还有花园，过着一种平静而安逸的生活。

M：但是交通拥堵太可怕了，如果住在郊区的话，每天早上我光花在公交车上的时间就有 1 个半小时。

R：那确实很恐怖。

M：我现在正打算买辆车呢。但是油价太贵了，开车又有点危险，而且在交通高峰时段我可能还是要等很久。

R：我倒是不介意等待。我真地很喜欢城区的那些摩天大楼。

### 核心词汇记一记

**Words Storm**

suburbs ['sʌbə:b] *n.* 郊区
apartment [ə'pa:tmənt] *n.* 公寓
downtown [daun'taun] *a.* 市中心的
peaceful ['pi:sful] *a.* 平静的
horrible ['hɔrəbl] *a.* 恐怖的
skyscraper ['skaiskreipə] *n.* 摩天大楼

**Phrases**

traffic jam 交通拥堵

**会话 2**

Chandler: I like being a farmer. I have a large farm and a lot of machines.

Liu Yang: But in China, a farmer doesn't have a large farm. The population is so large and the land is limited for cultivation. Besides, we don't have so many machines as you do. As a result, being a farmer means to toil and moil a lot.

C: In the US, most people live in the city, so there are large pieces of land left for us farmers. We usually have many machines for help, such as tractors, combine harvesters and so on. We sow quality seeds in the field, water them, and use fertilizers. In the right season we will have an abundant crop.

L: Exactly so, a farmer is always resolute and devoted. He provides us with food. Without farmers society would inevitably collapse.

C: Thank you for your compliment, and thanks for the biotechnology. Now the yield of my farm is much higher than before. Science helps us, saving a lot of manpower.

钱德勒：我喜欢当农民。我有个大农场，还有很多机器。

刘洋：但是中国的农民却没有自己的大农场。这个国家的人口太多了，耕地却十分有限。另外，我们也不像你们的农民那样有那么多的机器。因此，在中国，当一个农民就意味着艰苦的劳作。

C：在美国，大部分人都居住在城市里，因此为我们农民空出了很多大块的土地。通常我们有很多的机器来辅助我们劳动，如拖拉机、联合收割机等。我们把优质种子种在地里，浇水施肥，等到收获的季节里我们就会大丰收。

L：不管怎样，农民总是全心全意地辛勤劳作。他们为我们提供了食物。如果没有农民，社会就会垮掉。

C：谢谢夸奖。多亏了生物技术，现在我家农场的产量比以前高多了。科学帮我们节省了很多人力。

**核心词汇记一记**

**Words Storm**

| | | |
|---|---|---|
| cultivation | ['kʌlti'veiʃən] | *n.* 耕地 |
| toil | [tɔil] | *v.* 辛苦工作 |
| tractor | ['træktə] | *n.* 拖拉机 |
| harvester | ['hɑːvistə] | *n.* 收割机 |
| collapse | [kə'læps] | *v.* 垮掉 |
| compliment | ['kɔmplimənt] | *n.* 褒扬 |

**Phrases**

| | |
|---|---|
| as a result | 作为结果 |
| combine harvester | 联合收割机 |
| provide with | 供应 |

# 69. Culture Shock

## 文化冲击

### 知识链接 拓展视野，掌握背景知识

“文化休克”(Cultural Shock)是1958年美国人类学家奥博格(Kalvero Oberg)提出来的一个概念，是指一个人进入到不熟悉的文化环境中时，因失去自己熟悉的所有社会交流的符号与手段而产生的一种迷失、疑惑、排斥甚至恐惧的感觉。文化休克并不是一种什么疾病，而是一个学习的过程，一种复杂的个人体验。虽然期间自己可能会产生某种不舒服甚至痛苦的感觉，但它不会以同样的方式影响所有的人，甚至对同一个人在同样环境的不同时期也有着不同的影响。

### 难点点拨 知识难点看一看，情景实战热热身

1. get along well with 与……相处得好

   As a newcomer I don't know how to get along well with the local people.

   作为一个新来的人，我不知道如何同本地人相处。

2. adapt oneself to sth. 适应

   You have to adapt yourself to it.

   你必须让自己适应起来。

3. value 价值，价值观念

   The values I hold, the way I lead my life, become totally weird in this country.

   我的价值观，还有我的生活方式，在这个国家显得十分奇怪。

4. in low spirits 情绪低落

   I've been in low spirits since I came here.

   自从来这以后我情绪一直很低落。

5. When in Rome, do as the Romans do.

   入乡随俗（谚语）。

## 情景实战 跟着老外听一听，读一读，练一练

**会话 1**

Bruce: I am feeling a bit like a fish out of water. As a newcomer I don't know how to get along well with the local people.

Anna: That's called culture shock. You belong to your culture, which is totally different from this one. So you cannot adjust yourself within the new environment.

B: I cannot speak French. Even a small thing can be a great problem for me. When I go shopping, I find it hard to read the label and speak with the salesman.

A: You have to adapt yourself to it. You can get a textbook and learn the language.

B: It's not the only trouble. The values I hold, the way I lead my life, become totally weird in this country. I don't like other people staring at me as if were a monster.

A: I highly recommend that you go and visit some local families, get to know their way of life. Do you have some friends here?

B: Yes, but not many. I don't even know how to be invited. When I get there I feel fidgety and want to leave. It is very uncomfortable. Do you think I should bring them some gifts? I am not sure if I am supposed to do something beforehand as an act of courtesy?

A: You just go and see. Don't be too timid. They will understand you.

布鲁斯: 我感到很不适应。作为一个新来的人，我不知道如何同本地人相处。

安娜: 这被称之为文化休克，你属于你的文化，跟这里的完全不同，所以在新的环境里你无法调整好自己。

B: 我不会讲法语。即使一件小事对我来说都是大问题。当我去购物的时候，我发现很难读懂标签，跟售货员交流也很困难。

A: 你必须让自己适应起来。你可以找本书来学一下语言。

B: 这不是唯一的麻烦。我的价值观，还有我的生活方式，在这个国家显得十分奇怪。我不喜欢其他人像看怪物似的盯着我看。

A: 我强烈建议你去拜访一些当地的家庭，了解一下他们的生活方式。你在这儿有朋友吗？

B: 有，但是不多。我甚至不知道收到别人邀请时要怎样，我会变得不安，想尽快离开，很不舒服。要不要带点礼物去呀？我是不是应该预先做点什么以表示礼貌呢？

A: 你只管去。不要太羞怯，他们会理解你的。

### 核心词汇记一记

**Words Storm**

newcomer [njuː'kʌmə] *n.* 新来者
adjust [ə'dʒʌst] *v.* 调整
label ['leibl] *n.* 标签
weird [wiəd] *a.* 奇怪的
fidgete ['fidʒit] *v.* 坐卧不安
courtesy ['kəːtisi] *n.* 谦卑，礼貌

**Phrases**

culture shock 文化休克

### 会话 2

Kate: I've been in low spirits since I came here.

Steven: Lovesick or homesick?

K: Homesick, of course. Every night I dream of my family and I have a lot of problems here. I don't want to show up in public places and I don't like the way people do things.

S: For example?

K: For example, you hug and even kiss each other so often. It's so disgusting. I'm conservative, and I don't think it's right.

S: You have to get accustomed to it. It's our culture in which you are living. Have you heard the saying "When in Rome, do as the Romans do"?

K: You know, when I see local people, I think I belong to another species. We are so different. You are so white and tall and the majority of you all believe in a God. You have some strange traditions.

S: Don't be too serious about all this. Everything will be okay, you'll soon be assimilated into this culture, then you'll feel comfortable about living here.

K: I hope so.

S: But you should be bold and not limit yourself within the circle of your countrymen. Get to know the real local people, they are hospitable and will give you the warmest welcome.

凯特：自从来这以后我情绪一直很低落。

斯蒂芬：相思病还是思乡病?

K：当然是思乡了。每天晚上我都会梦到我的家人。我在这儿遇到很多问题。我不想在公共场合露面，我不喜欢这里的人做事的方式。

S：比如呢?

K：比如，你们经常拥抱甚至亲吻。这太恶心了。我很保守，我觉得这样是不对的。

S：你必须要适应。你现在生活在我们的文化里，有一句谚语"入乡随俗"你听说过吗?

K：你知道的，当我看到当地居民的时候，我就觉得我属于外来物种。我们太不一样了，你们又白又高，你们都信仰上帝，你们有一些奇怪的传统。

S：不要把这些看得太重。一切都会好起来的。你很快就会融入到这里的文化中，然后你就会觉得舒服了。

K：希望如此吧。

S：但是你应该勇敢些。不要把自己限制在同胞的圈子里，去认识一些真正的当地人。他们很好客，而且会给你最热烈的欢迎。

#### 核心词汇记一记

**Words Storm**

| | | |
|---|---|---|
| lovesick | ['lʌvsik] | a. 相思病的 |
| homesick | ['həumsik] | a. 思乡的 |
| disgusting | [dis'gʌstiŋ] | a. 恶心的 |
| conservative | [kən'səːvətiv] | a. 保守的 |
| assimilate | [ə'simileit] | v. 吸收 |
| countryman | ['kʌntrimən] | n. 同胞 |
| hospitable | ['hɔspitəbl] | a. 好客的 |

**Phrases**

| | |
|---|---|
| show up | 露面 |
| get accustomed to | 习惯于 |

# 70. Racial Equality

## 种族平等

### 知识链接 拓展视野，掌握背景知识

*美国黑人共有2600多万，大多是欧洲殖民主义者从非洲掳掠贩卖到美洲的黑人奴隶的后裔。这是一段浸满血泪和饱受屈辱的历史，自从被贩卖到美洲后，黑人只是奴隶主的财产和工具，受尽了非人的剥削和压迫。南北战争结束后，黑人虽然在法律上摆脱了被奴役的命运，但被歧视的现象依然十分严重。直到20世纪60年代，美国民权法、选举法的修定，黑人才获得了相对的平等权利。但在美国社会，对黑人的歧视一直隐性存在。*

### 难点点拨 知识难点看一看，情景实战热热身

1．protest against 反抗，抗议

In the 1950s and 1960s there was the "Civil Rights Movement" protesting against the government and white people's discrimination against the black.

在20世纪50年代和60年代有一场黑人民权运动，就是反抗政府和白人对黑人的歧视。

2．deliver a speech to 发表演讲

exert an influence upon sb. 对某人施加影响

He was murdered by a sniper while delivering his speech to the public, but his spirit of racial equality has already exerted a strong influence upon the whole American nation.

在一次发表公开演讲时他被狙击手暗杀了，可是他的民族平等的精神却一直深刻影响着整个美国。

3．thanks to 多亏

Thanks to his efforts, now the black can finally enjoy a relatively good position in the American society.

多亏了他的努力，现在美国黑人终于可以享受到相对自由平等的地位了。

## 情景实战 跟着老外听一听，读一读，练一练

**会话 1**

David: I feel puzzled about why the black people were discriminated.

Kate: I don't know, either. Maybe because the white thought the black ugly and stupid, but this is definitely not the truth.

D: I cannot imagine that. In my opinion, the idea of racial discrimination itself is ugly and stupid.

K: The black were deeply repressed. Once they were slaves before the civil war. After Lincoln, they got the so-called "freedom" but were still underprivileged in many ways. In the 1950s and 1960s there was the "Civil Rights Movement" protesting against the government and white people's discrimination against the black.

D: Yes, I know, Martin Luther King. His "I Have a Dream" is fantastic and enthralling.

K: He is a fighter of justice and great bravery. He was murdered by a sniper while delivering his speech to the public, but his spirit of racial equality has already exerted a strong influence upon the whole American nation. Thanks to his efforts, now the black can finally enjoy a relatively good position in American society.

大卫：我就不明白，为什么黑人以前总是受歧视呢？

凯特：我也不明白，也许是因为白人觉得黑人又丑又笨？可其实不是这样的呀。

D：我无法想象。在我看来，种族歧视这想法本身才又丑又笨呢。

K：黑人以前受打压太厉害了。在美国南北战争之前他们当奴隶，林肯之后的年月里他们虽说表面上自由了，实际上却仍旧遭受种种歧视。在20世纪50年代和60年代有一场黑人民权运动，就是反抗政府和白人对黑人的歧视。

D：是的，我知道，马丁·路德·金。他的演说"我有一个梦想"很棒，扣人心弦。

K：他是为正义而战的勇士，后来在一次发表公开演讲时他被狙击手暗杀了，可是他的民族平等的精神却一直深刻影响着整个美国。多亏了他的努力，现在美国黑人终于可以享受到相对自由平等的地位了。

### 核心词汇记一记

**Words Storm**

| | | |
|---|---|---|
| underprivileged | ['ʌndə'privilidʒd] *a.* | 弱势的 |
| enthralling | [in'θrɔːliŋ] *a.* | 引人入胜的 |
| bravery | ['breivəri] *n.* | 勇敢 |

**Phrases**

| | |
|---|---|
| racial discrimination | 种族歧视 |
| civil war | 内战 |
| exert an influence on/upon | 施加影响 |

### 会话 2

Justin: Do you know something about the Jews?

Tom: The Jewish people are an excellent nation, exceedingly smart and good at merchandising. In the Old Testament of the Bible, they were the chosen nation specially favored by God.

J: But I have heard a lot about the anti-Semitism, the hatred against the Jews.

T: Yes, in the past the Jewish people were discriminated against severely. In the 1930s, the Nazis shouted that all Jews should be eliminated from the earth. The Nazis persecuted them, and imprisoned them into concentration camps, where they were tortured and slaughtered.

J: I know there is an "Auschwitz Concentration Camp", which is the biggest slaughterhouse of Jews.

T: It's horrible indeed.

J: But it is comforting that they finally qot justice.

T: They have their own country Israel now, though a large number of Jews are still scattered all around the world. For example, in the US there are 5,300,000 Jews. The Jewish people have made a great contribution to the development of the whole world. Einstein, Marx, Spinoza and Freud are Jews, for example.

贾斯汀：你了解犹太人吗？

汤姆：犹太民族是个优秀的民族，非常聪明，善于经商。在《圣经·旧约》里，犹太民族是得到上帝垂青的。

J：可我听说过反犹主义，就是对犹太人的仇视。

T：对，在过去犹太人备受歧视。20 世纪 30 年代，纳粹叫嚣要把所有犹太人消灭掉。纳粹迫害犹太人，把他们关押到集中营，在集中营里犹太人受到折磨和杀戮。

J：我知道有个"奥斯维辛集中营"，是杀害犹太人最多的地方，简直就是个屠宰场。

T：简直太可怕了。

J：不过欣慰的是他们现在终于得到公正待遇了。

T：他们现在有了自己的国家，就是以色列。不过仍有大批犹太人散居在世界各地。比如在美国就有 530 万犹太人。犹太民族为世界发展作了巨大贡献。爱因斯坦、马克思、斯宾诺莎和弗洛伊德都是犹太人。

#### 核心词汇记一记

**Words Storm**

| | | |
|---|---|---|
| merchandise | ['mə:tʃəndaiz] | *v.* 经商 |
| persecute | ['pə:sikju:t] | *v.* 迫害 |
| slaughter | ['slɔ:tə] | *n./v.* 屠杀 |
| scatter | ['skætə] | *v.* 分散 |

**Phrases**

| | |
|---|---|
| imprison into | 关押 |
| concentration camp | 集中营 |
| make contribution to | 为……做贡献 |

# 71. Feminism

# 女权主义

## 知识链接 拓展视野，掌握背景知识

女权主义泛指妇女要求平等权利的社会思潮，是近代资产阶级启蒙思想运动和妇女解放运动的产物，提倡妇女在人类生活所有领域与男子具有同等权利。女权主义的观念基础是认为现时的社会建立于一个男性被给予了比女性更多特权的父权体系之上。现代女权主义理论主要出自于西方的中产阶级学术界。不同文化背景下的女权主义运动各有其独特性，并且会针对该文化背景下的女性来提出议题，比如苏丹的性器割除（genital mutilation，女性割礼）或北美的玻璃天花板效应（glass ceiling），而如强奸、乱伦等则是普遍的议题。

## 难点点拨 知识难点看一看，情景实战热热身

1．have prejudice against 对……有偏见

Many companies now still have their prejudice against women.

很多公司现在仍然对女性有偏见。

2．be supposed to 被当作，认为

In a family, the husband is still considered the master, and the wife is supposed to be the servant.

在一个家庭里面，丈夫仍然还是一家之主，而妻子则被认为是仆人。

3．a matter of course 理所当然的事

Nothing is a matter of course.

没有什么事情是理所应当的。

4．a heavy burden on sb. 对某人是沉重的负担

She thought having a baby is a heavy burden on woman.

她认为生小孩对女人来说是沉重的负担。

## 情景实战 跟着老外听一听，读一读，练一练

### 会话 1

Emily: Woman should not be enslaved by man.

Peter: Enslaved? What are you talking about? Women have already got what they want.

E: No, I disagree. Many companies, even today, still have their prejudice against women. They prefer male employees to females. In a family, the husband is still considered the master, and the wife is supposed to be the servant.

P: But at least women can do many more things than they could previously. They are allowed to enter nearly every field. Before the Second World War, if a woman wanted to get a job, she would only become a nurse or a teacher. But now she can even be a manager in a multi-national corporation if she wants to. In the US, the position of the Secretary of State seems to be reserved for female politicians, such as Condoleezza Rice and Hillary Clinton.

E: Yes. But we are still repressed in some sense. For example, it's always supposed that a woman should be passive and even conservative. Man can propose marriage to a woman, but why can't a woman do the same to a man? Man can be a soldier fighting a war, but why should woman stay at home cooking and taking care of babies?

P: You must be crazy. Women don't start wars. Men do that!

E: Nothing is a matter of course. What we should do is to completely reverse the situation. We should liberate ourselves.

艾米丽：女人不应该受男人奴役。

彼 特：奴役？你在说些什么呀？女人已经得到她们想要的了。

E：没有。很多公司现在仍然对女性有偏见。比起女性雇员，他们更喜欢男性雇员。在一个家庭里面，丈夫仍然还是一家之主，而妻子则被认为是仆人。

P：但是至少女人可以做的事情比以前多多了。她们可以进入几乎任何一个领域。在二战前，如果一个女人想得到一份工作，她只能成为一名护士或者教师。但是现在，你看，只要她们愿意就有可能成为一名跨国公司的职业经理人。在美国，国务卿的职位就像是专为女政治家而保留的，如赖斯和希拉里·克林顿。

E：是的，但是我们在某种意义上仍然是受打压的。比如，女人总被看作是被动的甚至是保守的。男人可以向女人求婚，但是为什么女人不能向男人求婚呢？男人能够作为一名士兵去打仗，但是为什么女人就只能待在家里做饭和照顾小孩呢？

P：你一定是疯了。女人才不打打杀杀的呢，那都是男人的事。

E：没有什么事情是理所应当的。我们应该做的是彻底改变这种情况。我们应该解放自己。

#### 核心词汇记一记

**Words Storm**

enslave [in'sleiv] *v.* 奴役
servant ['sə:vənt] *n.* 仆人
passive ['pæsiv] *a.* 被动的

**Phrases**

in some sense 在某种意义上
propose marriage to 求婚

**会话 2**

Allison: Do you know Simone de Beauvoir?

Joe: No. Who's she?

A: The lifelong partner of Sartre, the mother of Feminism.

J: Partner? She never got married with Sartre?

A: No. She is an independent woman. When young, she refused the marriage planned by her parents, and rebelled against some of the social codes.

J: I really admire what she did. What achievements has she got?

A: She wrote a very famous book titled *The Second Sex*. It's called "the Bible of modern feminism", and covers everything about woman, anthropologically, historically, literarily, sociologically.

J: Tough and knowledgeable. Did she have a child?

A: No. She thought that having a baby was too heavy a burden on a woman.

J: You know, in ancient China we have a saying "There are three unfilial behaviors, the worst of which is not to have a child". If a woman failed to give birth to a child, she would get a divorce and live alone for the rest of her life. Meanwhile, only a boy could carry on the family name, a girl didn't count for much. Now many people still firmly hold onto this ideal.

爱丽森: 你知道西蒙娜·德·波伏娃吗?

乔: 不知道，她是谁呀?

A: 她是萨特的终生搭挡，也是女性主义的始祖。

J: 搭挡? 难道她和萨特从来没结婚吗?

A: 嗯，她是一个很独立的女人。她年轻的时候拒绝了父母给她安排的婚姻，反对某些社会规范。

J: 我真佩服她做的事情。她取得了些什么成就呢?

A: 她写了一部非常著名的书，叫做《第二性》，它被称为“现代女性的圣经”。此书包揽了人类学、历史学、文学以及社会学上关于女人的一切。

J: 她一定很吃苦耐劳并且知识渊博。她有小孩吗?

A: 没有。她认为生小孩对女人来说是沉重的负担。

J: 你知道吗，在中国古代有句谚语是这么说的，“不孝有三，无后为大”。如果一个女人不能生小孩，她就会被休掉，孤独地度过余生。并且，只有男孩才能延续家族的香火，女孩是不算数的。现在很多人还是坚定地固守这个观念。

### 核心词汇记一记

**Words Storm**

feminism ['feminizəm] *n.* 女性主义

rebel ['rebl] *v.* 反叛

knowledgeable ['nɔlidʒəbl] *a.* 知识渊博的

unfilial [ˌʌn'filjəl] *a.* 不孝的

**Phrases**

social codes 社会规范

give birth to 生孩子

# 72. Animal Rights

## 动物权利

### 知识链接 拓展视野，掌握背景知识

动物权利或称动物解放，是人类发起的保护动物不被人类作为占有物来对待的社会运动。这是一种比较激进的社会思潮，其宗旨不仅要为动物争取被更仁慈对待的权利，更主张动物要享有精神上的基本“人”权，比如，和人类一样免受折磨的权利。在一些国家，已经立法保护动物权利。1992年，瑞士法律上确认动物为“生命”(beings)，而非“物”(things)。而批评者认为，由于动物无法对社会契约进行讨论或是做出道德判断，不能够顾及他人的权利，甚至根本对权力没有概念，因此不能被认为享有精神上的权利。

### 难点点拨 知识难点看一看，情景实战热热身

1. club...to death 用棍子打死

   I recently read news that in some places of China they are clubbing stray dogs to death.

   我最近看到一些新闻，说中国一些地区正在用棍棒杀害流浪狗。

2. protest against 抗议，反对

   Many people are protesting against this policy.

   很多人都在抗议这项政策。

3. euthanize 施行安乐死

   humane 人道的，少痛苦的

   In the US people also euthanize stray dogs. But their method is much more humane.

   在美国人们也常常对流浪狗施行安乐死，但这是比较人道的方法。

4. on the one hand...on the other hand... 一方面……另一方面……

   We human beings have dogs and cats as our friends on the one hand, then on the other hand we slaughter countless cows and pigs just for food!

   一方面，我们人类把狗和猫当做我们的朋友；而另一方面，我们却屠杀了不计其数的牛和猪来当做我们的食物。

## 情景实战 跟着老外听一听，读一读，练一练

### 会话 1

Kathy: I recently read news reports that in some places in China they are clubbing stray dogs to death—and this is the decision made by local governments! It's highly controversial. Many people are protesting against this policy.

Christine: Why should we kill those dogs? They are supposed to be men's best friends! This is a slaughter!

K: Stray dogs cause a lot of social problems. For example, they bark and bite and may carry the rabies virus. We need to solve the problem one way or another.

C: But we shouldn't torture them by clubbing them. We can put them into cages and control them. That would be better for all of us.

K: That's what I want to see happen also. In the US people also euthanize stray dogs. But their method is much more humane. They give the dog an injection so it will die painlessly.

C: That is much better method of tackling the problem, but I still think we shouldn't kill unnecessarily. Even animals should enjoy their rights and we should respect them. Human beings shouldn't be so arrogant.

K: I couldn't agree with you more.

凯西：我最近看到一些新闻，说中国一些地区正在用棍棒杀害流浪狗，这是一些地方政府的决定。这事情争议非常大。很多人都在抗议这项政策。

克里斯汀：我们为什么要杀死这些狗呢？它们是人类最好的朋友呀！这简直就是大屠杀！

K：流浪狗造成了很多社会问题。比如，它们狂吠和咬人，还可能带有狂犬病，我们总要解决这些问题的。

C：但是我们也不能用棍子来折磨它们呀！我们可以把它们关到笼子里控制起来。这样对谁都好。

K：我也是这样想的。在美国人们也常常对流浪狗施行安乐死，但这是比较人道的方法。他们会给狗打一针让它们没有痛苦地死去。

C：这种方法比较好。但是我还是认为我们不应该滥杀无辜。即使是动物也享有生存的权利。我们应该尊重它们，人类不该如此狂妄自大。

K：我太同意你的观点了。

#### 核心词汇记一记

**Words Storm**

club [klʌb] *v.* 棒打

controversial [ˌkɔntrə'vəːʃəl] *a.* 有争议的

protest [prɔ'test] *v.* 抗议

slaughter ['slɔːtə] *n.* 屠杀

rabies ['reibiːz] *n.* 狂犬病

humane [hjuː'mein] *a.* 人道的

**Phrases**

stray dog 流浪狗

## 会话 2

Alexandra: Have you noticed? We human beings have dogs and cats as our friends on the one hand, then on the other hand we slaughter countless cows and pigs just for food! Don't you think it's ridiculous and hypocritical?

Victor: But we need food. We have to eat something, or else we will starve.

A: We can eat vegetables. I'm a vegetarian. It's cruel to eat those animals. Why don't you eat your own pet?

V: I don't eat my dog because I love him. But this doesn't mean I love all the pigs. In my opinion, we rear them, so we have the right to deprive them of their lives.

A: Nonsense. Do you mean your mother has the right to kill you then?

V: Of course not. I just want to say…

A: Your mother kills you and eats you because she gives birth to you?

V: No. But we should eat meat. Without meat man cannot live.

A: I never eat meat. Am I dead now?

V: You are such a radical. Do you have to be so cynical toward me?

亚力山德拉：你注意到一件事了吗？一方面，我们人类把狗和猫当做我们的朋友；而另一方面，我们却屠杀了不计其数的牛和猪来当做我们的食物。你不认为这很可笑很伪善吗？

维克多：但是我们需要食物。我们要吃东西，不然会饿死的。

A：我们可以吃蔬菜呀！我就是个素食主义者。吃这些动物是很残忍的，你为什么不吃你自己的宠物呢？

V：我不吃我的狗是因为我爱他。但是这不代表我爱所有的猪。在我看来，我们饲养了它们，所以我们有权力剥夺它们的生命。

A：胡说。那照你的意思你母亲有权利杀你啰？

V：当然不是，我只是想说……

A：你母亲杀了你并且吃了你是因为她生了你？

V：不是。但是我们应该吃肉，没有肉人是不能活的。

A：我从来不吃肉，我现在死了吗？

V：你太激进了。你能不在我面前这么偏激吗？

### 核心词汇记一记

#### Words Storm

| | | |
|---|---|---|
| countless | ['kauntlis] *a.* | 数不清的 |
| hypocritical | [hipə'kritikl] *a.* | 伪善的 |
| vegetarian | [ˌvedʒi'tɛəriən] *n.* | 素食主义者 |
| nonsense | ['nɔnsəns] *n.* | 废话，胡说 |
| radical | ['rædikəl] *n.* | 激进分子 |

#### Phrases

in my opinion　在我看来

# 73. Democracy

# 民主制度

## 知识链接　拓展视野，掌握背景知识

民主的原则是由多数进行统治，通常被人与独裁政治相比较。目前自由民主制的国家数量是有史以来的最高点，而且仍继续增长。因此，许多人推测这波潮流会一直持续下去，直到自由民主制成为人类社会的普遍标准为止。

## 难点点拨　知识难点看一看，情景实战热热身

1．must 必须之物，名词

Do you think democracy is a must for human civilization?

你觉得民主对于人类文明来说是必须的吗?

2．do harm to 损害

They will only think of their own interests and do harm to our people.

他们只顾自己的利益而危害人民的利益。

3．approve of/ disapprove of 同意 / 不同意

I disapprove of what you say, but I will defend to the death your right to say it.

我不同意你所说的，但是我誓死捍卫你说话的权利。

4．coverage 覆盖，报道

They never showed a negative coverage of things, especially political issues.

他们从来不报道负面消息，尤其是对于一些政治事件。

5．broaden horizon 拓宽视野

You can broaden your horizons and see more of what is happening in the world.

你能拓宽自己的视野，看到世界上更多的事情。

## 情景实战 跟着老外听一听，读一读，练一练

**会话 1**

Andrew: Do you think democracy is a must for human civilization?

Bobby: Yes. Without it, the government will do whatever it wants, and get totally out of our control. That's a rather dangerous precedent.

A: So the government officials can do anything they want and because selfishness is an unavoidable part of human nature, they will only think of their own interests and do harm to our people.

B: Do you think you are enjoying democracy in your country?

A: Yes. In our country, every citizen has the right to vote. We have the right to express our own opinion and in turn the public's opinion has a great impact on the government's decisions.

B: It occurred to me that Evelyn Hall, the writer known for her biography of Voltaire, once wrote the phrase "I disapprove of what you say, but I will defend to the death your right to say it."

A: We can organize a mass gathering and demonstration to show our power and express our disagreement about things. We can publicly criticize what our government has done. This is good for the growth of the nation.

B: Yes. If one government fails to act properly, it will receive the due punishment. As a result, the government can get a lesson from it, and avoid repeating the same mistakes next time.

安德鲁：你觉得民主对于人类文明来说是必须的吗？

鲍 勃：是的，如果没有民主，政府就会为所欲为，完全脱离我们的控制。这是非常危险的。

A：如果那样的话，原则上政府官员就能为所欲为。因为自私是人性不可避免的一部分，他们只顾自己的利益而危害人民的利益。

B：你觉得你们国家民主吗？

A：民主。在我们国家，每个公民都有选举权。我们有表达自己意见的权利，公众舆论对政府决策有着非常重要的影响。

B：我想起一句话，写伏尔泰的传记而出名的女作家伊夫林·霍尔曾经写过，“我不同意你所说的话，但是我誓死捍卫你说话的权利”。

A：我们能够组织大众集会和游行，以显示我们的力量，表达我们对一些事情的不同意见。我们可以公开批评政府的所作所为，这有利于一个国家的成长。

B：是的。如果一个政府的行为不恰当，就会得到应有的惩罚，政府就会从中得到教训，然后避免下次再犯同样的错误。

### 核心词汇记一记

**Words Storm**

democracy [di'mɔkrəsi] *n.* 民主

selfishness ['selfiʃnis] *n.* 自私

unavoidable [ˌʌnə'vɔidəbl] *a.* 不可避免的

biography [bai'ɔgrəfi] *n.* 传记

demonstration [ˌdemən'streiʃən] *n.* 游行

criticize ['kritisaiz] *v.* 批评

**Phrases**

get out of control 失去控制

government official 政府官员

**会话 2**

Thomas: Have you noticed one thing about the Internet? It helps us to enhance our democracy!

Jenny: Why? What do you mean by that?

T: Before the Internet, we knew nothing other than what we saw on TV news and TV news can be very misleading. They never show negative coverage of things, especially political issues.

J: Nowadays things are the same. If we just watch TV, our mind will grow dull.

T: But the advent of the Internet changed this situation. Now you can easily get online, and see what's happening in the whole world. Instead of only a dozen channels, you have countless websites. So the blockade of information, as well as propaganda has become impossible.

J: So now you can broaden your horizons and see more of what is happening in the world.

T: Besides that the Internet offers you a channel to show your opinion. You can write almost whatever you want, to show your agreement or disagreement on things. It guarantees your right to speak. Meanwhile, the government may see what people have written in your blog or BBS, and gage public opinion better.

J: So it's both good for us and for the government. It will help those officials make decisions.

托马斯:你有没有注意到一件事情？互联网帮我们扩大了我们的民主！

珍 妮:为什么呢？你这么说是什么意思？

T: 在互联网产生前，我们除了电视上看到的新闻之外对世界一无所知。而电视新闻有时极具误导性。他们从来不报道负面消息，尤其是对于一些政治事件。

J: 如今也是这样。如果我们只看电视，我们的思想就会变得很单调。

T: 但是互联网的发展改变了这种状况。现在你很容易就能上网，看看世界上正发生着些什么。代替仅仅十几个频道的是数不清的网页。所以消息封锁和政治鼓动变得不再可能了。

J: 所以你能拓宽自己的视野，看到世界上更多的事情。

T: 除此之外，互联网还提供给你表达自己意见的渠道。你可以写下几乎任何你想说的事情，来表达你对此同意或反对的意见。它保证了你的话语权。同时，政府还可能看到人们写在博客和 BBS 上的东西，从而更好地评判公众舆论。

J: 因此,互联网对我们和政府都有益处。它可以帮助政府决策。

**核心词汇记一记**

**Words Storm**

| | | |
|---|---|---|
| misleading | [mis'li:diŋ] | *a.*误导的 |
| blockade | [blɔ'keid] | *n.*封锁 |
| propaganda | [ˌprɔpə'gændə] | *n.*宣传 |
| guarantee | [ˌgærən'ti:] | *v.*担保 |

**Phrases**

| | |
|---|---|
| negative coverage | 负面报道 |
| public opinion | 公众舆论 |

# 74. American Dream

## 美国梦

### 知识链接 拓展视野，掌握背景知识

美国梦（American Dream）产生于英国对美国的殖民时期，发展于19世纪，是一种相信只要在美国经过努力不懈地奋斗便能获得美好生活的理想，亦即人们必须通过自己的勤奋、勇气、创意和决心迈向繁荣，而非依赖于特定的社会阶级和他人的援助。许多欧洲移民都是抱着实现美国梦的理想而前往美国的。尽管有些人批评美国梦过度强调了物质财富在衡量胜利和快乐上扮演的角色，但许多美国人的确认为，这种获得成功的机会在世界上其他国家是找不到也并不存在的。《马丁·伊登》、《了不起的盖茨比》和《美国的悲剧》从不同的历史时期和角度揭示了“美国梦”的幻灭。

### 难点点拨 知识难点看一看，情景实战热热身

1. have fear doing sth. 害怕做某事

   We have no fear taking risks and facing challenges.

   我们不怕冒险，也不怕面对挑战。

2. regulate 控制，调控

   He made a detailed schedule to regulate his everyday life.

   他制订了很详细的时间表来规范自己的日常生活。

3. be rewarded with 收获到某物

   I fought hard only to be rewarded with failure.

   我努力奋斗，却失败了。

4. be sure to 肯定

   You are sure to fail.

   你肯定要失败。

## 情景实战 跟着老外听一听，读一读，练一练

**会话 1**

Allen: In the future I would like to be a great person.

Luke: Dream high! Anyone can be great if they strive hard enough. Have you heard of the "American Dream"?

A: Of course I have. We Americans, unlike people in many countries, are more energetic and motivated toward progress and change.

L: We are descendants of puritan pilgrims. On the one hand, we are influenced by puritan ideas, which say, "everyone should live in perfect discipline and strive hard for God's favor", on the other hand we inherited the pioneering spirit from our forefathers. We have no fear taking risks and facing challenges.

A: That's a reasonable claim I agree. In America anyone can become a government official, even become a millionaire. Have you seen the movie *The Pursuit of Happiness*?

L: Will Smith starred in it. He is a poor father, so poor that even his wife leaves him, but he strives with unrelenting tenacity and finally wins through. It's a typical motivational story.

A: It's quite inspirational and epitomizes the American ideology. It tells us that we should keep cool even in the face of adversity and then fight back to realize our dreams.

艾伦：我将来想做个伟大的人。

卢克：理想远大些好。如果努力奋斗，那么每个人都会成功。你知道"美国梦"吗？

A：当然。我们美国人和其他国家的人不一样，我们精力更加旺盛，而且更能适应社会进步和外部变化。

L：我们是清教徒朝圣者的后代。一方面，我们深受清教徒思想的影响，每个人都很自律，并且努力为得到上帝的恩惠而奋斗。另一方面，我们还从祖先那儿继承了开拓精神，我们不怕冒险，也不怕面对挑战。

A：很有道理。每个人都可以成为政府官员，每个人都能成为百万富翁。你看过电影《当幸福来敲门》吗？

L：威尔·史密斯主演的。他是一个贫穷的父亲，穷到他妻子因此而离开了他，但是他尽自己最大的努力去奋斗并且最终成功了。这是一个典型的励志故事。

A：这是典型的美国梦的故事，非常有激励意义。他告诉人们即使处在困境中也要保持冷静，然后奋力扭转局势，以实现自己的梦想。

### 核心词汇记一记

#### Words Storm

| | | |
|---|---|---|
| energetic | [ˌenəˈdʒetik] | *a.* 精力充沛的 |
| descendant | [diˈsendənt] | *n.* 后代 |
| puritan | [ˈpjuəritn] | *n.* 清教徒 |
| pilgrim | [ˈpilgrim] | *n.* 朝圣者 |
| inherit | [inˈherit] | *v.* 继承 |
| tenacity | [tiˈnæsiti] | *n.* 坚韧 |

#### Phrases

| | |
|---|---|
| pioneering spirit | 先锋精神 |
| in the face of | 面对 |

## 会话 2

Billy: I am reading *The Autobiography of Benjamin Franklin*. He is such a great person and has so many remarkable achievements to his credit. He made a detailed schedule to regulate his everyday life.

Dennis: It reminds me of a scene. In the story *The Great Gatsby*, Gatsby also designs a time table. But in that book it is a complete negation of the American dream. Personally I don't place any credence in that dream either.

B: Why not? Look at Franklin? He is the good example!

D: I'd rather believe in Naturalism, this philosophy donates that man is powerless in front of his destiny. Whatever he does to try to get change it is doomed to fail. Look at the character Gatsby, he bootlegs to gain money and dreams of his love Daisy coming back to him. Then look to the ending? He is a poor scapegoat, and no one loves him. He is just rich.

B: You are so pessimistic, buddy. The reality is that you have to fight hard, maybe you will fight hard only to be rewarded with failure, but at least there is always the possibility of success. But if you don't try then you are sure to fail.

D: You are right. But I still doubt the so-called "American Dream".

比 利：我正在读《本杰明·富兰克林自传》，他是个很伟大的人，取得了很多重大成就。他制订了很详细的时间表来规范自己的日常生活。

丹尼斯：这让我想到了另一个场景，在《了不起的盖茨比》里面，盖茨比也制作了一个时间表，但那本书却彻底否定了美国梦。就我个人来说也不太相信这个东西。

B：为什么？看看富兰克林，他就是个绝好的例子。

D：我更相信自然主义，我认为人在命运面前是渺小的。无论他做什么来改变命运的安排，他都注定要失败。看看盖茨比吧，他靠走私酒来挣钱，希望能够让黛西回到他身边，但是最后怎样？他成了可怜的替罪羔羊。没人爱他，他只是有钱而已。

B：哥们，你太悲观了。问题是你总要努力奋斗。可能你努力奋斗了，最后却失败了，但是起码还有成功的可能，但是如果你不去奋斗，那么你就必定失败。

D：是的，但是我还是对所谓的"美国梦"表示怀疑。

### 核心词汇记一记

#### Words Storm

autobiography [ɔːtəbai'ɔgrəfi] *n.* 自传
schedule ['skedʒuəl] *n.* 时间表
negation [ni'geiʃən] *n.* 否定
naturalism ['nætʃərəlizəm] *n.* 自然主义
bootleg ['buːtleg] *v.* 走私酒类
scapegoat ['skeipgəut] *n.* 替罪羊
pessimistic [ˌpesi'mistik] *a.* 悲观的

#### Phrases

be doomed to 注定

# Bits and Pieces 点点滴滴

## 75. Philosophy

## 哲学思潮

### 知识链接 拓展视野，掌握背景知识

所谓哲学，归根结底就是研究人类认识发展规律的科学。哲学的“有用”是因为它是统一切学问的万学之学；哲学的“无用”是因为它不直接致力于解决具体的问题。哲学的特征在于追问本质，不断反思。内容上，哲学的反思对象无所不包；深度上，哲学的反思是无穷无尽的。现实中，我们可以借用哲学的思维方式，但是不能照搬哲学的思维方式。

### 难点点拨 知识难点看一看，情景实战热热身

1. a bunch of 一群，一把

   A bunch of prisoners get their limbs tied up, standing in a cave.

   一群囚犯的腿脚都被绑了起来，站在一个山洞里。

2. speculation 思考，思索

   The ontological speculation may even exhaust you and frighten you.

   思考存在论的有关问题会让你筋疲力尽，惊恐不已。

3. the way of doing 做事情的方式

   The dialectical way of thinking, anyway, is great.

   不管怎样，辩证思想是很伟大的。

4. be borrowed from 从……借用而来

   His materialistic thoughts are borrowed from Feuerbach.

   他的唯物主义思想来自于费尔巴哈。

5. on one's own 自己做，独立完成

   You need to think on your own.

   你需要自己思考。

## 情景实战 跟着老外听一听，读一读，练一练

**会话 1**

Mike: Sometimes I doubt the reality of what I'm seeing.

Josh: You are great, buddy. You are just as great as *Plato* and *Cant*.

M: What do you mean?

J: Plato, in *The Republic*, gave a famous fable to explain his idea. A bunch of prisoners get their limbs tied up, standing in a cave. They face a wall and cannot turn their heads, while a campfire is burning behind them. What they can see, consequently, is only shadows on the wall. Then they mistake shadows for real things.

M: What's the meaning of it?

J: So what we see in our life might also be mere shadows. We cannot see the essence of things with our eyes. Kant also said that the thing in itself is unknowable. If you see it with your eyes, you get only a shallow image and cannot see what it was originally like, because your eyes themselves affect the vision.

M: It sounds metaphysical.

迈克：有时我会怀疑我所看到事物的真实性。

乔希：兄弟，你太棒了。你简直像柏拉图和康德一样伟大。

M：什么意思？

J：柏拉图在《理想国》里，讲了一个著名的寓言来阐释他的观点。一群囚犯的腿脚都被绑了起来，站在一个山洞里。他们面对着一堵墙，而且没法回头看，他们身后有一堆篝火在燃烧。结果他们所能看到的只是墙上的影子。于是他们就把阴影当成了真正的东西。

M：这个寓言背后有什么深意呢？

J：我们在现实生活中所看到的不过是一些影子。我们无法用眼睛看清事物的本质。康德同样认为事物本身是不可知的。如果你用肉眼来观察，你所得到的不过是表面的现象，而不能看到它本来的面目。因为你的眼睛本身就能影响视觉。

M：听起来好形而上学呀。

### 核心词汇记一记

**Words Storm**

cave [keiv] *n.* 洞穴

campfire ['kæmpfaiə] *n.* 篝火

consequently ['kɔnsikwəntli] *ad.* 因此

metaphysical [ˌmetə'fizikl] *a.* 形而上学的

**Phrases**

tie up 束紧，拴牢

**会话 2**

Vince: How do you like the Marxist Philosophy?

Jean: I think it's the most scientific one, but it still cannot explain some mysterious things such as the relationship between body and soul.

V: The dialectical way of thinking, anyway, is great.

J: It's borrowed from Hegel who believed that everything is a paradoxical entity comprising both positive elements and negative elements. Good and evil mingle together. However, Hegel didn't believe in materialism. He proposed a theory that the evolutionary history of human beings is indeed the consequence of the advance of "absolute geist".

V: So he admitted that it's spirit that decides material?

J: Yes. That's the reason why we call him an idealist.

V: I'm a little bit confused by all this. Who can give me the best answer?

J: There is no best answer in philosophy. Philosophers give their ideas. You can agree or disagree, but eventually you'll find none of them flawless and absolutely convincing. You need to think on your own.

文斯：你觉得马克思主义哲学怎么样？

琼：我觉得它是最科学的理论。但是它仍然不能解释一些神秘的事情，比如肉体和灵魂之间的关系。

V：不管怎样，辩证思想是很伟大的。

J：这是借鉴了黑格尔的一些理论。黑格尔认为所有的事情都是包含积极方面和消极方面的矛盾体，好的和不好的都混杂在一起。但是黑格尔不相信唯物主义。他提出了一个关于人类进化历史的理论，这是“绝对精神”进化的结果。

V：所以他承认精神决定物质啰？

J：是的。这就是我们称他为唯心主义者的原因。

V：我有点被这些东西搞糊涂了。谁能给我一个最佳答案？

J：哲学里是没有最佳答案的。哲学家们总是给出他们自己的思想观点。你可以同意，也可以不同意，但是最终你会发现，没有任何一个理论是没有瑕疵而绝对让人信服的。你需要自己思考。

### 核心词汇记一记

**Words Storm**

dialectical [daiə'lektikəl] *a.* 辩证的

materialism [mə'tiəriəlizəm] *n.* 唯物主义

flawless ['flɔːlis] *a.* 没有瑕疵的

convincing [kən'vinsiŋ] *a.* 令人信服的

**Phrases**

Marxist Philosophy 马克思主义哲学

paradoxical entity 矛盾体

# 76. The Meaning of Life

## 生命的意义

### 知识链接 拓展视野，掌握背景知识

生命的意义是一个深刻的哲学问题。这个概念通过许多相关问题体现出来，例如“我为何在此”、“什么是生命”、“生命的真谛是什么”等等。在历史长河中，它也是科学以及神学一直思索的主题。前人在不同的文化环境与意识形态背景下也给出了很多的多元化答案。阿尔贝·加缪指出，作为一个存在的人，人类用生命的价值和意义来说服自己：人的存在不是荒诞的。

### 难点点拨 知识难点看一看，情景实战热热身

1. This is the reason why... 这就是……的原因

   This is the reason why the Egyptians mummified the dead back in the days of the pyramids.

   这就是为什么埃及人早在修建金字塔的时期就制作木乃伊的原因。

2. give birth to sb. 生产，生育

   We preserve our body by giving birth to babies.

   我们通过繁育后代来延续我们的生命。

3. how come 怎么会……的?

   How come bad things are good to you?

   坏事情怎么会对你有好处呢?

4. a work of art 艺术品

   I take life as a work of art, say, a novel or a film.

   我把生活看做一件艺术品，比如一本小说，或者一部电影。

5. fall on/upon 降临

   If there is misfortune falling upon me, I'll just enjoy it and take it as a part of the story.

   如果不幸降临到了我身上，我就会欣然接受并且把这当成故事的一部分。

## 情景实战 跟着老外听一听，读一读，练一练

**会话 1**

Jesse: I'm confused as to why we live. By this I mean that every person must eventually die. So what's the point? Why are we fighting our way hard?

Laurie: Listen up and don't be silly. We're living because God has created us and he wants us to live happily. So you'd better stop thinking about this ridiculous thing.

J: You mean the meaning of life is ridiculous? No way, absolutely not! You want to hear my view?

L: Aren't you just confused?

J: I have my theory! I think a human being lives on earth only for a while, but he intends to prolong his life to reach eternity.

L: Nobody wants to die, that's true.

J: I didn't mean that. I mean, he wants to preserve both his body and his soul as long as he can.

L: This is the reason why the Egyptians mummified the dead back in the days of the pyramids.

J: You are just diverting the conversation. My meaning is that we preserve our body by giving birth to babies, and we preserve our soul by lecturing and writing books.

L: That sounds reasonable. But there are so many people who have never written a book.

杰西：我对于我们为何而生感到困惑。每个人最后都得死，那么活着是为什么？我们为什么要这么努力地奋斗呢？

劳里：听着，别傻了。我们活着是因为上帝创造了我们，他想要我们过得幸福。所以你最好别想这些可笑的问题。

J：你是说思考生命的意义很可笑？不，绝对不是的，你想听听我的想法吗？

L：你刚才不是说很困惑吗？

J：但是我有自己的理论。我觉得人活在世上只有一瞬间，但是他却想方设法延长生命至永恒。

L：没人想死，这是真的。

J：我不是那个意思。我是说，他想要尽可能长时间保存自己的肉体和灵魂。

L：这就是为什么埃及人早在修建金字塔的时期就制作木乃伊的原因。

J：你别转移话题啊。我是说，我们通过繁育后代来延续我们的生命，通过演说和写书来保存我们的灵魂。

L：听起来很有道理。但是从没写过书的人太多了。

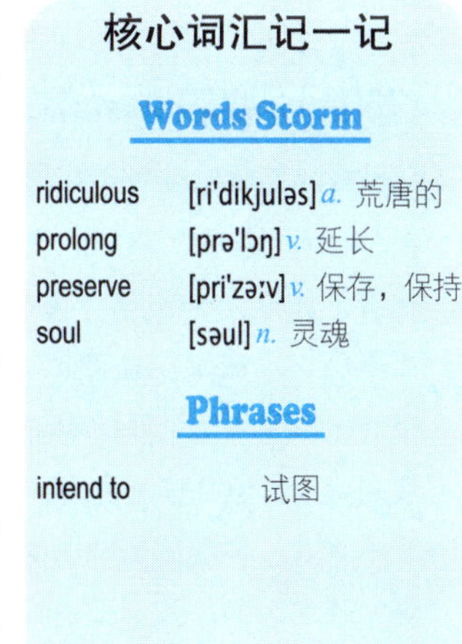

核心词汇记一记

**Words Storm**

ridiculous [ri'dikjuləs] *a.* 荒唐的
prolong [prə'lɔŋ] *v.* 延长
preserve [pri'zəːv] *v.* 保存，保持
soul [səul] *n.* 灵魂

**Phrases**

intend to 试图

**会话 2**

Tiffany: Many people feel their life meaningless. They become desperate and commit suicide.

Allison: But life is good, isn't it? Even bad things are good.

T: What? How come bad things are good to you?

A: I take life as a work of art, say, a novel or a film.

T: So what?

A: Even a tragic story can be a good one. If there is misfortune falling upon me, I'll just enjoy it and take it as a part of the story.

T: Few people can really do this and it's certainly easier to say than to do.

A: I'm a writer, you see. What I want is twists and turns in my life, rather than pure happiness. I need to suffer, so that I can see my life as a good story, and then write it all down.

T: I see. But you don't really love the suffering, surely?

A: I don't love the suffering, but appreciate it for the insights. When the unpleasant things fall into my life, I'll just smile, and say to myself. "Well then, another chance for me to get tougher!"

T: Life is always like that. I really admire your courage.

A: Hemingway once said, "A man can be destroyed, but not defeated." I think he is right.

蒂凡尼: 很多人觉得生命毫无意义。他们变得绝望，甚至寻短见。

艾莉森: 但是生活很美好，不是吗？即使坏的事情也是好的。

T: 什么？坏事情怎么会对你有好处呢？

A: 我把生活看做一件艺术品，比如一本小说，或者一部电影。

T: 那又怎样？

A: 即使是悲剧故事也是好故事呀！如果不幸降临到了我身上，我就会欣然接受并且把这当成故事的一部分。

T: 很少有人可以做到这样。说起来容易做起来难。

A: 你看，我是一个作家。我希望我的生活中充满酸甜苦辣，而不仅仅是快乐。我需要经受磨难，只有这样我才能把自己的生活当作一个好故事，然后记录下来。

T: 我知道了，但是你不是真地喜欢遭受痛苦吧？

A: 我不喜欢，但我感激痛苦，它让我看清了这个世界。当苦难来临的时候，我会笑着对自己说“好吧，另一个让你变得坚强的机会到来了”。

T: 生活总是那样的。我真地佩服你的勇气。

A: 海明威曾经说过“一个人可以被毁灭，但绝不可以被打败。”我觉得他说得很对。

### 核心词汇记一记

**Words Storm**

meaningless ['miːniŋlis] *a.* 没有意义的

misfortune [mis'fɔːtʃən] *n.* 灾祸

suffering ['sʌfəriŋ] *n.* 受苦

**Phrases**

commit suicide 自杀

twists and turns 迂回曲折

# 77. Historical Stories

## 历史故事

### 知识链接　拓展视野，掌握背景知识

“在从前无人到来的地方，我们希望移植一个民族。”17世纪初，英国开始向北美殖民。最初的北美移民主要是一些失去土地的农民、生活艰苦的工人以及受宗教迫害的清教徒。定居后，英国对北美殖民地采取剥削、压制政策。由于美国资本主义的蓬勃发展，民族意识逐渐觉醒，殖民地人民和英国殖民者之间爆发了激烈的战争，美国取得胜利，获得了民族独立。随后的美国内战废除了奴隶制，为资本主义的发展扫清了障碍，为美国经济的腾飞奠定了基础。

### 难点点拨　知识难点看一看，情景实战热热身

1．mistake sth. for sth. 把某物误当作某物

He mistook it for India, and called the local inhabitants “Indians”.

他误以为到了印度，所以称当地居民为“印度人”。

2．convert sb. into Christianity (a religion) 使某人信仰基督教

They wanted to convert local “barbarians” into Christianity, and share the favor of God with them.

他们想要把本地的“野蛮人”改造成基督徒，与他们一同分享上帝的恩惠。

3．gratitude to sb. 对某人的感激之情

On that day we eat turkey and express our gratitude to those forthcoming Indians.

在那天我们吃火鸡来表达对好心的印第安人的感谢。

4．the cause of sth. 某事的原因

What do you think is the major cause of the civil war in America?

你觉得美国内战的主要原因是什么？

5．be accompanied by 伴随着

The founding of America was not accompanied by the emancipation of the black.

美国的建立并没有伴随黑人的解放。

## 情景实战 跟着老外听一听，读一读，练一练

**会话 1**

Kenny: Can you tell me something about early America?

Raymond: Of course. In 1492, Christopher Columbus sailed westward and found the American continent. He mistook it for India, and called the local inhabitants "Indians".

K: That's a funny mistake. He thought the earth was round, but much smaller than it actually is.

R: After the discovery of America, European people wanted to sail and settle there. In 1620, the ship called "Mayflower" reached the east coast of America. The settlers opened up a place of their own. They were Puritans and they regarded this voyage as a pilgrimage. They wanted to convert local "barbarians" into Christianity, and share the favor of God with them.

K: So they had contact with local Indians?

R: After their arrival, they met harsh problems and had nothing to eat. Many of them died. The kind-hearted Indians then came to their help by giving them life necessities and teaching them how to hunt animals and grow crops.

K: So they should really thank the Indians. They were so good to them.

R: That's why we have Thanksgiving Day now. On that day we eat turkey and express our gratitude to those forthcoming Indians.

肯尼: 你能告诉我一些关于早期美国的事情吗?

雷蒙德: 当然。1492 年，克里斯托弗·哥伦布向西航行，并且发现了美洲大陆。他误以为到了印度，所以称当地居民为"印度人"。

K: 这个错误挺好玩的。他认为地球是圆的，但是他想象中的地球比实际要小很多。

R: 美洲发现后，欧洲人就想定居在这里。1620 年，"五月花"号抵达美洲东海岸，殖民者们开辟了一块属于他们自己的领土。他们都是清教徒，把这次航行看做一次朝圣。他们想要把本地的"野蛮人"改造成基督徒，与他们一同分享上帝的恩惠。

K: 所以他们和本地的印第安人就有了接触?

R: 他们到达后，遇到了严峻的问题，没有吃的东西。很多人都饿死了。好心的印第安人帮助了他们，给了他们生活必需品，并且教他们如何狩猎和种地。

K: 所以他们应该好好感谢印第安人啰！因为印弟安人对他们太好了。

R: 这就是感恩节的由来。在那天我们吃火鸡来表达对好心的印第安人的感谢。

### 核心词汇记一记

**Words Storm**

westward ['westwəd] *ad.* 向西

pilgrimage ['pilgrimidʒ] *n.* 朝圣

barbarian [bɑː'bɛəriən] *n.* 野蛮人

Christianity [ˌkristi'ænəti] *n.* 基督教

forthcoming ['fɔːθ'kʌmiŋ] *a.* 好心的

**Phrases**

open up 开发

of one's own 属于某人自己的

## 会话 2

Juliet: What do you think was the major cause of the civil war in America?

Tom: After the British people settled on the continent, they fought for independence from Britain, and founded a new country, America.

J: I know that. Just go straight to the point.

T: OK. What I just wanted to say is that the founding of America was not accompanied by the emancipation of the black people. The black men or Negros still remained in America as slaves. Later, in the North slavery was abolished, and northerners demanded southerners to do the same thing.

J: So you think the abolition of slavery is the cause of the war?

T: Not exactly. It's just superficial. There is another reason. The northern industrial economy and the southern plantation economy clashed. The North needed raw materials from the South, where slavery was seen as an obstacle. Northerners then wanted to end slavery and liberate all black people.

J: Was the war fierce?

T: Yes. Many people lost their lives in the war. Finally the North won, and the black men had their freedom, at least it was the beginning, but the 'civil rights movement' later became another issue.

朱丽叶：你觉得美国内战的主要原因是什么？

汤 姆：英国人定居这片大陆之后，他们想要脱离英国的统治取得独立，建立一个全新的国家——美国。

J：我知道，切入重点就行。

T：好。我刚才想要说的是美国的建立并没有伴随黑人的解放。黑人仍然还是奴隶。之后，北方的奴隶制度废除了，然后北方的黑人要求南方殖民者也这么做。

J：所以你觉得奴隶制的废除是导致这次战争的原因？

T：也不全是，这只是表面原因，还有另一个原因。北方的工业经济和南方的种植园经济发生了冲突，北方需要来自南方的原料，而南方的奴隶制度被看做是一种障碍。北方人于是就想结束奴隶制，解放所有的黑人。

J：那场战争激烈吗？

T：激烈。很多人都战死了。最后北方赢了，黑人得到了自由，至少是初步自由吧。后来我们又有了民权运动，进一步解放了黑人。

### 核心词汇记一记

**Words Storm**

emancipation [i,mænsi'peiʃən] *n.* 解放

slavery ['sleivəri] *n.* 奴隶制

abolish [ə'bɔliʃ] *v.* 废除

**Phrases**

industrial economy 工业经济

plantation economy 种植园经济

# 78. King and Queen

# 国王和王后

## 知识链接 拓展视野，掌握背景知识

在君主立宪制国家，国王或王后不再享有决定国家大事的权利，而是作为一个国家的象征，是身份和地位的象征。很多小报都喜欢八卦王室的各种事情，震惊世界的戴安娜王妃的车祸事件就与狗仔队的追踪不无关系。

## 难点点拨 知识难点看一看，情景实战热热身

1．hold power over sb. 对某人有权力

In earlier times the King held absolute power over his subjects.

在以前，国王对他的臣民拥有绝对权力。

2．in the grip of 在某人手中

The real power is in the grip of the British Parliament.

真正的权力掌握在英国国会的手里。

3．participate in 参加

They participate in a lot of important social activities as prominent figures.

他们作为重要人物出席很多重要的社交活动。

4．ascend the throne 登基

Now they even want Prince William, the son of Charles, to ascend the throne instead of his father.

现在他们甚至想让查尔斯的儿子威廉王子代替他登上王位。

5．graduate from 从……毕业

He graduated from Eton, and joined the Royal Air Force as a pilot.

他从伊顿中学毕业后就参加了皇家空军，成了一名飞行员。

## 情景实战 跟着老外听一听，读一读，练一练

**会话 1**

Rice: Does the British Queen still enjoy political power?

Ted: Technically not. In earlier times the King held absolute power over his subjects. He could decide almost everything about the fate of the kingdom. After the Glorious Revolution and the Bill of Rights, the old feudal forces were in some sense eliminated and a new government was established. Britain stepped into democracy.

R: But now Queen Elizabeth II is still the titular leader of the whole kingdom as well as the British Commonwealth of Nations.

T: Yes, but only titular. The real power is strongly in the grip of the British Parliament. Technically, it's the Queen who appoints ministers and other officials, but actually it's the Prime Minister and the dominant party in the Parliament whose words really count.

R: So now the royal family must feel depressed, because they have lost their power.

T: Not at all. They are rich, have no worries about their life and they participate in a lot of important social activities as prominent figures.

R: They should shoulder some social responsibilities. They are supposed to always do the right thing and keep their grace. This is politics.

赖斯：英国国王现在还享有政治权力吗？

泰德：实际上没有。在以前，国王对他的臣民拥有绝对权力。他可以决定关乎王国命运的一切事务。但是自从光荣革命制订了《权利法案》后，古老的封建势力在某种程度上被肃清了，一个新政府取而代之。英国由此步入了民主时代。

R：但是现在女王伊丽莎白二世依然是整个王国和英联邦国家名义上的领袖。

T：是的，但也只是名义上的。真正的权力掌握在英国国会的手里。理论上来说，是由女王来任命部长和其他官员，但是实际上说了算的是首相和国会的执政党。

R：所以现在皇室一定觉得很沮丧吧，因为他们失去了曾经的权力。

T：一点都不。他们很富有，不用为生活而发愁。他们作为重要人物出席很多重要的社交活动。

R：他们应该负起一些社会责任。他们总是要做正确的事情并且保持优雅。这就是政治。

### 核心词汇记一记

**Words Storm**

subject ['sʌbdʒekt] *n.* 国民
fate [feit] *n.* 命运
feudal ['fjuːdəl] *a.* 封建的
eliminate [i'limineit] *v.* 除去
titular ['titjulə] *a.* 有名无实的
appoint [ə'pɔint] *v.* 委任
dominant ['dɔminənt] *a.* 支配的
prominent ['prɔminənt] *a.* 显著的

**Phrases**

political power 政治权力
absolute power 绝对权力
step into 进入

**会话 2**

Markus: Who will be the King of England after Queen Elizabeth II?

Ronald: Charles, the Queen's eldest son.

M: Was he the husband of Princess Diana?

R: Yes. Diana was the princess of Wales. They got married in the early 1980s, but later they got a divorce.

M: I remember that! Charles got another woman, and Diana was saddened. What a pity. She died in a car crash. The whole world was shocked.

R: Many people put the blame on Charles, thinking of him as a betrayer. Now they even want Prince William, the son of Charles, to ascend the throne instead of his father.

M: William! I love him. He is so handsome.

R: Indeed he is quite popular. He graduated from Eton, and joined the Royal Air Force as a pilot. Then he graduated from the University of St. Andrews. He got a bad reputation for flying military helicopters to visit his friends. But most people still love him.

M: His love stories with girls are also in the public spotlight.

R: Yes. The general public has a great interest in whom will become his Princess in the future.

马库斯：伊丽莎白二世之后谁会成为英国的国王呢？

罗纳德：查尔斯，他是王后的长子。

M: 他是戴安娜王妃的丈夫吗？

R: 是的，戴安娜是威尔士的公主，他们在 19 世纪 80 年代早期结婚了，但是后来他们离婚了。

M: 我知道。查尔斯有了另外的女人，戴安娜很伤心。真是可惜！她死于一场车祸，整个世界都震惊了。

R: 很多人都指责查尔斯，认为他是个背叛者。现在他们甚至想让查尔斯的儿子威廉王子代替他登上王位。

M: 威廉！我很爱他，他好帅的！

R: 他确实很受欢迎。他从伊顿中学毕业后就参加了皇家空军，成了一名飞行员。后来他又从圣安德鲁斯大学顺利毕业。他也因为驾着军用直升机去拜访朋友而有些坏名声，但是大部分人还是很喜欢他。

M: 关于他和一些女孩的爱情故事也暴露在公众的聚光灯下。

R: 是的，公众们对于将来谁能成为王妃是很感兴趣的。

**核心词汇记一记**

**Words Storm**

sadden [sædn] *v.* 悲哀
betrayer [bi'treiə] *n.* 背叛者
ascend [ə'send] *v.* 登上
throne ['θrəun] *n.* 王位
reputation [ˌrepju'teiʃən] *n.* 名声
spotlight ['spɔtlait] *n.* 聚光灯

**Phrases**

car crash 车祸
put blame on 责怪

# 79. Anecdotes

# 趣闻轶事

## 知识链接 拓展视野，掌握背景知识

名人轶事一直以来都是人们津津乐道的话题。从科学家到文学家，从音乐家到政治领袖，人们仿佛有无穷无尽的话题可以挖掘，而且一传十，十传百，越传越玄乎，恨不得把这些名人的私生活也搞得跟他们的丰功伟绩一样伟大而神奇。有些名人轶事可能被人们妖魔化了，但是无风不起浪，事情不能是空穴来风，透过这些轶事我们还是可以从一个侧面窥探到名人的个性和生活方式。

## 难点点拨 知识难点看一看，情景实战热热身

1. at the age of... 在几岁的时候

   He was able to play harpsichord at the age of four.

   他 4 岁就能弹古式钢琴了。

2. gain/lose popularity 获得 / 失去名气

   When he grew older, he lost his popularity.

   当他再大些的时候，就不那么出名了。

3. cut off 割掉

   He cut off one of his own ears.

   他割掉了自己的一只耳朵。

4. all kinds of... 各种各样的

   Once she hurled all kinds of abuse at Socrates, and the poor husband could do nothing but listen timidly.

   有次她向苏格拉底破口大骂，这位可怜的丈夫除了乖乖地听着什么也不能做。

5. giant 巨人，某一领域的大师

   A giant of philosophy died in such a misery. History is always so cruel.

   一位哲学大师就这样凄惨地死去。历史总是如此残酷。

## 情景实战 跟着老外听一听，读一读，练一练

**会话 1**

Nick: Do you know, Mozart was a genius even in his childhood.

Alex: Mozart the composer?

N: Yes. He was able to play harpsichord at the age of four. He even wrote a concerto for a band in the same year.

A: Incredible. When I was four I couldn't even read well.

N: At the age of 17 he began to travel around Europe to compose music and play musical instruments for the royal families and other aristocrats. He was just like a star.

A: What a genius!

N: But when he grew older he lost his popularity. After marriage he and his wife lead a poor life. One wintry evening a friend who came to visit him saw the couple dancing in the house through the windowpane, but when he entered the house he found they danced only because they didn't have enough money to make a fire.

A: It is terrible. Many great artists were ignored by the public when they were alive. Do you know Vincent van Gough?

N: Yes. His paintings were not acknowledged. He was frustrated in his relationships with women and had mental problems as well. He cut off one of his own ears. Finally he committed suicide.

尼　克: 你知道吗，莫扎特在童年时期就是个天才。

阿历克斯: 你是说作曲家莫扎特?

N: 是的，他 4 岁就能弹古式钢琴了，同年甚至还为乐队写了协奏曲。

A: 太不可思议了。我 4 岁的时候还不怎么识字呢。

N: 他 17 岁的时候开始环游整个欧洲，为皇室和其他贵族撰写乐曲并且演奏乐器，就像明星一样。

A: 好一个天才!

N: 但是当他再大些的时候，就不那么出名了。结婚后他过着清贫的生活。一个寒冷的晚上，他的一个朋友去拜访他，从窗外发现夫妻俩在房子里跳舞，但是等他进了屋才发现他们跳舞仅仅是因为没钱生火太冷了。

A: 太糟糕了！很多伟大的艺术家生前都被大众所忽略，你知道文森特・梵高吗?

N: 知道。他的画作当时得不到人们的认可。他为情所困，精神出了问题，割掉了自己一只耳朵，最后自杀了。

### 核心词汇记一记

**Words Storm**

| | | |
|---|---|---|
| genius | ['dʒiːnjəs] | *n.* 天才 |
| composer | [kəm'pəuzə] | *n.* 作曲家 |
| concerto | [kən'tʃəːtəu] | *n.* 协奏曲 |
| aristocrat | ['æristəkræt] | *n.* 贵族 |
| popularity | [pɔpju'læriti] | *n.* 名气 |
| wintry | ['wintri] | *a.* 寒冷的，冬季的 |
| windowpane | ['windəupein] | *n.* 窗玻璃 |

**Phrases**

| | |
|---|---|
| play musical instrument | 演奏乐器 |
| royal families | 皇室 |
| make a fire | 生火 |

**会话 2**

Kevin: Do you know Socrates was henpecked?

Sandie: Really? You mean the great philosopher?

K: Yes. His wife was quite a shrew. Once she hurled all kinds of abuse at Socrates and the poor man could do nothing but listen timidly. Then she poured a basin of cold water over him, soaking him completely. Guess what he said? He said "I knew that after thunder there would be rain!"

S: Ha ha. He was really henpecked. But in my view it's more of respect than fear. Man will never fear a woman if he doesn't love her.

K: Maybe you're right. But his life was a tragedy none the less. He was considered as guilty for "misleading the young men of Athens", and was sentenced to death. He remained composed at the last moment, and talked calmly with his wife, friends and relatives. After that he drank the cup of hemlock, which is a poison, and died soon after. Before death, he told his friends that he had eaten a chicken of his neighbor, and wanted his friends to pay for it.

S: What a moving scene. A giant of philosophy died in such a misery. History is always so cruel.

凯文：你知道吗？苏格拉底怕老婆。

桑迪：真的吗？你是说那个大哲学家？

K：是的。他的老婆是个泼妇。有次她向苏格拉底破口大骂，这位可怜的丈夫除了乖乖地听着什么也不能做。然后她还向他老公泼了一脸盆冷水，弄得他全身都湿透了。然后你猜猜他说了什么，他说“我就知道雷声过后必有倾盆大雨”。

S：哈哈，他真是个“妻管严”。但是在我看来，与其说是怕老婆，更应该说是尊重老婆。如果一个男人不爱一个女人的话，他是不会怕她的。

K：可能吧。但是他的一生可是个悲剧。他以“误导雅典的年轻人”为罪名被判了死刑。他直到生命的最后一刻都保持着镇静，和他的妻子以及亲朋好友们平静地谈话。然后他就服毒而死。在他死之前，他告诉朋友说他吃了邻居家一只鸡，想让朋友帮他把钱还了。

S：多么令人感动的一幕啊！一位哲学大师就这样凄惨地死去。历史总是如此残酷。

### 核心词汇记一记

**Words Storm**

henpecked ['henpekt] *a.* 怕老婆的
philosopher [fi'lɔsəfə] *n.* 哲学家
shrew [ʃruː] *n.* 泼妇
abuse [ə'bjuːz] *n.* 辱骂
timid ['timid] *a.* 胆怯的
composed [kəm'pəuzd] *a.* 镇静的
hemlock ['hemlɔk] *n.* 毒芹

**Phrases**

in one's view 在……看来
be considered as 被当作

# 80. Library

## 恋上图书馆

## 知识链接 拓展视野，掌握背景知识

在传统意义上图书馆是收藏书和各种出版物的地方。然而，现在信息保存已经不只是保存图书，还包括DVD光盘等一些资料。因此，现代图书馆愈加被重新定义为能够无限制地获取多种来源、多种格式的信息的地方。另外，高校图书馆除了提供知识外，还有更为重要的作用，即形成校园文化，造就一种文化氛围。高尚的图书馆文化是一种强大的潜在教育力。

## 难点点拨 知识难点看一看，情景实战热热身

1. at a time 一次，同时

   The new library can accommodate more than a thousand people at a time.

   新图书馆能够同时容纳1000多人。

2. keep 持有，拿在手，保存

   How long can we keep a book borrowed there?

   我们借的书能看多久啊？

3. as long as 只要

   Anyone can borrow any book he wants as long as he is a citizen living in this city.

   只要是住在这个城市的公民，都可以去借他喜欢的书。

4. reference 参考文献

   I want to get some useful articles as the references of my term paper.

   我想为我的学期论文查找一些有用的文章作参考。

5. be familiar with 熟悉

   It seems I'm not quite familiar with this system.

   我好像对这个系统不太熟悉。

6. interlibrary loans 馆际互借

   We can get books through interlibrary loans.

   我们还可以通过馆际互借借到书。

## 情景实战 跟着老外听一听，读一读，练一练

**会话 1**

Willie: Have you been to the new library?

Alexandra: Yes, it is fantastic! The new library can accommodate more than a thousand people at a time. It has more than three million books. As a city library, it is enough for us to use.

W: How long can we borrow a book for?

A: A month. Anyone can borrow any book he wants as long as he is a citizen living in this city, but after one month the book must be returned, or else the borrower would be fined.

W: Books cannot be renewed there?

A: Yes, you can renew it three times. This way you can keep the book as long as three months.

W: Good, next Sunday I will go there and borrow a novel to read. Can you go with me? I don't know how to find the right book.

A: It's easy, you can use the computer catalogue to find the number of the novel, then go straight to the right section and the right bookshelf to get it. I can go with you next weekend and show you.

W: Thank you. You know I am very fond of reading.

A: You're welcome.

威利：你去过新图书馆吗？

亚历山德拉：去过呀，非常棒！新图书馆能够同时容纳 1000 多人，藏有 300 多万册图书。作为一座城市图书馆，足够我们用的了。

W：我们借的书能看多久啊？

A：一个月。只要是住在这个城市的公民，都可以去借他喜欢的书。但是必须在一个月之内把书还了，不然就得交罚款。

W：难道不能续借吗？

A：可以的，你可以续借 3 次。所以你最长可以保管 3 个月。

W：太好了。下周日我要去借一本小说。你能跟我一起去吗？我不知道如何找到我想要的书。

A：很简单的，你可以用电脑目录查找小说的编码，然后直接到指定的分区和书架去找。下周我会跟你一起去的。

W：太感谢了。你知道我很爱读书的。

A：不客气。

### 核心词汇记一记

**Words Storm**

accommodate [ə'kɔmədeit] v. 容纳
citizen ['sitizn] n. 公民
renew [ri'njuː] v. 更新
catalogue ['kætəlɔg] n. 目录
bookshelf ['bukʃelf] n. 书架

**Phrases**

be fond of 喜欢

**会话 2**

Tom: Hey, Jack, what are you doing here?

Jack: I'm trying to use this database. I need to find some useful articles as references for my term paper. Could you help me? I'm not familiar with this system.

T: Oh. Just input the key words here, choose the right topic, and click here. You will have a long list of articles, many of which are written by famous scholars in this field. Then go through some of them to get the information you need. I'm going to return my books, but I'm afraid they are two weeks overdue. I will have to sweet-talk the librarian there and pay the fine. Hopefully she will go gently on me!

J: Good luck.

T: Then I'll go search for some periodicals myself. I'm also writing a research paper on Chinese history.

J: Maybe I can help you. You just go ahead to do your business, and I'll find something for you here.

T: Thanks.

J: If you cannot find what you need, you can try the libraries of other universities. Maybe they will have what you need. We can get books through interlibrary loans.

T: Good. See you later.

汤姆：嘿，杰克，你在这儿干吗呢？

杰克：我在用数据库呢。我想为我的学期论文查找一些有用的文章作参考。你能帮一下我吗？我好像对这个系统不太熟悉。

T：你只需要把关键词输进去，选择正确的话题，然后点击这儿就行。你会得到一长串的文章题目列表，很多都是这个领域的著名学者写的。然后浏览一下选择你需要的信息就行了。顺便说一下，我正要去还书，但是已经过期两周了，我得去讨好下图书管理员，因为我需要交一下罚金。希望她对我温柔点。

J：祝你好运。

T：然后我还要去查些期刊，我现在也在写一篇研究论文呢，是关于中国历史的。

J：也许我能帮帮你。你赶快先去办你的事情吧，我在这儿可以帮你找一下资料。

T：谢谢了。

J：如果你找不到需要的资料，就试试其他学校的图书馆，也许能找到需要的书。我们还可以通过馆际互借借到书。

T：太好了，再见。

**核心词汇记一记**

**Words Storm**

database ['deitəbeis] *n.* 数据库
reference ['refərəns] *n.* 参考
input ['input] *v.* 输入
scholar ['skɔlə] *n.* 学者
overdue ['əuvə'dju:] *a.* 过期的
periodical [ˌpiəri'ɔdikl] *n.* 期刊

**Phrases**

term paper 学期论文
pay the fine 交罚金

# 81. How to Learn Foreign Language

## 这样学外语

### 知识链接 拓展视野，掌握背景知识

20世纪80年代中国有句叫得很响的口号叫做“学好数理化，走遍全天下”。而现代中国社会，则讲究外语、驾照、计算机样样精通，这才算得上合格的新时代人才。神州大地各种各样的外语补习班如雨后春笋般涌现出来。去补习班学外语真的有必要吗？外语究竟要怎样才能学好呢？我们一起来看一下吧。

### 难点点拨 知识难点看一看，情景实战热热身

1．have a grasp of sth. 掌握某事

You need to have a good grasp of those most commonly used words.

你需要好好掌握这些最常用的单词。

2．stick to 坚持

It would be good for you if you stick to a plan to review what you have learned.

如果你能每天坚持复习学过的内容的话就会好一些。

3．in the first place 首要的

Language, in the first place, is for oral communication.

学习一门语言，最重要的就是口头交流。

4．endow sb. with sth. 赋予某人某物

Just following your textbook will endow you with enough sense of French.

你只要跟着课本来就能够找到学法语的感觉。

5．a word of 一点（语言）

Now I cannot speak a word of it.

现在我已经一个单词都不会说了。

## 情景实战 跟着老外听一听，读一读，练一练

**会话 1**

Teddy: I'm learning French at the moment, but I can never remember those irregular conjugations. Besides, I have to memorize many new words, some of which are so complicated in spelling.

Andrew: Begin with simple words—prendre, entendre, etudier... You need to have a good grasp of those most commonly used words.

T: And I often forget what I have learned. That's a big problem.

A: It would be good for you if you stick to a plan to review what you have learned. Reviewing old knowledge helps you hold it fast.

T: And I find it's hard for me to speak those words. I'm confused about the pronunciation.

A: You have to read them aloud repeatedly. Language, in the first place, is for oral communication. Speaking and listening are the most important. Reading and writing are not as urgent as that.

T: Do I need a better textbook? This book seems rather old-fashioned.

A: Sure, the newer a textbook is, the better it helps you. Try some famous textbooks such as *Reflets*, they are more scientifically designed compared with some books that are less authoritative.

泰 迪：我最近在学习法语。但是我实在记不住那些不规则的变位。而且，我每天都要记好多新单词，这些单词的拼写都很复杂。

安德鲁：那就从一些简单的单词开始嘛，像"prendre"，"entendre"，"etudier"什么的。你需要好好掌握这些最常用的单词。

T：我还经常忘记学过的单词。这是个很大的问题。

A：如果你能每天坚持复习学过的内容的话就会好一些。复习旧的知识会帮助你更快地掌握它。

T：而且我发现这些单词读起来很难，我都被那些发音搞糊涂了。

A：你必须要大声地反复来朗读。学习一门语言，最重要的就是口头交流，听和说是最重要的，而读和写则不像听说那样紧迫。

T：我是不是需要一本更好的教科书？这本书看起来很过时。

A：是的。教科书的版本越新，对你的帮助就越大。试试诸如《Reflects》之类的经典法语教材。这种教材比起那些不太权威的书来说，在编辑组织上更加科学。

### 核心词汇记一记

**Words Storm**

| | | |
|---|---|---|
| irregular | [i'regjulə] | *a.* 不规则的 |
| conjugation | [ˌkɔndʒu'geiʃən] | *n.* 变位 |
| urgent | ['əːdʒənt] | *a.* 紧急的 |
| authoritative | [ɔː'θɔritətiv] | *a.* 权威的 |

**Phrases**

| | |
|---|---|
| oral communication | 口头交流 |
| compare with | 与……相比较 |

**会话 2**

Celia: Should I buy a good dictionary if I want to learn French?

Allison: Of course. *Le Petit Larousse* is a good one. It covers tens of thousands of words, with explicit explanations and sentence examples. You can really learn a lot from it.

C: Shall I get a grammar book? I find French more complex than English.

A: I don't think you need one. Just following your textbook will endow you with enough sense of French. Later you will see French as more or less the same with English in basic structure. Have you learned some other European languages before?

C: Yes. When I was young, my father once taught me Latin because he thought Latin is the most valuable thing for a man to learn. I went through the whole *Wheelock's Latin*. But now I cannot speak a word of it. It is even much harder than French.

A: So you have had some experience of learning a foreign language already. I think it'll be easier for you to learn French this time.

赛莉娅：如果我想学法语的话，需不需要买一本好字典？

艾丽森：当然需要了。《小拉鲁斯字典》就是一本不错的字典。它涵盖了好几万单词，并配有清晰的解释和例句。你真的可以从中学到很多东西。

C：那我需要买一本语法书吗？我觉得法语比英语复杂好多哦。

A：我觉得不需要。你只要跟着课本来就能找到学法语的感觉。再往后你就会发现法语跟英语在基本结构上还是基本相似的。你以前学过其他的欧洲语言吗？

C：学过。我小时候我爸爸教过我拉丁语，因为他认为拉丁语是一个人能学到的最宝贵的东西。我学习了整个《韦洛克拉丁语》教程，但是到现在我已经一个词都不会说了，它比法语还要难。

A：这么说来你在学习外语方面还是有一定的经验的，那我觉得这次你学法语会相对轻松些。

### 核心词汇记一记

**Words Storm**

explicit [ik'splisit] *a.* 清楚的

complex [kəm'pleks] *a.* 复杂的

**Phrases**

tens of thousands of 好几万的

grammar book 语法书

# 82. Chinese and Western Medicine

## 中医和西医

### 知识链接 拓展视野，掌握背景知识

中医学是一种起源于中国并且以古代中国人的医学实践为主体的传统医学，至今已有数千年的历史。它具有整体观念、辨证论治等特点。狭义的中医，指的是汉医。而广义的中医则还包括藏医、蒙医、苗医等。现代医学即通常说的西医学，在约1840年之时由德国医学界首创，将科学实验室方法导入医学界，对于急性病症成效极佳，正式成为现代化医学的起点。西医治疗针对病症部位下药，具有见效快、疗效好的特点，但是容易复发，被诟病为“头痛医头，脚痛医脚”。

### 难点点拨 知识难点看一看，情景实战热热身

1．more and more 越来越

The traditional Chinese medicine is becoming more and more reputable these years.

传统的中医近些年来越来越受到好评了。

More and more people begin to find the disadvantages of western medicine, so they turn to Chinese medicine for help.

越来越多的人开始发现西医的不足了，所以他们开始转向中医治疗。

2．aim at 致力于，目标是

Chinese medicine aims at finding the real cause of the sickness.

中医旨在发现疾病的真正原因。

3．take care of 保养

It teaches us how to take care of our bodies to avoid diseases, rather than try to cure the diseases.

它教我们如何保养身体以防治疾病，而不是试图治愈疾病。

4．come into effect 见效，有用

Many people complain that Chinese medicine comes into effect so mild and slow that they cannot wait.

很多人都抱怨中药见效太慢了，他们等不及。

## 情景实战 跟着老外听一听，读一读，练一练

**会话 1**

Alice: The traditional Chinese medicine is becoming more and more reputable these years.

Mark: Yes. More and more people begin to find the disadvantages of western medicine, so they turn to Chinese medicine for help.

A: What's the major difference?

M: The principle of western medicine is to treat the affected part only. For example, if you have a pain in the stomach, the doctor prescribes bottles of pills and capsules to dull your pain and to reduce inflammation.

A: And to completely cure the pain, we should not only use antibiotics and painkillers and focus on the stomach. What we should do is to track down the real cause of the sickness, which is often the disorder of one's life.

M: Yes. Chinese medicine aims at finding the real cause of the sickness. It teaches us how to take care of our bodies to avoid diseases, rather than try to cure the diseases.

A: So it is more about the prevention than the treatment?

M: You are smart. We should take the human body as a whole, and well nourish it. This is the main principle of Chinese medicine.

艾丽斯：传统的中医近些年来越来越受到好评了。

马 克：是的，越来越多的人开始发现西医的不足了，所以他们开始转向中医治疗。

A：它们最主要的不同是什么呢？

M：西医的原则是针对病症部位下药。举例来说，如果你胃疼，医生就会给你开几瓶药丸或者胶囊来帮你缓和疼痛，消除炎症。

A：要彻底治愈病痛，我们不仅要用抗生素和止痛片来治疗胃疼，更应该找到引起疾病的真正原因，往往是个人生活失调紊乱所致。

M：正是。中医旨在发现疾病的真正原因。它教我们如何保养身体以防治疾病，而不是试图治愈疾病。

A：所以中医更多是关于预防而不是治疗了？

M：你很聪明嘛！我们应当把人体当作一个整体来看待，然后好好保养。这就是中医的精华。

### 核心词汇记一记

**Words Storm**

| | | |
|---|---|---|
| prescribe | [pris'kraib] | v. 开药 |
| capsule | ['kæpsju:l] | n. 胶囊 |
| dull | [dʌl] | v. 缓和 |
| inflammation | [ˌinflə'meiʃən] | n. 炎症 |
| antibiotic | [ˌæntibai'ɔtik] | n. 抗生素 |
| painkiller | ['peinˌkilə] | n. 止痛片 |
| nourish | ['nə:riʃ] | v. 滋养 |

**Phrases**

as a whole 作为一个整体

**会话 2**

Jerry: Many people complain that Chinese medicine comes into effect so mild and slow that they cannot wait. So they would rather turn to western medicine for help.

Mike: Chinese medicine puts more emphasis on the care of the whole body. Its side effects are slighter than those of western medicine. And most importantly, Chinese medicine helps you build up your body and become healthier.

J: The western medicine is often poisonous. Many pills are purely chemical. They come from laboratories rather than nature. By comparison, Chinese herbal medicine mainly comes from plants growing in the wilderness, so it's much healthier.

M: Yes. But sometimes we have to admit that the western medicine has its own advantages. For example, blood transfusion and surgery can help millions of people and save their lives. Western medicine pays more attention to the physical mechanism of the human body, including organs, limbs, and blood vessels. They compare a human body to a machine.

J: But Chinese people don't believe in this traditionally. They think of man as a creature of nature. As a result, man has to obey nature, and keep equilibrium of Yin and Yang.

杰瑞：很多人都抱怨中药见效太慢了，他们等不及。所以他们宁愿选择西药。

迈克：中药更注重全身的调理。它的副作用比西药要小。最重要的是，中药能帮你调理好身体，使你变得更健康。

J：西药毒性比较大，很多药片都是纯化学产品。它们来自实验室而不是大自然。对比来说，中草药主要来自野生的植物，所以更健康一些。

M：是的。但是有时我们得承认西医有它自己独特的优势。如输血和手术拯救了数以百万计的人。西医更注重人体的物理机制，包括器官、肢体，还有血管等。他们把人的身体比作一台机器。

J：但是传统的中国人不信这个。他们认为人是自然的创造物。因此，人们要顺从自然，保持阴阳的平衡。

**核心词汇记一记**

**Words Storm**

| | |
|---|---|
| slight | [slait] *a.* 轻微的 |
| laboratory | ['læbrətəri] *n.* 实验室 |
| comparison | [kəm'pærisn] *n.* 比较 |
| equilibrium | ['iːkwi'libriəm] *n.* 平衡 |

**Phrases**

| | |
|---|---|
| side effect | 副作用 |
| blood transfusion | 输血 |
| blood vessel | 血管 |

# 83. About the Army

## 军事漫谈

## 知识链接 拓展视野，掌握背景知识

军队是国家安全的保障，是国家机构重要组成部分。当今世界各大军事强国都努力依靠科技研发新一代武器，训练更优秀的军事人员。但是我们应当认识到，这一切都应当是为了和平，而不是战争。当下，各国在军事上完全有合作的可能和必要，来打击海盗、恐怖组织等共同的敌人。

## 难点点拨 知识难点看一看，情景实战热热身

1. the same...as... 与某物在某方面相同
   Of course it is only a model, but it is the same size and material as a real one.
   当然这是个模型玩具，不过它跟真枪在大小和材料上都一样。
2. professional 常用来形容某人很专业
   You are quite the professional.
   你很专业嘛！
3. this is why... 这就是为什么……
   This is why I like to collect so many stamps.
   这就是我喜欢收集这么多邮票的原因。
4. the end of... 结束，终止
   There is no end of arms race if we don't want peace.
   如果我们不想寻求和平的话，军备竞赛就会永远无休无止。
5. may...do/be... 但愿，希望
   May peace last forever.
   希望和平永存。

## 情景实战 跟着老外听一听，读一读，练一练

**会话 1**

Adam: Look. I've got a new rifle, an M4A1 carbine. It's quite a realistic one, handy and smart.

Bill: Where did you get it? It looks like a real one.

A: Of course it is only a model, but it is the same size and material as a real one. It is a gift from my brother, who is now working in a toyshop. He says this toy rifle is quite expensive for it is an authentic model of good quality for guys who love military equipment like me.

B: Can you shoot something with it?

A: Yes, it uses small plastic bullets. A little bit dangerous. But it is quite accurate, and has a good power and a long range.

B: Now you can play an American soldier finally.

A: Yes. Look what I have—helmet, combat suit and boots, M4A1 carbine, a backpack of military gadgets. Besides, I have an MP5 submachine gun, and a M9 pistol.

B: Binoculars, camelbak, flashlight, combat knife and a first aid kit, night vision goggles as well! You are quite the professional.

A: Just for fun. When you imagine yourself as a strong soldier with weapons, you feel quite excited and satisfied—this is why I like to collect so many military things.

B: Have fun then, GI Joe.

亚当：看，我有支新的步枪了，M4A1 卡宾枪，非常漂亮，手感好，很灵活。

比尔：从哪儿弄的？跟真的一样。

A：当然这是个模型玩具，不过它跟真枪在大小和材料上都一样。这是我在玩具店工作的哥哥送我的，他说这支枪很贵，是专门为军事迷精心制作的。

B：可以打子弹吗？

A：可以，用的是小塑料子弹。这枪有点危险，但非常准，劲儿大，射程也远。

B：现在你终于可以扮演美国大兵了。

A：是啊。看看我都有什么——头盔，军装和军靴，M4A1 卡宾枪，一背包的军用小玩意儿。另外我还有一把 MP5 冲锋枪和一把 M9 手枪。

B：望远镜、水袋、手电、军刀、急救包，还有个夜视仪！你很专业嘛。

A：就是好玩而已。你要是想象自己是拿着武器身强体壮的士兵，你会很激动很满足的。这就是我喜欢收集军用品的原因。

B：好好玩吧，大兵。

### 核心词汇记一记

**Words Storm**

rifle ['raifl] *n.* 步枪
carbine ['kɑːbain] *n.* 卡宾枪
handy ['hændi] *a.* 手感好的
helmet ['helmit] *n.* 头盔
gadget ['gædʒit] *n.* 小配件
pistol ['pistl] *n.* 手枪

**Phrases**

a little bit 有点

**会话 2**

Simon: I've recently read a passage saying that China has become the second most powerful country in the world military power ranking.

Carl: Do you believe it?

S: Yes. You see, China has the largest army in the world—so many soldiers, more than two million. The US has only more than one million now. Besides, China now has developed many advanced weapons, such as J-11B fighter plane, T-99 tank, and DF-31 intercontinental ballistic missile.

C: In modern warfare we cannot depend on the number of soldiers. By the way, the US has the best weapons, such as F-22, M1A2, aircraft carriers and better missiles. Russia is another country which has powerful weapons.

S: There is no end of arms race if we don't want peace. We must know we are not enemies of each other—the international terrorism is now the only enemy of both of us. The US and China have to cooperate to fight against it.

C: May peace last forever.

西蒙：最近我看了些材料，说中国已经跻身为世界第二大军事强国。

卡尔：你相信吗？

S：相信啊。你看，中国拥有世界上最庞大的军队，兵员多达 200 万，而美国只有 100 万多一点。除此之外，中国现在还研制开发出了很多像 J-11B 战斗机、T99 坦克，还有 DF-31 洲际弹道导弹那样的高端武器。

C：在现代战争中，我们是不可能依靠兵员的数目庞大来致胜的。美国拥有一批最先进的武器装备，如 F-22 战斗机、M1A2 坦克、航空母舰和一些更加精良的导弹。俄国也是军事强国。

S：如果我们不想寻求和平的话，军备竞赛就会永远无休无止。我们必须要明白中美彼此之间不是敌人，国际恐怖主义才是我们唯一的共同的敌人。中美两国必须要合作起来对抗恐怖主义势力。

C：希望和平永存。

**核心词汇记一记**

**Words Storm**

intercontinental [ˌintəˌkɔntiˈnentl] *a.* 洲际的

warfare [ˈwɔːfɛə] *n.* 战争

terrorism [ˈterəˌrizəm] *n.* 恐怖主义

cooperate [kəuˈɔpəreit] *v.* 合作

**Phrases**

international terrorism 国际恐怖主义

fight against 对抗

# 84. The Ivy League

## 常青藤联盟

### 知识链接　拓展视野，掌握背景知识

常青藤盟校或常青藤联盟（Ivy League）指的是由美国东北部的8所高等学府组成的体育赛事联盟。这8所学校有着许多共同的特点：它们都是美国最顶尖、最难考入的大学，也是全世界接受捐款最多的学府，拥有优秀的学生与师资，许多著名的科学家、政界要人、商界精英都毕业于此。此外它们也是美国历史上最悠久的大学——8所学校中的7所是在英国殖民时期建立的。常青藤盟校包括：布朗大学、哥伦比亚大学、康乃尔大学、达特茅斯学院、哈佛大学、宾州大学、普林斯顿大学、耶鲁大学。

### 难点点拨　知识难点看一看，情景实战热热身

1. get admission to 准许（入学）

   Only top students can get admission to these universities.

   只有顶尖的学生才能被这些大学录取。

2. rather than 而不是……

   We value one's perseverance and diligence rather than creativity.

   我们更加珍视一个人的恒心和勤奋，而不是创造性。

3. pursue one's studies 深造

   Now I'm pursuing my studies at Harvard.

   现在我正在哈佛大学深造。

4. fall behind 落后

   Competition nowadays is so fierce. If you don't move forward, you'll soon fall behind.

   如今的竞争这么激烈，如果你不前进，就会落后。

5. be curious about 感到好奇

   I'm curious about your life at Harvard.

   我对你在哈佛的生活感到很好奇。

## 情景实战 跟着老外听一听，读一读，练一练

**会话 1**

Peter: There are some exchange students from Yale in our university. They share the same dormitory building with us.

Coby: Really? I envy you. Yale is such a great a university, one of the Ivy League!

P: Ivy League? I know of this, a bunch of famous universities in the United States. Such as Harvard, Yale, Princeton, Cornell, Columbia, Brown, and…

C: The University of Pennsylvania and Dartmouth College. There are so many famous graduates—politicians, businessmen and scientists—they have a great impact on the fortune of America.

P: Yes, they are the best. Only the top students can get admission to these universities. The gaining of knowledge is not the only concern. They are supposed to think independently and creatively, and be able to handle great pressure.

C: I dream that one day I can visit these universities.

P: By comparison, we Chinese universities are totally different. We value one's perseverance and diligence rather than creativity. If a student can memorize all the professor has taught, he can secure a high mark in the exam.

C: To memorize blindly is a waste of time. Today we have the Internet, and we can get whatever information we want, so we don't need to learn useless details by heart any longer.

皮特：我们大学来了一些耶鲁的交换生。他们跟我们住同一个宿舍楼。

科比：真的吗？我好羡慕你呀，耶鲁大学很不错呢，是常青藤联盟院校。

P：常青藤联盟校？我知道的，是美国的一些著名大学，如哈佛大学、耶鲁大学、普林斯顿大学、康奈尔大学、哥伦比亚大学、布朗大学，还有……

C：宾夕法尼亚大学和达特茅斯大学。这些学校有很多著名的毕业生，包括政治家、商人还有科学家。他们对美国的命运有举足轻重的影响。

P：是的。这些是最好的大学。只有顶尖的学生才能被这些大学录取。知识并不是他们唯一关心的，学生们必须有独立思考能力和创造性，还要能在重压下游刃有余。

C：我梦想有一天能够去参观一下这些大学。

P：相比之下，我们中国的大学完全不同。我们更加珍视一个人的恒心和勤奋，而不是创造性。如果一个学生能够记住教授讲的所有知识，那么他在考试中就能得高分。

C：盲目的背诵是在浪费时间。今天我们拥有了互联网，可以从上面得到所有我们想知道的信息。我们已经不再需要背诵这些没用的细枝末节了。

### 核心词汇记一记

**Words Storm**

dormitory ['dɔːmitəri] *n.* 宿舍

perseverance [pəːsi'viərəns] *n.* 坚持，恒心

diligence ['dilidʒəns] *n.* 勤奋

memorize ['meməraiz] *v.* 记住

**Phrases**

exchange student 交换生

Ivy League 常青藤联盟

**会话 2**

Erica: I heard you are a graduate of Peking University.

Robin: Yes, I graduated from PKU in 2006. Now I'm pursuing my studies at Harvard.

E: Goodness! You are so great! Harvard is one of the best in the world.

R: One has to fight hard. Competition nowadays is so fierce. If you don't move forward, you'll soon fall behind. In a few years I'll receive my degree and start my own business.

E: I'm curious about your life in Harvard.

R: You have compulsory courses and elective courses to gain enough credits. You attend some parties and make friends. There are also many programs for you to join.

E: So you don't like it?

R: I've been accustomed to this lifestyle. A scholar's life should be like this and in Harvard I still keep the old habits.

E: But why did you choose Harvard?

R: I am majored in business, and Harvard is the best business school.

艾丽卡：我听说你是北京大学毕业的。

罗宾：是的，我 2006 年毕业于北京大学。现在我正在哈佛大学深造。

E：天啊！你太出色了！哈佛是全世界最好的大学之一。

R：得努力奋斗呀！如今的竞争这么激烈，如果你不前进，就会落后。再过几年我就能拿到学位，创办自己的企业了。

E：我对你在哈佛的生活感到很好奇。

R：你必须上必修课和选修课来取得足够的学分。然后参加一些聚会，交一些朋友。还有许多活动可以参加。

E：那么你喜欢吗？

R：我已经习惯这种生活方式了。一个学者的生活就是这样的。在哈佛我还是保持原来的习惯。

E：但是你为什么选择哈佛呢？

R：我的专业是关于商务方面的，而哈佛有最好的商学院。

**核心词汇记一记**

**Words Storm**

pursue [pə'sjuː] *v.* 追求
fierce [fiəs] *a.* 激烈的
elective [i'lektiv] *a.* 选修的
credit ['kredit] *n.* 学分
accustom [ə'kʌstəm] *v.* 习惯于

**Phrases**

fight hard 努力奋斗
move forward 前进

# 85. American English and British English

## 英语和美语

### 知识链接 拓展视野，掌握背景知识

*顾名思义，美式英语是主要在美国使用的英语，而英式英语是指主要在英国使用的英语。两者在发音和拼写方面都有所不同。美式英语发音混杂了来自不列颠群岛的各种方言特色，并形成了自己独特的发音方式。*

### 难点点拨 知识难点看一看，情景实战热热身

1．difference between A and B　A 与 B 的区别

What's the major difference between American English and British English?

美式英语和英式英语的最主要的区别是什么？

2．especially when 特别是……的时候

We very often use retroflex sounds in American English, especially when there's the letter "r" in a word.

在美式英语里，我们经常发翘舌音，尤其是有字母"R"的单词。

3．it sounds... 听起来

I like American pronunciation because it sounds modern and lively.

我喜欢美式发音是因为它听起来比较具有现代气息且活泼生动。

4．take... as... 把……看作

They take everything European as superior to the American model.

他们觉得欧洲的一切都超过了美国。

5．learn about 学习关于……的知识

We should learn more about American things.

我们应该更多地了解美国。

## 情景实战 跟着老外听一听，读一读，练一练

**会话 1**

Vernasa: What's the major difference between American English and British English?

Serena: It's the pronunciation. We very often use retroflex sounds in American English, especially when there's the letter "r" in a word. But in British English, the retroflex sound is rare and considered clownish.

V: So they vary quite a lot in pronunciation.

S: Very often, most British people consider the American way of speaking as "uncultivated", whereas the American people laugh at the British English as "outdated".

V: But we should acknowledge both ways. I like American pronunciation because it sounds modern and lively. But I also appreciate traditional British for its elegance.

S: This also reflects the difference between these two cultures. Many critics are so cynical that they never love anything American, and they declare that America is a country without history and culture. They love the good old Europe, and take everything European unconditionally as superior to the American model.

V: I don't agree with those people. In my view, America is now having the greatest impact upon the world, so we should learn more about American things.

瓦纳莎：美式英语和英式英语的最主要的区别是什么？

瑟琳娜：是发音。在美式英语里，我们经常发翘舌音，尤其是有字母"r"的单词。但是英式英语里的翘舌音非常少，而且你要是发这种音，别人就觉得你很滑稽。

V：所以它们在发音上有很多不同。

S：通常情况下，英国人认为美式发音"没教养"，而美国人嘲笑英式英语"过时"了。

V：但是我们对两种发音都接受。我喜欢美式发音是因为它听起来比较具有现代气息且活泼生动，但是我也欣赏传统的英式发音，因为它听起来很优雅。

S：这也反映了这两种文化的不同吧。很多批评家太愤世嫉俗了，他们不喜欢美国的任何东西。他们称美国是一个没有历史和文化的国家。他们喜欢美好的老欧洲，无条件地认为欧洲的一切都超过了美国。

V：我不能赞同这些人的看法。在我看来，美国现在正在对全球产生巨大影响，所以我们应该更多地了解美国。

### 核心词汇记一记

**Words Storm**

pronunciation [prənʌnsi'eiʃən] *n.* 发音

clownish ['klauniʃ] *a.* 滑稽的

disdain [dis'dein] *v.* 蔑视

whereas [hwɛər'æz] *conj.* 然而，但是

acknowledge [ək'nɔlidʒ] *v.* 承认

elegance ['eligəns] *n.* 优雅

**Phrases**

retroflex sound 翘舌音

## 会话 2

Angela: American English and British English use different words to express the same thing.

Sam: Yes. For example, American people say "pants", while British people say "trousers". There are lots of words in this case—"movie" and "film", "sick" and "ill", "baggage" and "luggage", "can" and "tin", "candy" and "sweets", "couch" and "sofa", "fall" and "autumn"... So many of them.

A: So can they understand each other?

S: No problem. These differences are never an obstacle to their communication.

A: Any other differences?

S: In spelling. American English uses "er" while British English uses "re". For example, "center" and "centre", "meter" and "metre", "theater" and "theatre".

A: So they vary in many ways—pronunciation, diction, and spelling. How can we memorize so many differences?

S: You don't have to memorize all of them. You just need to know them, and understand them. That will do.

A: If I talk to an American, am I supposed to use American words only?

S: Not necessarily. He will understand every word of yours if you speak good English, whether American or British.

安吉拉: 美式英语和英式英语用不同的单词表达同一个事物。

山姆: 是的。举例来说吧，美国人说裤子是"pants"，而英国人说"trousers"，还有很多这样的词汇，如"movie"和"film"（电影），"sick"和"ill"（生病），"baggage"和"luggage"（行李），"can"和"tin"（罐），"candy"和"sweets"（糖果），"couch"和"sofa"（沙发），"fall"和"autumn"（秋天）等，好多呢。

A: 那他们能听懂对方说话吗?

S: 没问题。这些区别从来不会成为交流的障碍。

A: 还有其他区别吗?

S: 拼写方面。美式英语用"er"，而英式英语用"re"。举例来说，如"cente 和"centre"，"meter"和"metre"，"theater"和"theatre"。

A: 所以它们在很多方面都不太一样咯？如发音、措辞和拼写。我们怎样才能记住这么多不同呢?

S: 你不需要把所有的都记住。你只需要知道并且理解就好。

A: 如果我和一个美国人交谈，我是不是只能用美式单词?

S: 没必要。如果你英语说得好，他会听懂你说的每个字，不管你说的是美式还是英式英语。

### 核心词汇记一记

**Words Storm**

pants [pænts] *n.* 裤子
baggage ['bægidʒ] *n.* 行李
vary ['vɛəri] *v.* 不同
diction ['dikʃən] *n.* 措辞
memorize ['meməraiz] *v.* 记住

**Phrases**

be supposed to 应该做……

# 86. Luxury Goods

## 奢侈品

### 知识链接 拓展视野，掌握背景知识

奢侈品是在市场上无论是质量还是价格都是最高档次的商品。不同的市场也有各自不同的奢侈区间，譬如轿车、葡萄酒，甚至巧克力。因为其高利润回护严格控制着品牌。奢侈品市场被认为对于经济的起落有比较高的敏感度。路易·威登 (Louis Vuitton Moet Hennessy) 集团是世界上最大的、拥有五十多个品牌的奢侈品供应商。其他的市场领导者包括古驰集团 (Gucci Group) 和历峰集团 (Richemont)。在大众文化或者公众印象中，一些商品已经成为了奢侈的代名词，包括鲟鱼子酱、劳斯莱斯轿车等等。这些都被认为是地位的象征以及用来突显购买者的财富。

### 难点点拨 知识难点看一看，情景实战热热身

1. a waste of money 浪费钱

   But for me, it's rather a waste of money.

   但是对我来说，这简直就是浪费钱。

2. try one's best to do 尽力做某事

   I'll try my best to save money.

   我会尽我最大努力来攒钱的。

3. enrich one's mind 充实头脑

   To be attractive, you need to enrich your mind and broaden your horizon.

   要想变得有魅力，你要丰富你的头脑，拓宽你的眼界。

## 情景实战 跟着老外听一听，读一读，练一练

**会话 1**

Lucas: Why do people love luxury goods?

Grace: It is just a matter of vanity. They simply want to show off. If you have an LV handbag, others will envy you and admire you. But in reality this is not really the case because many people dislike those who love to show off.

L: Luxury goods are often high quality products and you can use luxury goods to show your distinctiveness—that you have good taste.

G: Not for me, I think it's rather a waste of money. Why should I spend so much on those useless things? I'd rather save the money and invest it.

L: Some luxury goods can be seen as a way of investment, because their values may rise as time passes. For example, a vintage car that has a good price now, and will increase its value over time.

G: True enough I guess. You can collect some luxury goods if you have enough money.

L: Luxury goods are often quite beautiful. They are often designed and crafted by famous artisans, and a source of delight and satisfaction.

G: But I still cannot understand why they are so expensive.

L: Have you heard of "brand value"? They are expensive because they are good brands.

卢卡斯: 大家为什么喜欢奢侈品呢?

格雷斯: 这是一种虚荣。他们只是想炫耀罢了。如果你有一个LV的手袋，其他人就会嫉妒和羡慕你。但是并不总是这样的，很多人不喜欢爱炫耀的人。

L: 但是奢侈品经常意味着高品位。你可以用奢侈品来显示你的与众不同，那就是你的品位不错。

G: 但是对我来说，这简直就是浪费钱。为什么我要花这么多钱来买这些没用的东西？我宁愿存起来进行投资。

L: 一些奢侈品也可以成为投资对象呀，因为它们随着时间可能会增值。比如，一辆老爷车现在可以卖个好价钱，而且还会变得越来越值钱。

G: 是呀，如果你有足够的钱，也可以去收集奢侈品。

L: 奢侈品一般都很漂亮，它们都是由一些著名的艺术家设计而成，很讨人喜欢，让人满足。

G: 但是我不理解它们为什么如此之贵。

L: 你听说过“品牌价值”吗？它们贵是因为都是好牌子。

### 核心词汇记一记

**Words Storm**

| | | |
|---|---|---|
| vanity | ['væniti] | *n.* 虚伪 |
| handbag | ['hændbæg] | *n.* 手袋 |
| distinctiveness | [di'stiŋktivnis] | *n.* 独特性 |
| investment | [in'vestmənt] | *n.* 投资 |
| vintage | ['vintidʒ] | *a.* 古老的 |

**Phrases**

| | |
|---|---|
| luxury goods | 奢侈品 |
| show off | 炫耀 |

**会话 2**

Ava: I'm working hard these days. I want to save enough money to buy a Chanel Chance.

Joe: Why? I know it's really expensive. How much is it?

A: About one thousand yuan. I'll try my best to save money.

J: But you don't really need it, do you? Why do you want to spend so much money on it?

A: I don't know why. My roommate got one from her boyfriend as a gift. I need one too.

J: Don't be silly! You need money to do many other things and a very expensive bottle of perfume can give you nothing.

A: Maybe I can use it to find a wealthy boyfriend. I'll become attractive. I also want some other expensive accessories such as a handbag and sunglasses.

J: Find a wealthy boyfriend first; maybe he'll get them for you! Besides, to be attractive, you need to enrich your mind and broaden your horizon. You will not need to depend on luxury goods.

A: So can you give me some suggestion?

J: You need to read more books, and talk with real intelligent people. See some classic movies instead of soap operas. They will improve your demeanor and outlook, that way men will find you interesting and will enjoy talking to you.

爱娃: 这些天来我工作很努力，我想要存些钱来买一瓶香奈儿的“邂逅”香水。

乔: 为什么？这对你来说太贵了。多少钱呀？

A: 大约 1000 元。我会尽我最大努力来攒钱的。

J: 但是你并不真的需要它吧，是吗？你为什么要花这么多钱在这上面呢？

A: 我不知道为什么。我室友的男朋友给她买了一瓶作为礼物。我觉得我也需要一个。

J: 别傻了。你需要钱来做其他的事情。一瓶这么贵的香水什么都不能给你。

A: 也许我可以用它来找到一个有钱的男朋友。我会变得很有吸引力。我还想要一些其他的小饰品，比如手袋和太阳镜。

J: 那还不如先找个有钱的男朋友然后叫他给你买呢！而且要想变得有魅力，你就要丰富你的头脑，拓宽眼界，不能靠奢侈品。

A: 那你能给我一些建议吗？

J: 你需要多读一些书，跟一些真正有知识的人交谈。看一些经典电影而不是肥皂剧。这些都会提升你的举止和视野，这样男人就会觉得你有趣，然后喜欢你啰。

### 核心词汇记一记

**Words Storm**

| | | |
|---|---|---|
| perfume | ['pəːfjuːm] *n.* | 香水 |
| accessory | [ək'sesəri] *n.* | 附加物 |
| attractive | [ə'træktiv] *a.* | 吸引人的 |
| demeanor | [dɪ'miːnə] *n.* | 举止 |
| sunglasses | ['sʌn,glaːsiz] *n.* | 太阳镜 |

**Phrases**

save money 存钱